HISTORIOGRAPHY AND SPACE IN LATE ANTIQUITY

The Roman Empire traditionally presented itself as the centre of the world, a view sustained by ancient education and conveyed in imperial literature. Historiography in particular tended to be written from an empire-centred perspective. In Late Antiquity, however, that attitude was challenged by the fragmentation of the empire. This book explores how a post-imperial representation of space emerges in the historiography of that period. Minds adapted slowly, long ignoring Constantinople as the new capital and still finding counter-worlds at the edges of the world. Even in Christian literature, often thought of as introducing a new conception of space, the empire continued to influence geographies. Political changes and theological ideas, however, helped to imagine a transferral of empire away from Rome and to substitute ecclesiastical for imperial space. By the end of Late Antiquity, Rome was just one of many centres of the world.

PETER VAN NUFFELEN is Professor of Ancient History at Ghent University, where he leads an European Research Council–funded team on late ancient historiography. His recent publications include *Rethinking the Gods: Philosophical Readings of Religion in the Post-Hellenistic Period* (Cambridge University Press, 2011), *Orosius and the Rhetoric of History* (2012) and *Penser la tolérance durant l'Antiquité tardive* (2018).

HISTORIOGRAPHY AND SPACE IN LATE ANTIQUITY

EDITED BY

PETER VAN NUFFELEN

Ghent University, Belgium

CAMBRIDGE
UNIVERSITY PRESS

CAMBRIDGE
UNIVERSITY PRESS

University Printing House, Cambridge CB2 8BS, United Kingdom

One Liberty Plaza, 20th Floor, New York, NY 10006, USA

477 Williamstown Road, Port Melbourne, VIC 3207, Australia

314–321, 3rd Floor, Plot 3, Splendor Forum, Jasola District Centre,
New Delhi – 110025, India

79 Anson Road, #06–04/06, Singapore 079906

Cambridge University Press is part of the University of Cambridge.

It furthers the University's mission by disseminating knowledge in the pursuit of
education, learning, and research at the highest international levels of excellence.

www.cambridge.org
Information on this title: www.cambridge.org/9781108481281
DOI: 10.1017/9781108686686

© Cambridge University Press 2019

First published 2019

Printed and bound in Great Britain by Clays Ltd, Elcograf S.p.A.

A catalogue record for this publication is available from the British Library.

ISBN 978-1-108-48128-1 Hardback

Contents

Contributors

TIM GREENWOOD is Reader in the Department of Mediaeval History at the University of St Andrews. He is the author of numerous studies on the political, social and cultural history of late antique and medieval Armenia and has recently published *The Universal History of Step'anos Tarōnec'i* (2017), the first English translation and commentary of this early-eleventh-century Armenian text.

MARK HUMPHRIES is Professor of Ancient History and Head of the Department of Classics, Ancient History and Egyptology at Swansea University. He has published widely on various aspects of history, literature and religion in late antiquity. He is one of the general editors of the series Translated Texts for Historians.

SCOTT JOHNSON is Associate Professor of Classics and Letters at the University of Oklahoma. He studies the literary and cultural history of the late antique world. His book *Literary Territories: Cartographical Thinking in Late Antiquity* was published in 2016.

ANTHONY KALDELLIS is Professor and Chair of Classics at The Ohio State University. He has published many books and articles on aspects of Byzantine history, literature and culture, including many translations of Byzantine sources.

HARTMUT LEPPIN is Professor of Ancient History at the Goethe University Frankfurt am Main and Principal Investigator of the Leibniz prize project Polyphony of Late Antique Christianity. His main research areas are the history of political ideas and the history of Christianity in antiquity. He recently published *Die frühen Christen. Von den Anfängen bis Konstantin* (2018) and with S. Alkier (ed.), *Juden, Christen, Heiden. Religiöse Inklusion und Exklusion in Kleinasien bis Decius* (2018).

PETER VAN NUFFELEN is Professor of Ancient History at Ghent University. He publishes on philosophy and religion of the Roman Empire, Early Christianity and the history and literature of Late Antiquity. His most recent book is *Penser la tolérance durant l'Antiquité tardive* (2018). With Lieve Van Hoof, he is publishing a translation of Jordanes in the Translated Texts for Historians series, a *Clavis Historicorum Antiquitatis Posterioris*, and an edition of fragmentary Latin historians of Late Antiquity (Cambridge University Press).

PHILIP WOOD is Associate Professor at the Aga Khan University, Institute for the Study of Muslim Civilisations, in London. His research deals with minority groups in the Roman and Sasanian empires and in the Umayyad and Abbasid caliphates, from the fifth to the ninth centuries. He has published two monographs on this subject: *We Have No King but Christ: Christian Political Thought in Greater Syria on the Eve of the Arab Conquests (c. 400–585)* (2010) and *The Chronicle of Seert: Christian Historical Imagination in Late Antique Iraq* (2013). He is currently working on a book on Christians in the ninth-century Jazira.

Acknowledgements

This volume originates in a conference called Historiography and Space in Late Antiquity, held in Ghent on 15–17 January 2015. It was the first conference organised within the Research Project 'Memory of Empire: The Post-Imperial Historiography of Late Antiquity', funded by the European Research Council (under the European Union's Seventh Framework Programme (FP/2007–2013)/ERC Grant Agreement n. 313153). I wish to thank the entire project team and in particular Marianna Mazzola, who organized the conference. Several chapters were written especially for this volume and I wish to thank the contributors for their willingness to engage with the theme. My sincerest thanks also to Cambridge University Press in the person of Michael Sharp for the smooth collaboration that allowed the genesis of this volume.

Introduction
From Imperial to Post-Imperial Space in Late Ancient Historiography

Peter Van Nuffelen

If time is the first dimension of history, then space is its second, so the saying goes. Time is the more obvious axis against which to plot histories, but historians obviously have to make choices as to which geographical areas to cover. A traditional conundrum for historians of antiquity was how to reconcile a variety of theatres of war with the single course of time. For the narrative to remain coherent, a continuous account was required, but this entailed shifts in geographical focus that threatened the narrative's clarity.[1] One solution was to divide the story into geographical sections, seen in its most explicit form in the *Wars* of Procopius (mid-sixth c.). His first seven books are composed of three units that follow events in Persia, Africa and Italy with hardly any overlap between the books. This choice of structure involved a judgement on the importance of these various theatres in relation to others that did not receive separate treatment. A. Sarantis, for example, has argued that Procopius's presentation results in a modern underestimation of the importance of the Danube border during the reign of Justinian (527–65).[2] Indeed, book 8 of Procopius's *Wars*, which updated the first seven books and offers a single narrative about the various fronts, succeeds in giving a better idea of what happened outside these three major regions, in particular the Danube area. Modern accounts of Justinian's wars of conquest are indeed highly dependent on the literary choices Procopius made, choices that imply a judgement on where history was really happening. As this example shows, for all the importance documentary sources hold, historiography still strongly shapes the geographical focus of the narratives modern scholars offer of the ancient world.[3]

---

[1] Cf. Purves 2010; de Jong 2012; Maier 2016.   [2] Sarantis 2016.

[3] Cf. Humphries 2017 on how modern ancient historians are still dependent on the imperial perspective of their sources. For other attempts to shift the geographical focus of modern narratives, see, e.g., Reed 2009; Fowden 2014 and Frankopan 2015.

While Procopius's example suggests that we are at the mercy of the idiosyncrasies of individual authors, his choices were also shaped by the cultural, social and political conditions of his time. This is the aspect of spatiality in ancient historiography that the present volume is interested in: How do histories reflect the changing space of the later Roman Empire? How does the shifting balance between centre and periphery shape histories? How does the increasing importance of the church affect representations of imperial space? How is the ecclesiastical representation of space shaped by imperial space?

With the Roman dominance over the Mediterranean, historiography became closely linked to the empire: history was written *from* the centre – that is, Rome – and *for* that centre. The correlation between office-holding, social position and literary activity was strong during the empire, and was especially visible in historiography. Tacitus and Cassius Dio are just the most obvious examples of this link. Social status and career, education and literary tradition conspired to produce a culture that had its geographical centre in Rome. P. Gautier Dalché puts it aptly: 'This culture of an ideological nature was a vital condition of building a career in the bureaucracy and grounding administrators' actions in a perception of the unity of the empire'.[4] As analysed by C. Nicolet, the creation of an empire implied not just physical control of a territory but also the claim to knowledge about that territory and what lies beyond – an activity that was directed and perceived from the centre.[5] Developing this idea, S. Benoist has emphasised how a tension always existed between the concept of the empire as a stable entity limited by frontiers, on the one hand, and the idea of permanent conquest, on the other. The empire always laid an implicit claim to what was beyond it.[6] This 'imperial habitus' made historians writing during the Roman Empire imperial historians in three senses: they wrote during the empire, about the empire and from the perspective of the empire.[7] This is true even for historians with

---

[4] Gautier Dalché 2014: 182: 'Cette culture de nature idéologique était une condition indispensable pour faire carrière dans la bureaucratie et pour donner à l'action des admininistrateurs un sens fondé sur la perception de l'unité de l'empire'. See Lozovsky 2006 for a similar argument relating to the Carolingian period. Note that Witakowski 2007: 221 explains the absence of geographical literature in Syriac by the fact that Syriac speakers did not have an empire to run.

[5] Nicolet 1991. See further Brodersen 1995; Clarke 1999; Hänger 2001; Talbert and Brodersen 2004; Woolf 2011 (who explores further nuances of the link between empire and knowledge); Geus and Rathmann 2013; Rimell and Asper 2017. See Yarrow 2006 on how provincial histories are affected by the Roman Empire; Liddel and Fear 2010 on universal history.

[6] Benoist 2016: 53.

[7] The focus on the emperor, expressed in a biographical format for imperial historiography, is another illustration of how the empire shaped historiography: Zimmermann 1999.

a provincial standpoint. Eunapius, for example, writing towards the end of the fourth century, complains that it was hard for him, a sophist living in Sardis in Asia, to access information about the West[8] and his account reveals his distance to the court. At the same time, his history has as much an imperial perspective as, say, the *breviarium* of Festus written a couple of decades earlier to advise the emperor Valens on his dealings with the Persians. To give a later example: the history of Pseudo-Joshua the Stylite, written in Syriac, narrates the conflict between Rome and Persia between 502 and 506 from the viewpoint of border society, but its ideological centre is Rome.[9]

This volume asks what happened to the imperial representation of space in late ancient historiography. In brief, the crucial question for each chapter is: Where is the centre located? We understand space here in the sense of geographical space mediated through narrative. This means that other forms of representing or experiencing space, like travel and urban space, figure only marginally in this book. Through a series of case studies that take us from Constantinople to Armenia and from Spain to the Euphrates, it uses historiography as a lens through which to study what happens to the imperial representation of space in a world where that empire is losing its grip on the Mediterranean. We contend that because historiography tended to be written from the centre, it is a particularly well-suited lens to trace how the imperial representation of space slowly changed under the impact of the transformation of empire. Works of geography, like *Expositio totius mundi et gentium* and the account of Cosmas Indicopleustes, therefore, only feature occasionally here, but we hope that the results of this volume will be of interest for historians of geography also.

Much like ancient historiography, late antique historiography is a large body of text and this volume only offers a series of case studies. However, we contend that the changes these case studies allow us to trace have wider validity. We shall see that the imperial habitus was slow to die – indeed, if it really died before being resurrected in the Carolingian Empire and at the Byzantine court of Constantine Porphyrogenitus (913–59).[10] At the same time, there were many factors that shed doubt on the stability of the empire

---

[8] Eunapius of Sardis, *History* F55 and F66 (Blockley 1981–2).
[9] Trombley and Watt 2000. Other examples of the distinction between a provincial standpoint and the imperial perspective are the *Philotheos historia* by Theodoret of Cyrrhus (Perrin 2001) and the chronicler Hydatius, on whom see Chapter 2 by Van Nuffelen. See also Perrin 1997 on Gregory of Tours.
[10] Cf. Lozovsky 2006; Treadgold 2013: 153–96.

and its centre, not least the fragmentation of the West and the rise of the church, which was both closely aligned with the empire and represented a potential alternative focus. Indeed, late ancient culture, as reflected in historiography, can already be said to reflect a post-imperial perspective before the end of empire: the empire remained the major point of reference, but its centrality was no longer a mere matter of fact. The centre was destabilised and challenged by alternatives (successor kingdoms, the church, the major rival Persia). This volume is interested in the dynamic that this post-imperial situation generated in historiography.

The Imperial Habitus in Late Antiquity

Let me start by noting that the 'ideological culture' sketched by P. Gautier Dalché remained largely in place in late antiquity. There is an abundance of geographical literature from the period, most of which reproduces 'classical' knowledge and is aimed at a school context. The surviving works of Julius Honorius, Vibius Sequester, Ampelius, Solinus, Martianus Capella and the Latin translation of Dionysius Periegetes by Priscian bear clear witness to their role in rhetorical training, as does the continued popularity of Pomponius Mela.[11] These texts unfailingly reproduce the imperial perspective of their sources or, in the case of Pomponius Mela, of their time of writing. Another indication of the imperial habitus' continued vitality is that one easily finds references in late ancient literature to claims to world rule, often but not always directly emanating from or directed at the court.[12] Ethnography was still a continuous presence within late ancient historiography. Establishing the nature of the difference between the empire's insiders and outsiders, it made it possible for foreign peoples to be integrated into the imperial perspective, allowing, for example, a place to be found for the hitherto unknown Huns.[13] Ethnography underscored the superiority of the empire, even if (or especially when) foreign peoples were used as a positive foil for the moral decline of the empire, as Tacitus had done in the *Germania*.[14] Even a late ancient

[11] Cf. *Panegyrici Latini* 9 (4) 20.2, mentioning a geographical map at rhetoric school. See Wolska-Conus 1978; Humphries 2007; Maas 2007; Johnson 2012. For overviews of Christian texts, see Inglebert 2001; Günther 2007 (emphasising decline); Schleicher 2014.
[12] E.g., *Panegyrici latini* 10 (11)7.7, cf. 8(5) 20.2; Corippus, *Ioannis* 2.382–3, 3.5–10. See further Inglebert 2015: 21–2: Traina 2013 and 2015; Chapter 2.
[13] Eunapius of Sardis, *History* F41 (Blockley); Ammianus Marcellinus 31.2. Cf. Dagron 1987: 215 for the idea that writing meant stabilising the flux that marks late antiquity.
[14] See Kaldellis 2013: 1–25 for an overview. On Ammianus, see Vergin 2013. Maas 2003: 156 argues that Christians do not do ethnography, but see Stevenson 2002–3. On its resurrection in the Carolingian period, see Lozovsky 2006.

innovation, the geographical surveys of the world, with which the historians Orosius and, in his wake, Jordanes opened their histories, betrays a perspective centred on the empire.[15] Besides education and an elite identification with the empire, which remained the major conduit for social advancement, travel has been highlighted as a factor in fostering a view of the empire as a unity and hence identification with the imperial perspective.[16] Travel is indeed well documented for this period, beyond the rise of pilgrimage.[17] Trade was important, but other forms of travel are plentifully attested for the later empire, too: embassies travelled back and forth to foreign rulers, spies infiltrated the enemy, refugees left their homes, exiles were sent to distant corners and officials moved around the empire.[18] Connectivity, as much as education, was a product of empire that sustained the imperial habitus.

Challenges from Within and Without

While this ensured that Rome continued to be seen as the centre of the world, that centrality was destabilised by various factors. The first challenge came from within. The tetrarchical regime of multiple travelling emperors meant an inexorable decline in Rome's political importance. The strong emphasis of the tetrarchs on political and filial unity obviously sought to counteract possible centrifugal tendencies.[19] While the return to single imperial rule in 325 eliminated one challenge to unity and hence to the centrality of Rome, Constantine's decision to found Constantinople set in motion a process that would create a new centre for what moderns tend to see as a new empire, the Byzantine one. As Anthony Kaldellis shows in Chapter 1, Constantinople was very slow to occupy the central place in late ancient historiographical narrative that modern accounts tend to attribute to it from the late fourth century onwards on political grounds. Indeed, it was the perceived fall of Rome in 476 that seemed to open up space in the mental geography of the late

---

[15] Merrills 2005. This is true, even if Orosius shows a post-imperial awareness of the possible end of the empire (cf. Orosius, *Histories* 5.2; Van Nuffelen 2012: 170–86). For further integrations of geographical accounts and historiography, see book 1 of the *Excerpta latina barbari*, the Syriac *Chronicle of 724*, and book 12 of Pseudo-Zachariah's *Church History*.

[16] Perrin 1997.

[17] Newbold 1983; Adams and Laurence 2001; Macrides 2002; Ellis and Kidner 2004; Dietz 2005. On the relative ease of movement within the empire and some restrictions, see Tacoma 2016 and de Ligt and Tacoma 2016.

[18] Lounghis 1980; Lee 1993; McCormick 2001; Gillett 2003; Nechaeva 2014; Washburn 2012; Hillner 2016.

[19] Van Dam 2007: 35–78.

Roman elite,[20] leading them to embrace and represent Constantinople as the centre of the empire. Once in this position, Constantinople was as hard to dislodge as Rome had once been. Writing at a time of persecution for his Miaphysite church at the end of the sixth century, and doing so in Syriac, not a language of the imperial elite, the church historian John of Ephesus still wrote from an 'imperocentric' perspective with Constantinople at its heart, as Hartmut Leppin shows in his contribution (Chapter 5).[21]

The imperial habitus was shaken but not immediately brought down by the exogenous shocks that characterise late antiquity from the fifth century onwards. The barbarian invasions, especially from the fifth century onwards, set in motion a process that eventually resulted in the dismemberment of the empire in the West. While the empire soon lost effective control over important parts of Africa, Spain and Gaul and these processes were instantly recorded in historiography, they were slow to impact on the mental geography. Even dramatic events like the sack of Rome in 410 may have had less of an impact than often thought.[22] The chronicles of the West retain an imperial perspective, be it sometimes a disenchanted one as in the Gallic *Chronicle of 452*.[23] Alternative conceptions are slow to emerge but become tangible towards the end of the sixth and the beginning of the seventh century. In Chapter 4, Mark Humphries describes how the Visigothic chronicler John of Biclaro suggested the transferral of centrality from the Roman Empire to the Visigothic Kingdom, built on the perceived lapse of the empire into heresy and the conversion of the kingdom to Catholicism under Reccared I (586–601). Ecclesiastical ideas about a nation's chosen status thus helped to break the hold of the empire – a process that can be seen in even more developed form in the historiographical oeuvre of Isidore of Seville.[24]

If the West was, by the end of the sixth century, largely lost to the empire, the East was shaken too. External threats by the Goths, Huns and Persians were matched by internal ones, such as the ever-restless Isaurians. In the fifth century, they rose to a force to be reckoned with, allowing Zeno to become emperor. His death in 491 and the Isaurians' attempt to retain power against the new emperor Anastasius generated a backlash: in a war

---

[20] Praet 2018 studies the effect of the 'fall' on sixth-century elites in Constantinople.
[21] See Wood 2010 for the very slow move away from the Roman Empire among Syriac speakers.
[22] Van Nuffelen 2015 with further references.   [23] See Van Nuffelen's Chapter 2 on Hydatius.
[24] Wood 2012. Although a study of identity, Reimitz 2015 shows how historiography in Gaul from the sixth century onwards develops from a post-imperial genre to one that acquires a new imperial focus on the Carolingian family.

that lasted until 498, Anastasius rooted out any meaningful Isaurian opposition once and for all.[25] The most enduring opposition to the Roman Empire came from Sasanian Persia. Warfare was intermittent, especially in the sixth century, with the sack of Antioch in 538 as the most important event in symbolic terms. While fourth-century warfare is accompanied by a proliferation of historical works recalling past victories over the Persians, including those of Alexander the Great,[26] the sixth century imagines the relationship of the two powers on a more equal footing. After Justinian closed the Athenian Academy in 529, the historian Agathias tells us, seven philosophers travelled to the Persian king Chosroes in 531 to practice their philosophy in freedom.[27] In the story, the Persian king appears as a possible equivalent to the Roman emperor. Narrating events of the same decade, Procopius depicted Chosroes as assuming the role of emperor during his occupation of Apamea, presiding over chariot races and meting out justice, yet the presentation is skewed to show how unreliable he is.[28] In both cases, Chosroes fails to live up to the expectations Romans project onto him, and Agathias and Procopius thus reject the equality that their stories initially suggest. In a letter to the emperor Maurice, Chosroes II described Rome and Persia as the two eyes of the world, a vision of equality that Roman sources record but do not endorse.[29] Even so, there now seems to be an alternative to the Roman Empire. The proliferation from the fourth century onwards of the term *Romania* to designate the territory held by Rome indicates an awareness of its limitations and creates a strict parallel with other territories, such as *Gothia* or *Germania*.[30] Rome now can become just one of many regions of the world. In Chapter 2, Peter Van Nuffelen argues we see another sign of this doubt concerning the empire in sixth-century historiography produced in Constantinople. Procopius and Jordanes in particular have an interest in the margins of the world, especially distant islands. This can be read as a reaffirmation of the power of the centre faced with the pressure that peoples coming from the margins put on the empire. Such signs that alternatives to *Romania* are possible are important in the light of the

---

[25] Cf. Meier 2009; Feld 2012.
[26] Esp. Julius Valerius, *The History of Alexander the Great* and the *Itinerarium Alexandri*; Festus, *Breviarium*, with Lane Fox 1997.
[27] Agathias, *Histories* 2.30.3–4, with Watts 2006: 138–42; Börm 2007: 277–83.
[28] Procopius, *Wars* 2.11.36–8. For the context, see Börm 2007: 251–68.
[29] Theophylact Simocatta, *Ecumenical History* 4.11.2, with Dignas and Winter 2007: 238–9. See Canepa 2009: 34–52; McDonough 2011 for positive Roman views about the Sasanians.
[30] Inglebert 2015: 21–2 for references. Wolfram 1979: 27 notes that through this usage Rome becomes one *gens* among many.

tendency for imperial discourse to be exclusive and to claim world dominance. This is one of the themes in Tim Greenwood's chapter (Chapter 3) on Armenian conceptions of space. Armenia was split between Rome and Persia. Armenian discourse from Persian Armenia tended to envisage Armenia as an autonomous entity and/or part of Ērānšahr. This orientation towards the East was not changed by the conversion to Christianity. Moreover, no sources from Roman Armenia survive and Greenwood suggests that that discourse, expressing possibly the same autonomy, was silenced by Roman imperial power.

Christianity and Imperial Space

The rise of Christianity is the other major feature of late antiquity, and research has often emphasised that it created new perceptions of space that differ from the imperial one. Christianity attributed symbolic centrality to holy places and in particular Jerusalem, the centrality of which was emphasised by literary means through pilgrimage literature.[31] Leaving one's home could be a spiritual experience.[32] Much as the reading of classical literature generated the need for geographical training, the Bible conveyed its own geography that needed to be understood and explained.[33] The movements of apostles, tracked in traditional and apocryphal gospels, created an alternative geography that spanned the known world.[34] The emphasis on God's activity everywhere could turn purely local events into universal ones.[35] Places at the margins, like the desert or Mount Sinai, could assume centrality by virtue of being the scenes of God's favour. In a famous formula, monasticism brings the desert into the city: it blurs and confirms the border lines. Furthermore, Philippe Blaudeau has meticulously explored how the various church historians project different centres of orthodoxy, depending on their own geographical standpoint and their doctrinal preference. Besides the Constantinopolitan focus of Socrates, there is the Antiochene one of Theodoret of Cyrrhus and the Alexandrian one of Zachariah Scholasticus. Coining the term 'geo-ecclesiology', Blaudeau ties these representations to the policies and visions of the sees, all of which pursued strategies to achieve centrality in their own

---

[31] See, e.g., Maraval 1985; Elsner 2000; Humphries 2007: 43 and further literature cited in Chapter 7 by Johnson.
[32] E.g., the priest Bachiarius in Gennadius, *De viris illustribus* 24.   [33] Stenger 2016.
[34] Johnson 2011, 2015.
[35] E.g., Elishe, *History of Vardan Mamikonean* 7, p. 192 on how local Armenian events are depicted as having universal importance. See also van der Vliet 2006: 54–5; Muehlberger 2015.

understanding of ecclesiastical geography.[36] This type of analysis can be usefully extended to other ecclesiastical authors: Dionysius of Tell-Mahre, as shown in Chapter 6 by Philip Wood, succeeded in depicting his own Syrian Orthodox church as the only Christian church in the East from Alexandria to Baghdad, thus effectively obliterating his Nestorian and Greek Orthodox counterparts.

As this brief survey shows, there can be little doubt that Christian literature offers a more varied representation of space than that found in secular literature. However, Christian representations of space complicated imperial geography but did not contradict it. As is well known, the institutional geography of the church was largely modelled on that of the empire and the geo-ecclesiology described by Blaudeau plays out within the empire, with sufficient imperial involvement: the pentarchy established by Justinian, which balanced the five patriarchal sees, was an imperial construction. Pilgrimage literature is a predominantly Latin genre and altogether absent in Syriac, as observed by Scott Johnson in Chapter 7: it may be as much an imperial as a Christian type of text and therefore it may be dangerous to read the genre as reflecting 'the' Christian conception of space. Scholars have emphasised the universalism inherent in the Christian urge to convert all nations, sometimes suggesting that this marks a difference to the localised empire and that Christianity remodelled the frontiers. Yet, as we have seen, the empire also laid claim to world dominion, meaning that Roman imperialism and Christian universality were not necessarily mutually exclusive.[37] The Christian reimagination of the edges of the world was not unrelated to earlier imperial conceptions, as the association of the biblical Gog and Magog with the Alexander legend illustrates.[38]

The best indication of the entanglement of ecclesiastical and imperial conceptions of centrality is that political change was needed as a trigger for alternative conceptions, which were underpinned by ecclesiastical visions, to take hold. As stated in the preceding text, the idea of transferral from Rome to Visigothic Spain expressed by John of Biclaro is the product of the loss of the empire's grip on the West and the conversion of Spain to Catholicism. As illustrated by Wood's chapter, it was only when the Arab conquest cut Syriac speakers off from the empire that alternative

[36] Blaudeau 2006, 2017.
[37] E.g., Maas 2003; Nasrallah 2005; Fürst 2007; Humphries 2007; Maier 2011; Pollmann 2011. For further discussion of Christian universality, as attributed to Christian historiography, see Van Nuffelen 2010; Inglebert 2014.
[38] Van Donzel and Schmidt 2010: 15–49.

conceptions were developed. While Melkite and Maronite histories from the early Islamic period continued to look towards the West, in Syriac Orthodox ('Miaphysite') histories there are remnants of the preceding ecclesiastical geography, especially in the concentration on the sees of Alexandria and Antioch as the heartlands of orthodoxy. Yet the story is now focused on councils and bishops that contributed to a 'Syriac' identity. The Islamic empire did not replace the Roman one as a focal point, but – as the neglect of territories farther east shows – the geographical emphasis lay on the Middle Eastern centre from which the elite who wrote these histories stemmed. Indeed, in a context where the empire still stood, as in the case of John of Ephesus analysed by Hartmut Leppin, even persecution did not lead an abandoning of the empire.

Creating Space in Narrative

So far we have been looking at historiography as a reflection of changes in the political and mental geography of the Roman Empire. Yet texts never simply reflect their cultural context, they also engage with it: they are creative and sometimes idiosyncratic ways of imparting meaning to reality. The spatial setting is a crucial element in the representation of an event and an important clue to how the historian hopes his narrative will be understood. It is no accident that Procopius narrates an episode in which the Persian king Chosroes presides over games in the hippodrome: the hippodrome was the place where interaction between ruler and subjects took place in Constantinople. [39] To give another example: Rufinus's description of the so-called destruction of the Serapeum has the pagans residing artificially many days in the temple where they perform human sacrifices, thus having pagans do archetypally pagan things in this archetypally pagan place. [40] While these are examples of adjusting the setting for the narrative, creativity sometimes went further. When Constantinople emerges as the central place in historiography, that is, the early sixth century, accounts of the city's mythical and distant past start being recorded, *in casu* by Hesychius of Miletus. [41] This reflects a mechanism also seen in the production of late ancient patria. These celebrations of local history tend to be written for cities that achieved new importance in the reordered empire of Diocletian and Constantine, which created new 'corridors of empire'.

---

[39] Pfeilschifter 2013: 294–355.
[40] Rufinus, *Ecclesiastical History* II.22–3 with Van Nuffelen 2018: 133–41, with further references. Isele 2010 is a fine analysis of the role of space in religious conflict.
[41] See Chapter 1 by Kaldellis.

New-found wealth and an increased prominence demanded a respectable history.[42] Ultimately, this is the same mechanism that underpins the creation of long genealogies for peoples that gained importance in late antiquity, like the Goths (as attested in Jordanes) or the Isaurians (as found in Candidus).[43] While the distant past was one focal point of creativity, geographical distance was another. Van Nuffelen argues that the histories of Jordanes and Procopius attribute renewed importance of islands like Thule and Scandza that form the traditional edges of the world. Their geographical distance is collapsed with the difference in civilisation and morality in relation to the empire, which appears – albeit momentarily – to be threatened by the peoples coming from the rim of the earth.

Meaning can also be conveyed by absence, which plays an important role in several chapters. Kaldellis shows how Constantinople was consciously ignored in parts of fourth-century literature, defying the emergent centrality of Constantine's foundation. Greenwood suggests that the voice of Armenians living in the Roman part of Armenia was silenced, possibly because it did not fully turn its gaze towards Rome. Syriac Orthodox ecclesiastical historiography, which was written from a strongly clerical and hierarchical point of view, ignores the Christian Arabs and the Christians in the East, even though they were part of their church. As Wood underlines, such ignorance is more surprising than the general absence of other confessions and the lack of interest in other, non-Miaphysite churches to the West. That absence can be understood as the result of the focus on the sees of Alexandria and Antioch, a focus that was inherited from the geo-ecclesiology of the empire. Indeed, as Leppin's chapter shows, centrality attributed to a particular place tends to result in the neglect of or even disregard for other claimants to centrality: John of Ephesus ignores Persia, even though he was well informed about places close to the border. Finally, Johnson asks about the absence of a genre: we have every reason to expect the existence of the genre of pilgrimage literature in Syriac, which flourished in Latin and, to a lesser degree, in Greek. As we have seen in the preceding text, this parahistoriographical genre was one in which the traditional political geography of the empire was refashioned to take the new religious centres into account. As there is sufficient proof for religious travel in Syriac literature, this absence cannot be due to a difference in travel culture. If Johnson's answer is aporetic, one

---

[42] Focanti 2018a, 2018b.
[43] For Candidus, see Meier 2014; for Jordanes, the discussion in Van Hoof and Van Nuffelen forthcoming a.

factor may have been the same control by the clerical hierarchy noted by Wood: pilgrimage literature in Latin was often composed by laymen and their independent travels and accounts may have clashed with a desire to control more strictly where holiness was to be located in Syriac society. Yet we do well to recall that such control need not have been more conscious than the imperial habitus that had shaped the accounts coming from within the Roman Empire.

The story told in this volume is, then, one of inertia and slow change. The characters in the story are authors and texts that both reflect the wider changes and shape them. The plot is what happens to the centre: how the old order is challenged, reaffirmed and replaced, and how it partially survives. Borders, a well-studied topic,[44] are therefore of less interest to us than the question of where the centre is located. The volume opens with a focus on the first 'recentring' of late antiquity, away from Rome: the foundation of Constantinople, with Kaldellis's analysis of why the city only achieved a central position in historiography in the sixth century. Van Nuffelen argues that histories from that century actively engage with the borders of the world with the aim of reaffirming the traditional imperial claim to world dominance and the centrality of Constantinople. Studying Armenian perceptions of space, Greenwood shifts the focus to how the imperial claims to which smaller nations were subjected impacted on their representation of geography and space. The Persian Empire, Rome's major late ancient rival, here assumes the role played by Rome in the earlier chapters. In the subsequent chapters, the volume shifts towards the rise of alternative centres. Humphries shows how John of Biclaro attributed centrality to Visigothic Spain, on the basis of an ecclesiastical argument about heresy and orthodoxy. With Leppin's chapter we turn to ecclesiastical historiography. Contrary to what one might expect, the Miaphysite Syriac speaker John of Ephesus writes an 'imperocentric' ecclesiastical history, illustrating the strength of the imperial habitus at the end of the sixth century. That pull is largely absent in later Miaphysite historiography, written after the Muslim conquests, as shown by Wood. Yet it is not replaced by a new imperial centre in, say, Baghdad. Rather, an ecclesiastical perspective, which inherits some features of the late Roman mental map, dominates the story. Whether there is indeed something like a Syriac perspective on space is one of the questions asked by Johnson in his chapter on the absence of pilgrimage literature in Syriac. While his answer is aporetic, the question reveals we should not simply assume that literary

[44] E.g., Brauer 1995; Pohl, Wood and Reimitz, eds. 2001; Curta 2006; Zadeh 2011; Eger 2015.

genres merely reflect social practices and ideas. Indeed, this introduction started by noting that late ancient historiography was by its very nature focused on the Roman Empire and presupposed its centrality. The change in geographical focus this volume has traced is thus one way of chronicling the transformation of historiography in late antiquity: by the time Rome and Constantinople have become just two of many possible centres, we may have entered the Middle Ages.

CHAPTER I

Constantinople's Belated Hegemony

Anthony Kaldellis

By the end of the fourth century, Constantinople, New Rome, had been endowed with a constellation of monuments that collectively signified the City's centrality in imperial space, in conceptions of time, and the very ordering of the physical world. The Milion, a *tetrapylon* (or *quadrifrons*) built by Constantine at the end of the Mese boulevard, stood as a symbolic "zero point" in the geography of empire, analogous to Elder Rome's *Miliarium Aureum*.[1] The Milion had a clock, called the "clock of the City," attached to it, thus marking time in addition to space.[2] Another massive *tetrapylon* stood between the fora of Constantine and Theodosius I, and was likely built by the latter: this one featured a huge bronze weathervane at the top of its pyramid in the form of a winged woman, and so was called Anemodoulion, or the "servant of the winds." Its carvings included images of the personifications of the winds and the tamed natural world, which the monument mapped and measured.[3] Valentinian I, or more likely his brother Valens, set up the bronze Modion ("Measure"), a monument that functioned as a measuring standard for grain volumes.[4] Equipped with these and other instruments, Constantinople surveyed, ordered, and measured the world: it was a kind of architectural metronome of the empire and cosmos. The fourth-century orator Themistius already called the City an *omphalos*, or navel, an image that had a long history ahead of it.[5]

The City certainly succeeded in becoming the hub of its own civilization, which we name Byzantium after it. The beginning of Byzantine history is traditionally dated to the inauguration of Constantinople in AD 330, and the City eventually became so important to the eastern empire that a historian has flatly asserted in a title

---

[1] Milion: Müller-Wiener 1977: 216–18.
[2] Lydus, *On the Magistracies* 3.35; Malalas, *Chronicle* 18.85; see Anderson 2014.
[3] For the main sources and previous bibliography, see Anderson 2011.   [4] Lenski 2002: 269.
[5] Themistius, *Oration* 18.222c; see Magdalino 2005.

that "Byzantium = Constantinople."[6] The Byzantine empire can even be compared to a city-state, especially in its middle and late phases.

However, Constantinople's centrality to the governance and identity of the eastern empire and its placement at the center of a cosmos of sorts was only belatedly recognized in late antique historiography, a problem that will be the focus of this chapter. Specifically, it is not until the *sixth* century that historiography comes around to placing Constantinople at the center of its geographical and political view of the world. It is also in the sixth century that auxiliary genres and literary modalities such as antiquarianism and mythography were deployed to flesh out the backstory of Constantinople's rise and prominence, to naturalize its centrality in retrospect, long after it had been accomplished in fact, and to make it seem inevitable. But why did it take two centuries for Constantinople to become a conceptual center around which narratives were structured? After all, it had been founded from the beginning to be a counterpart and "branch office" of Rome in the east.[7] Emperors did not reside there in person for the first fifty years or so,[8] but after Theodosius I (379–395) it became their permanent residence and also the most important political center in the Roman world, both east and west, especially as Elder Rome declined during the same period. It was the eastern empire and the regime in Constantinople that intervened in the affairs of the west in the fifth century, not the reverse. So why did its importance not translate into a corresponding conception of historiographical space until the sixth century, by which point the eastern empire was reconquering the west?

The problem is not limited to historiography but extends to many aspects of our knowledge of early Constantinople, which is sparse, no matter the genre. For example, it is not until the works of Zosimus, Hesychius, and John Malalas – in the early sixth century – that we have quasihistorical texts that pay focused attention to the monuments and topography of Constantine's foundation (rather than the merely incidental asides that we find earlier). It is only from John Lydus (sixth century) that we learn about the pagan rituals that accompanied the inauguration of the City. Only in the sixth century are we told that Constantine moved the famous Palladium from Rome to Constantinople, placing it beneath the famous porphyry column in his forum. In a striking reversal of the normal sequence, then, pagan accounts of the foundation (Zosimus, Hesychius, John the Lydian) appear later than Christian ones (found in ecclesiastical history, from Eusebius on). Neither type of account, of course, can be fully trusted on the religious aspect. Therefore, scholars

---

[6] Magdalino 2010.   [7] Grig and Kelly 2012: 3–30; Lenksi 2014.   [8] Discussed by Van Dam 2014.

researching the foundation of the City have to cope with the late prove-
nance and uncertain value of this material.[9] It is methodologically impossible to know whether it was invented during the two-century interval or
whether it did in fact derive from the foundation but only happened to be
reported later in our surviving sources. Regarding early Constantinople,
then, Roman historiography kept it in the margins for too long and found
its focus too late, leaving us with an unsatisfactory and ambiguous record.

A methodological problem with apparent silences must be acknowledged at the outset. A great deal of fourth- and fifth-century literature did
not survive or was later subsumed and superseded by its successors. For
example, we know that there were stand-alone accounts of the reign of
Constantine produced in the fourth century (e.g., by Praxagoras and
Bemarchius) that may have covered the foundation of Constantinople in
detail, but tracing their influence on the later tradition is almost
impossible.[10] Yet this problem is not debilitating. Our main focus is on
historiography, not on any kind of text that may have included discussions
of Constantinople, and the trajectory from its absence in the fourth
century (in many texts) to its centrality in the sixth (again, in many
texts) holds reasonably well. The fifth century represents our largest gap
in the historiographical record, but that may be because fewer texts were
produced in that period and we can form relatively clear impressions of the
contents of those that were. They will be discussed individually in what
follows.

This chapter will start at the end point, the sixth century, to establish
a heuristic benchmark for the eventual centrality of the City in historiographical space. It will then go back to the start and trace its gradual
emergence in preceding centuries.

The Sixth Century: Constantinople's Rise to Centrality

The first extant text that shines the spotlight directly on Constantinople
and grants it a central historical role is the *Patria* of Hesychius of Miletus
(writing in ca. 520). This brief extract traces the ancient history of
Byzantium through its various transformations as a Greek, Roman, and
finally Constantinian city, a history that Hesychius models directly on that
of Republican Rome. In his vision, New Rome was prepared by history,
even destined, to inherit the torch of Elder Rome and continue on as an

---

[9] For all the topics mentioned, see Dagron 1974.   [10] Janiszewski 2006: 352–80; Krallis 2014.

imperial capital in its place. At the very start of the *Patria*, he makes the cryptic statement that, by the time of Constantine, Elder Rome had "reached its limit" (τῶν πραγμάτων αὐτῆς ἤδη πρὸς πέρας ἀφιγμένων), which may mean that it had reached its maximum extent as an empire or, more likely, that its historical destiny had run its course.[11] The literary effort made in the sixth century to place Constantinople at the center did not, then, neglect to look back and flesh out its pre-Constantinian past, balancing its refoundation by Constantine and its imperial future with a matching background. The foundation thus sits at the nexus of ancient Byzantium's long, distinguished, and quasi-Republican past (on the one hand) and its Roman imperial future (on the other). Therefore, the City's centrality is posited here as temporal too, not only spatial-imperial. The *Patria* is likely an excerpt from Hesychius's lost *Roman and General History* (in six books), whose narrative framework was the history of Rome. Its fifth book ended with the foundation of Constantinople, while the sixth went down to the reign of Anastasius (491–518). Thus, by the end of the work, time too was aligned with Constantinople, as the western empire had ceased to exist. Imperial time and space were henceforth assumed to be Constantinopolitan time and space.

This same structuring of time is found in John Lydus, who read Hesychius. At the start of his work *On the Magistracies of the Roman State* (ca. 554), Lydus divides time into the same Roman-defined periods as are found in Hesychius, the last of which begins with "the foundation of this here most fortunate City."[12] Its foundation was not just one event recorded among others in a linear sequence, but rather it marked a new phase of Roman history, "from the foundation of Constantinople to the present." The potential for this view of history probably emerged in the later fifth century, as the eastern empire grew aware that it was the only one left,[13] and was then realized in the early sixth. We can observe the process in the Latin (but Constantinopolitan) chronicle of Marcellinus *comes*, written at the court of Justinian (ca. 530). Marcellinus was continuing Jerome's version of Eusebius's chronicle, which went down to 378. In his preface, Marcellinus notes that Eusebius's original version went from Creation to Constantine, and Jerome then continued it to Valens. Marcellinus now proposes to extend this down to the present but "following the eastern

[11] Hesychius, *Patria* 1; ed. Preger 1901: 1–18; and see also the entry in Photius, *Bibliotheke* cod. 69; in general, Kaldellis, 2005; tr. and commentary: idem in BNJ 390. For ancient ideas of Rome's prophesied demise, see Olbrich 2006.

[12] Lydus, *On the Magistracies* 1.2; ed. and tr. Bandy 1983; see, in general, Wallinga 1992.

[13] Kaegi 1968.

empire." Chronology is henceforth explicitly attached to one branch of the empire (Marcellinus surveys both western and eastern events, though he focuses on eastern ones).[14] And to mark the accession of his patron Justinian, he calculates the number of years since the foundation of Constantinople (197 years in AD 527).

The three works of Procopius of Caesarea (ca. 550) provide another useful index for tracking Constantinople's rise to dominance in historical geography. In fact, more than an index, they may have been the first works of historiography to reflect a Constantinopolitano-centric perception of the world, a fact that may partially explain their popularity among later Byzantine readers. Constantinople's hegemony over the structure of time is not so much an issue in Procopius because his works cover a relatively compressed time frame, the first thirty years or so of Justinian's reign. But in spatial terms, they present an interesting aggregate profile. The *Wars* is often seen as a "doughnut," in which the narrative takes places mostly along the periphery with almost nothing in the center. Yet this shape emphasizes the center just as much, or even more, than if the doughnut were filled in. The heart of Procopius's world is Justinian, who is men-tioned in the first sentence of the preface of the *Wars* as responsible for the wars against the barbarians, and throughout the work he is stationed at the center of a web of agents, diplomats, and armies. Moreover, when Procopius recounts the most dramatic event that affected the entire empire, the plague, he does so from a Constantinopolitan perspective. Granted, this was in part because he was there. However, he, a native of Caesarea in Palestine, was there because it was the center of his world, as it was for most imperial historians of his age. A map of their birthplaces and workplaces consists of spokes radiating upward from the provinces to the capital.[15]

The "hole" at the center of the *Wars* has another explanation. Procopius intended to fill that jelly-core separately with a dossier that eventually became the *Secret History*. He may have intended to merge the two works, but that could be done only after a regime change, and Justinian was showing no signs of dying.[16] Making the best of this situation, Procopius arranged it so that, while the *Wars* covered what we might call

---

[14] The *Chronicle of Marcellinus*, ed. and tr. Croke 1995; a full-length study in Croke 2001. Marcellinus wrote a separate work on Constantinople and Jerusalem, attested by Cassiodorus (but lost): Croke 1984; Van Hoof and Van Nuffelen forthcoming.

[15] Treadgold 2007: 380–1.

[16] Cf. Greatrex 2000. Many theories circulate about the motives behind the work, but they are only interesting conjectures; e.g., Börm 2015. For the making of the *Secret History*, see Kaldellis 2009.

the empire's "foreign history," the *Secret History* was its "domestic history."[17] Now, most of the *Secret History* concerns Constantinople, of which it provides a fascinating ethnography. The capital is the only place in the work whose life we glimpse in a relatively full way, whereas other places inside the empire appear only in anecdotes or asides. (Even so, Procopius exhibits more interest in provincial affairs than do later Byzantine historians, so the narrowing of spatial focus to the capital and military frontier is not yet so extreme as it would later become.)

A more integrated view of the empire is presented in the *Buildings*. This work is not primarily historical, but it confirms the spatial outlook of the chief historian of the age. The first book, its gateway, is devoted to Constantinople and contains Procopius's most impressive rhetorical demonstrations, including the ekphrasis of Hagia Sophia. His choice of words is significant. He says that Justinian's buildings in Byzantium, better than any of the others, will provide "the foundation (*krepis*) of his account," and then he quotes Pindar's *Olympian Ode* 6, according to which one must set a shining face on any work that is just beginning.[18] Byzantium is thus the shining face of the entire world in the *Buildings*. And insofar as the work is a textual representation of the entire world, Constantinople emerges as its "foundation," an expression analogous to Ammianus's *templum mundi totius* – the temple of the entire world – only he had used it in reference to Elder Rome.[19] The distance that separates the face and foundation from the rest of the world is emphasized again at the start of book 2, where Procopius takes us from the capital to the "farthest limits of Roman territory,"[20] i.e., the military frontier. This replays the center-periphery polarity of the *Wars* and *Secret History*, only in reverse order.

Our third and final sixth-century author is John Malalas. His bizarre chronicle, which survives only in a later epitome, remains one of the most poorly understood and yet still important texts of this period. I set aside here the issue of his (possibly invented) sources and his fantastic versions of both mythology and history and look only at his shift in narrative focus, which, in circa 530, moves from a largely Antiochene perspective to a Constantinopolitan one. The author is accordingly presumed to have moved from Antioch to Constantinople, where he later updated his

---

[17] Procopius, *Secret History* 1.1; *pace* Haldén 2012: 282, who believes the distinction was unthinkable before modernity.
[18] Procopius, *Buildings* 1.1.18–19; Pindar, *Olympian Ode* 6.4.
[19] Ammianus Marcellinus, *Res Gestae* 17.4.13; see below for Ammianus.
[20] Procopius, *Buildings* 2.1.2.

chronicle possibly as late as into the 570s (though I am skeptical of this biographical reconstruction).[21] Whether this shift in perspective resulted from the author's physical move or the addition of a supplement by a later author (and thus the creation of a composite text), it nicely exemplifies the gradual "corralling" of historiography into the Constantinopolitan fold. Between the years 528 and 529, where one of the seams in the work has been postulated, Malalas engages in a chronological computation, as if to mark the shift, tallying up the years to the reign of Justinian starting from (1) the Creation, (2) the foundation of Rome, and (3) the foundation of Constantinople. Thus Constantinople and the reigns of its emperors henceforth define the passage of time. In this matter, Malalas was probably echoing Justinian, who also calculated the passage of Roman time from its origin down to himself. And the last book of the chronicle, which covers the reign of Justinian, seems to have been partially based on official notices issued by the court.[22] Here, then, it is not only Constantinople but, more narrowly, the palace's view of history that comes to prevail.

Let us briefly look forward from here. Once in place, this outlook centered on Constantinople dominated Byzantine historiography, which focused on emperors in the City and on the military frontier. One rarely finds information in it about life in the provinces, for which we have to turn to other genres such as hagiography. Some works of Byzantine historiography are so tightly focused even within the City that, unless the reader knows intimately the layout of the imperial palace, it is hard to follow the narrative.[23] The great exception is the *Chronicle* of Theophanes the Confessor (ca. 813), which used Near Eastern materials through various intermediaries and therefore presents a more multipolar view of the world, though Constantinople predominates overall.[24]

We must now turn back to the period between the foundation of Constantinople and the reign of Justinian. How and why did it take Roman historiography two centuries to place Constantinople in the middle of its mental geography? As things that did not happen are difficult if not impossible to explain, we must be precise about what the question is. For example, Procopius tells us in the preface of the *Secret History* why Constantinople is generally missing from his *Wars*: it was because he was afraid of the regime and could not tell the truth about what it was doing

---

[21] Croke 1990b; Treadgold 2007.
[22] Malalas, *Chronicle* 18.8; ed. Thurn 2000; tr. Jeffreys et al. 1986; cf. Justinian, prefaces to the *Tanta* and *Deo auctore* (in the *Novellae*); see Wallinga 1992: 365–72; last book: Scott 1985: 99–109.
[23] Featherstone 2012.
[24] Mango 1988–9. The debate about those intermediaries is ongoing. The latest salvo is Conterno 2014.

there. Thus fear explains the doughnut shape of the *Wars*. But here we are investigating the broad mental geography that shaped the writing of history between 330 and circa 520. By 400, Constantinople was the permanent home of the imperial court that governed the eastern empire (and, at times, the western one too). It was legally equivalent to Rome, monumentally its equal, and outpacing it demographically. So why did it not sooner generate histories that placed it in the middle comparable to those that had told the story of Rome? And, conversely, what happened in the sixth century that such histories were produced? Facing such questions, we can only identify factors, not propose definitive explanations. After all, the appearance (or not) of a historical text covering a certain period was an unpredictable event, stemming from mostly personal initiative and so governed by private motives. There was no "official historiography."[25]

The Fourth Century: The Absent Capital

The "mobile empire" of the third and fourth centuries already had a decentering effect. Ray Van Dam has cleverly shown how the Roman Empire turned "inside out": emperors largely ceased to reside in Rome and moved to the frontiers; the armies were politically more powerful than the political and civic institutions in the capital; and the extension of citizenship after 212 turned the provinces into a vast Roman world (*orbis*) that, in the long run, outweighed the Roman city (*urbs*). "Second Romes" began to proliferate along the former periphery wherever emperors resided, from Trier and Sirmium to Nicomedia and Antioch. Constantinople, for all that it was conceived on a grander scale, was at first only the latest in a series of such provincial Romes-for-a-day.[26] Byzantium, in Thrace, went from being near the frontier to being the new capital, and Rome went from being the capital to, after 476, being on the frontier. Under Justinian, Rome was even conquered by Roman armies from New Rome.[27] Cassius Dio and Herodian were the last historians who could assume a conception of imperial space of which Rome was the center. It was appropriate that the latter author gave wonderful expression to this decentering with the phrase "Rome was now wherever the emperor was," the late antique sequel to Tacitus's famous *arcanum imperii* that the emperor could be *made* elsewhere than at Rome.[28] Now not even Rome was at Rome. In the early third century it was destabilized and dispersed throughout the provinces, and it

[25] Cf. Kaldellis 2010.   [26] Van Dam 2007: 35–78.   [27] Van Dam 2010: 50.
[28] Herodian, *Events after Marcus Aurelius* 1.6.5; Tacitus, *Histories* 1.4.2.

was not until the 380s that it regrouped and coalesced again in the east, when Constantinople began to emerge as a fixed center of imperial governance. Even then, however, contemporaries could not take it for granted that this new configuration would endure, far less that it would create an entire world centered on itself (which we call Byzantium). The struggle of Constantinople for hegemony in historiography was the same as its struggle to impose order on this decentered late Roman world, but politically and symbolically. Judging by the historiography of this period, it would appear that this struggle lasted until the reign of Justinian.

The surviving portion (353–378) of the history of Ammianus Marcellinus reflects this more dispersed, frontier-oriented Roman world, defined by itinerant emperorship. To be sure, Ammianus holds Rome to be the crucible and mother of empire, but this is a symbolic position of honor. It is the vision of a past greatness that Ammianus sees reflected in the Eternal City. His treatment of its current residents and especially its aristocracy can be sarcastic and bitter. Moreover, Gavin Kelly has astutely noted that Ammianus is curiously silent about Constantinople, failing to mention it where logic demanded it, and these silences seem even to be scornful.[29] It is not possible to fully explain them, but they may correlate with identifiable trends in the fourth century that may have delayed the onset of Constantinopolitan hegemony. Specifically, some later Romans were devoted to the memory and traditions of Rome and were unwilling to recognize its counterpart in the east as a peer, and there were others who were hostile to Constantinople because it exemplified the empire's Christian turn, or because it diminished the relative standing of other cities in the east, or both.

The first group included the historians Ammianus and Aurelius Victor (a Roman senator) and the Latin poets Ausonius and Claudian, the last of whom found himself representing the western court in moments of tension with the eastern one. All these western-oriented, Latin writers made little or no effort to adjust their perception of the world to accommodate the weird phenomenon of a New Rome in the east.[30] So whereas the prior dominance of Elder Rome in historiography entailed a consensus by all provincial elites about its centrality, including on the part of eastern writers, no one in the late Roman *west* made room in their conception of the world for Constantinople. It was up to easterners to generate such

[29] Kelly 2003: 588–607.
[30] Ibid.: 588–9; and "Claudian and Constantinople," in idem and Grig 2012: 241–64; for the pointed scorn of the *Expositio totius mundi*, see Dagron 1974: 53–4.

a conception, but some of them too were wedded to old Romano-centric ideas. One example from historiography is Zosimus (ca. 500), a career bureaucrat in Constantinople. His work may have been called the *New History* but the logic of its narrative of Roman decline was focused on Old Rome and especially on the loss of its pagan traditions. Zosimus's talk about the decline and fall of the empire, culminating in events such as the sack of Rome in 410, and his failure to articulate a model for how the eastern empire might have represented a continuation or successor to the now-fallen west, have led some historians to conclude that he imagined himself as living in a post-Roman era.[31] This goes too far, but Elder Rome is certainly central to his notion of Roman identity.[32] (We will discuss Zosimus's awkward inclusion of Constantinople below.)

The second group, attested only in the fourth century, consisted of eastern writers who looked askance on the rise of Constantinople because it soaked up people, elites, careers, food, taxes, prestige, and monuments from other eastern cities. In addition to (possibly) Ammianus, this group included Libanius and Eunapius, and it is likely that their distaste was amplified by religion, as they were pagans alienated by the empire's Christian turn. For them, Constantinople likely epitomized this revolution, though they were in no position to see it as final, for the process of its establishment had just begun.[33] These three men were probably more closely connected than we can reconstruct. Libanius corresponded with his fellow-Antiochene Ammianus in Rome, who had possibly read the *History* of Eunapius, who had, in turn, read the orations of Libanius.[34] This is significant because it implies the existence of an anti-Constantinopolitan attitude among precisely those *eastern* intellectual circles who were likely to produce histories of the eastern empire in the classical tradition; and this particular circle happened to include the two most important historians of the later fourth century. We have only fragments of Eunapius's *History*, which was much used by his contemporaries, but not enough to form an impression of its conception of space; for example, did it focus on specific regions or the careers of specific men? Most of the fragments concern barbarian and civil wars, and Constantinople is rarely mentioned, even

---

[31] Goffart 1971, and some of his followers.

[32] For a close reading of Zosimus on Rome and Constantinople, see Kruse forthcoming.

[33] Libanius, *Orations* 1.279, 30.37, 18.177: see Dagron 1974: 56, 64–5, 135; Cameron 2011: 656–7; but see the skeptical reading of Libanius's professed distaste by Van Hoof 2011. Eunapius, *Lives of the Philosophers* 462, 490, 495: see now Hartmann 2014. Religious motives are tentatively postulated for Ammianus by Kelly 2012: 589–90, 607.

[34] For Libanius and Ammianus, see Kelly 2008 passim (index for Libanius); for Ammianus and Eunapius, see Cameron 2011: 670–8; for Eunapius and Libanius, see Watts 2014: 217–18.

though the work must have had an eastern focus (at one place Eunapius admits that he was not able to obtain information about events in the west). It is, however, likely that Eunapius had the same negative attitude toward Constantinople in the *History* that he expressed in his surviving work, the *Lives of the Philosophers*. He was certainly alienated from the Christian court of the Theodosian dynasty, criticizing almost all its members.[35]

In sum, in the fourth century Constantinople faced an uphill struggle on many fronts merely to be recognized even by Roman writers in the east as important, far less as an equal to Rome, or the center of its own world. The only eastern intellectual making the case for its parity to Rome was Themistius, the pagan spokesman for the Christian emperors, who entrusted him with important aspects of the City's development, especially the recruitment of local elites into its Senate. Themistius wove his pride for the new City into his orations, although he did not write a history and was criticized as a sellout in the east by those who were suspicious of the new capital and its court.[36] Yet it was his outlook that would ultimately prevail, and this may partly explain the survival and popularity of his orations later on. He projected pride in Constantinople and a pagan but accommodating philosophical message that was amenable to Christian rule, i.e., just what later Byzantines wanted.

The Multipolar World of the Fifth Century

During the fifth century, Constantinople grew in size, population, and political importance as Rome declined, and the eastern empire flourished while the western one dissolved. The eastern emperors began to reside permanently at Constantinople. Yet Constantinopolitan hegemony still did not emerge in historiographical discourse. In many ways, the empire of the fifth century still remained a multipolar world that resisted the hegemony of a single city. I survey, in turn, ecclesiastical and secular historiography.

Ecclesiastically Constantinople was hardly dominant in the fifth century. That era's Church politics present a geographical configuration strikingly reminiscent of the Hellenistic age: Alexandria, Antioch, Rome, and Jerusalem – plus Constantinople, the only Patriarchate lacking

---

[35] Text and tr. of the fragments of the *History* in Blockley 1981–3, v. 2: 2–150; west: F66.2. See n. 33 for his *Lives*.
[36] Dagron 1968, 1–242; Vanderspoel 2012.

a Hellenistic past. The deeply political conflicts among the great prelates of these cities are well known. In the fifth century, the bishops of the other cities could join forces to take down the Patriarch of Constantinople, and it was not certain that even the emperor would support him. Also, while the Councils of Constantinople (381) and Chalcedon (451) decreed that New Rome was to be elevated above other sees in rank and brought almost to the level of Rome, this met with considerable resistance in practice. Ecclesiastical relations between Rome and Constantinople in particular inhibited a Constantinopolitano-centric theory of the Church, assuming that anyone was inclined to produce one. So while we have histories written in the eastern capital (by Socrates and Sozomen) that are laudatory of its resident emperor, Theodosius II, their tableau of Church politics is multipolar, almost confusingly so. The bishops and monks who played leading parts in the history of the Church came from all over the empire, and so these works' narrative focus shifts from Alexandria and Constantinople to the desert, Rome, and Antioch, as the Church historians tried to weave it all into a coherent tapestry. In their later books, however, covering the early fifth century, Socrates and Sozomen sharpen their focus on Constantinople.[37] Ecclesiastical historians may have generally tended to favor one see over the others in the relative extent and quality of their coverage (e.g., as Evagrius did with Antioch in the later sixth century), but the world of the Church was nowhere near as centralized as that of imperial authority. Whatever advantage Constantinople gained from its canonical standing and from being the seat of imperial power was implicitly contested by narratives that emanated from its peers (or rivals). The *Liber Pontificalis*, which was begun in the sixth century, promoted the claims of Rome in literary format that replaced the lives of emperors with those of popes, and some similarly self-assertive projects emanated from Alexandria.[38]

Secular historiography in the fifth-century east is problematic because the texts survive only in fragments and quotations, which, even in aggregate, are not necessarily representative of their original outlook and contents. Olympiodorus of Thebes published his history in circa 426, Priscus of Panion in circa 476, and then we have a cluster around circa 500, including Zosimus (who may in fact be placed decades earlier or later), Malchus of Philadelphia (ca. 480?), Candidus (who wrote about the Roman-Isaurian wars and so will not concern us here),[39] and Eustathius

---

[37] For geo-ecclesiology, see Blaudeau 2006, 2012; for a reading of Roman-Constantinopolitan relations, see Demacopoulos 2013. For the historians, see Van Nuffelen 2004.

[38] Camplani 2015: 85–120.

[39] The development of local identities in historiography may have been responding to a reaffirmed Roman identity at the center: Meier 2014: 171–94.

of Epiphania (ca. 506?, whose lost chronicle has become a major point of contention,[40] and will also not be discussed here). It is mostly in Olympiodorus and Priscus that we must trace our theme through the fifth century.

The history of the pagan Olympiodorus was a major source for the Church historians and Zosimus. It was dedicated to Theodosius II and reflects the eastern court's point of view, but it covers only western affairs. Constantinople figures in it hardly at all. Peter Van Nuffelen has convincingly explained this "paradox," as the history culminates in the restoration of the western emperor Valentinian III by the force of eastern arms in 425. It is a work of eastern imperial triumphalism, for all that it takes places entirely in the west. Part of its purpose is to show how the western court had done everything poorly and needed to be set right by the east.[41] Van Nuffelen's interpretation poses a hermeneutical issue that must be made explicit, specifically the issue of how to interpret silence, which we touched on previously. The eastern court may be largely absent from Olympiodorus's narrative, but the latter cannot be understood without taking it into account, indeed without our making it the key for understanding western events. For the failing west is the negative mirror of the flourishing east, the point of reference for the work, even if it is absent. Constantinople, then, is marked by an "overwhelming absence." This may be an example of the rhetorical strategy in ancient literature of emphasizing something by pointedly omitting it.[42] We are perhaps, then, closer to a view of empire centered on Constantinople, except we are seeing it here for the first time in photonegative. Put differently, Olympiodorus's work culminates in an eastern invasion of Italy, prefiguring Procopius's *Gothic War*. In this case, however, the lead-up is the entire work, with the invasion coming only at the end, i.e., the narrative inverse of Procopius's *Gothic War*.

We have to wait fifty years for the next historian, Priscus of Panion. His extant fragments cover the years 438–471 but, if it was a continuation of Olympiodorus, it would have started in 425. The narrative covers both halves of the empire, and the surviving extracts are not unduly biased in favor of eastern coverage. Constantinople does not appear much, nor is it singled out in any way. This silence, at any rate, may be explained by the process of selection. Much of Priscus survives in the volume of the tenth-century *Excerpta* of Constantine VII dealing with embassies, of which

---

[40] Treadgold 2007: 316; *contra*: Croke 2010: 133–5.
[41] Van Nuffelen 2013. For the text and translation, Blockley 1981–2 v. 2: 151–220.
[42] Ahl 1984: 174–208.

Priscus accompanied many (to Attila, Rome, and Egypt). Thus the focus on foreign affairs may be only apparent.[43] Still, even within these limitations we observe some interesting developments. First, the previously loose distinction between the eastern and the western "parts" of the Roman Empire has by now crystalized and hardened into a firm distinction between a western empire, western emperor, and western Romans on the one hand, and an eastern empire, eastern emperor, and eastern Romans, on the other. What were previously only loose geographical regions within a single empire have now been "reified," though for all that they have separate identities and rulers these two parts still together constitute "the empire of the Romans."[44] This balanced, bipolar articulation of imperial space contrasts with the multipolar world of contemporary Church politics. It is also important to note that for Priscus the eastern Romans are as just as Roman as the western ones: the Roman Empire consists of two distinct parts, both equally Roman. "Indeed, the zealous attachment to Rome of Greek-speaking inhabitants of the eastern provinces . . . at a time when Rome could no longer dominate the Greeks was a remarkable tribute to the empire's persistent ability to assimilate subject peoples and transform them into Romans."[45]

Under such circumstances, we can well imagine that the eastern Romans, governed by Constantinople, would be moving toward formulating a distinct identity, even if only inchoately. Inside Priscus's history they appear as "the Romans of the east" or "the eastern Romans." But the reported title of his work makes an interesting move. According to the *Souda*, Priscus's *History* was subtitled *Byzantine (Byzantiake)* and *The Dealings with Attila*; the Constantinian *Excerpta* calls it the *Gothic History*, i.e., dealing with the Huns. Let us assume that *Byzantiake* was in the original title, which is reinforced by the fact that Malchus (roughly a contemporary) also entitled his history the *Byzantiaka*.[46] *Byzantiake historia* pointed to a conception of history that took its lead from the ancient name of Constantinople, Byzantium, which writers of this period used as an archaism (just as they sometimes called Romans "Ausonians," and so on). It is conventional in Byzantine studies to say that the terms "Byzantium" and "Byzantine" were invented in the early modern period to refer to the eastern Roman Empire, while in Byzantium they were

---

[43] Text and translation in Blockley 1981–2 v. 2: 221–400; another edition by Carolla 2008; in general, see Treadgold 2007: 96–103. For the Constantinian *Excerpta*, see Kaldellis 2015a: 35–46.

[44] Priscus, *History* F17 (p. 302), 20 (p. 304), 31 (pp. 332–4), and passim.

[45] Kaegi 1968: 112–13: For the eastern, Greek-speaking world as Roman, see Kaldellis 2007, ch. 2.

[46] Text and translation in Blockley 1981–2 v. 2: 401–62, here 402 (from Photius, *Bibliotheke* cod. 78).

archaisms that referred only to inhabitants of Constantinople, not to the empire as a whole (the Byzantines as a whole were otherwise just "Romans," down to and after 1453). But in the title of these two works we face the prospect of "Byzantine" being used to refer to the eastern empire as a whole, not just to the City. In them, the City lent its archaic name to a conception of imperial history that also covered the west. The works of Priscus and Malchus were not "local" histories focusing on Constantinople. In them, the City, as "Byzantium," was extending its name and identity to an eastern empire that would soon find itself without a western partner. What would it become, then, after 476?

Byzantiaka turned out to be a nonstarter as a name for the eastern empire.[47] After circa 500, Byzantine historians called their works either generically a History (or Chronicle or whatever) or a Roman History. The first known writer of the newly independent eastern empire to call his work a Roman History was Hesychius of Miletus, discussed previously. So now that we have closed the circle, we can return to the early sixth century and look again at the outlook of its historiography. Why the sudden burst of interest in the City and its Romanness?

Explaining the Centrality of Constantinople

The intensive and multipronged project to Romanize Constantinople in the sixth century, I propose, stemmed in part from the existential challenge of carrying on as an (eastern but now sole) Roman Empire, without Rome, and in part from political developments internal to the regime at Constantinople (which I touch on at the end of this chapter). In 330, New Rome made sense only against the template provided by Rome. In terms of its buildings, names, and institutions, its standing as an imperial capital was anchored in the living model set by the Eternal City, for all that Byzantion lacked a proper imperial history. But after the fall of the western empire in 476, and then again after the 520s, when relations soured between Constantinople and the Goths who were ruling Italy ostensibly in the name of the eastern emperors, it became a more pressing issue to define how Constantinople was "the" surviving Roman capital in a world in which Rome was a marginal city on the imperial periphery. The deep interest in ancient Rome, especially in the Republican period, that we observe in so much sixth-century eastern literature was part of a project of

---

[47] Stephanus of Byzantium, Ethnika, s.v. Gotthoi, refers to another (?) Byzantiaka; ed. and tr. Billerbeck, 2006 vol. 1: 434–5 (possibly a City chronicle).

Roman reinvention, an attempt to explain how a predominantly Greek-speaking city could be even more Roman than Rome. The new City already had the requisite monuments: what it needed were the more intangible accoutrements, especially historical, religious, and cultic. This had the dual effect of Romanizing the history of Constantinople and recentering Roman history on Constantinople.

Justinian was many things – conqueror, theologian, and builder – but it is not well known that he was also a historian, of sorts. In the prefaces to many of his *Novels* and other legal enactments, he justified his laws, reforms, and policies by appealing to Roman history, both ancient and recent. Justinian claimed to be revitalizing ancient virtues to roll back the losses incurred by recent emperors, i.e., what we call the fall of the western empire. Thanks to Justinian's codification of Roman law, we do not have the prefaces to the laws of previous emperors, so we do not know whether they too had regularly appealed to Roman history in this way or whether Justinian was innovating. As Justinian's view of history and the responses to it by writers of the period will be treated in a separate study by Marion Kruse,[48] I set it aside here to concentrate on other historical projects of the sixth century, including antiquarian research.

Hesychius of Miletos endowed ancient Byzantium with a parallel Roman past of its own. His project has two fascinating aspects. First, he constructs this quasi-Roman past for Constantinople out of *Greek* mythical and historical components. Second, it is thoroughly pagan. Hesychius endows the history and topography of Constantinople, even its current Christian sites, with pagan cultic backgrounds. What mattered to him about Rome was not just its ancient history but also its rich pagan matrix, the way in which sites and memory could be linked to ancient founders through cultic and mythological associations. John Lydus, who knew Hesychius's work, pursued a parallel project that was both pagan-cultic and historical. Lydus worked for the prefecture of the East and taught Latin in Constantinople. His work *On the Magistracies of the Roman State* traces the history and genealogy of the offices of the eastern empire back to the period of the Republic and, beyond even that, to the kings. One goal of the work is to criticize the changes to the administration that were being introduced by Justinian and his officials, including the gradual switch from the use of Latin to Greek. These changes, he believed, were taking the empire away from its authentic Roman roots. But at the same time, Lydus follows previous Greek scholars in tracing the origins of Rome back

---

[48] Kruse forthcoming.

to Greek roots, specifically to Aeolia (perhaps not coincidentally, Lydus was from Aeolian Philadelphia). Thus he too, like Hesychius, was reinventing Roman traditions on a Greek bedrock. The most striking aspect of his politics is his nostalgia for the "free" Republic and his argument that emperors, *all* of them by virtue of their office, were basically illegitimate tyrants. In pursuit of Roman authenticity, Lydus was willing to go deep and far. He was appalled at the changes that Justinian was introducing in the name of Roman tradition.[49]

This political stance may be linked to the fact that Lydus was a devotee of Rome in the field of religion too. His work of research on the Roman calendar, *On the Months*, survives in fragments and extracts and has generally been neglected in modern times. At first sight, most of it does not deal directly with Constantinople, but we need to look closer. The work provides a philosophical and cultic *interpretatio Graeca* of the Roman calendar that was then in use in the east. And if we look more closely, we find many equivalents of Hesychius's "paganization" of the topography of Constantinople. For example, Lydus explains the origins and pagan associations of the hippodrome at Rome, but in the course of his exposition it becomes clear that he is also, or primarily, talking about the one in Constantinople. Likewise, he explores the pagan backgrounds of the triumph, the imperial vestments, and even the vestments of the archbishop of Constantinople. Lydus was creating a cultic backstory for the City by drawing from Roman paganism, which, in turn, derived for him from Greek paganism. In a passage that has troubled many modern scholars of Constantine, Lydus alludes to the pagan rites that accompanied the foundation of Constantinople: the two protagonists in his story are a Roman senator and a Greek Platonist philosopher.[50] These two figures nicely stand in for the twin basis of Lydus's antiquarian project.

Just as Constantinople was moving to dominate eastern historiography, these writers were actively paganizing its past. I have argued elsewhere that they belonged to the surviving pagan intellectual circles of the eastern empire, and were not Christians dallying with classical traditions (though for the purposes of this inquiry it makes no difference).[51] We saw in the

[49] Aeolia: Lydus, *On the Magistracies* 1.5; in general, see Maas 1992; for his politics, see Kaldellis 2005.
[50] Lydus, *On the Months* 1.2, 1.12, 1.20, 1.21, 4.2, 4.30. For the foundation rites, cf. Watts 2014: 71, 246 nn. 73–4, with Barnes 2011: 126–31.
[51] For Lydus's religion, see Kaldellis 2003: 300–16. There is in fact much more evidence for Lydus's paganism than is offered there, which I intend to present separately. The alternative model would be like that argued for Macrobius by Alan Cameron, most recently in *The Last Pagans* (2011), a study from which paganism and especially the gods are strikingly absent; its pagans are all Christians-in-

preceding text that pagan writers in the fourth-century east had spurned Constantinople. Here we have sixth-century eastern writers who were fascinated with ancient paganism embracing Constantinople, but only after they had reinvented it on pagan terms. The lateness of this pagan embrace of the City, which took place long after Constantinople had been invested with Christian associations in Church circles, is one of the reasons why we will never know the truth about the "original" character of its foundation. I personally suspect the foundation was neither pagan nor Christian in an overt or unambiguous way – Constantine was a master of calculated ambiguity. But by the sixth century, it had been endowed with parallel foundation narratives in each religious tradition.

A possible source for the information that we find in Hesychius, Lydus, and Malalas about early Constantinople was the *patria* tradition, basically city-focused chronicles that provided accounts of origins (often fantastic).[52] Many such texts were written in late antiquity on a variety of cities, though most are lost. We happen to know of one on Constantinople written in circa 500 by the poet Christodorus (who wrote the *Ekphrasis of the Statues in the Zeuxippos Baths = Greek Anthology* II). Geographically each of these texts was centered on one location, but together, as a corpus, they would have presented a pluricentric view of the empire similar to that found in ecclesiastical history, for the *patria* highlighted local traditions and histories. A related genre were "city chronicles." The snippets of the history of Constantinople that we find in Malalas and the seventh-century *Paschal Chronicle* may have come from such a text or set of texts.[53] More work needs to be done on their common sources and transmission before they reached surviving texts. It is possible that the invention of a Roman background for the new eastern capital took place in such texts, from where they were taken by our surviving sources, which reveal curious correspondences that cannot all or easily be explained by their use of each other.

For example, Constantine's transfer of the Palladium from Rome to Constantinople is mentioned in Malalas, Procopius, and the *Paschal Chronicle*.[54] Tales about Apollonius of Tyana (the first-century AD sage) protecting the City against various animals are in Hesychius and Malalas.[55]

---

waiting. Cameron has more recently (2015) pushed back against my readings of sixth-century intellectuals as pagans, to which I will respond in detail, though probably not soon.

[52] Janiszewski 2006: ch. 2, esp. 265–81. The present paragraph benefited greatly from an exchange with Paul Magdalino.

[53] Whitby and Whitby 1989: xvii–xxii; Croke 1990a: esp. 182–6, 193–4.

[54] Malalas, *Chronicle* 13.7; Procopius, *Wars* 5.15.8–14; Paschal *Chronicle* s.a. 328.

[55] Hesychius, *Patria* 25; Malalas, *Chronicle* 10.51; see Dagron 1984: 103–15; Madden 1992: 120–1.

Malalas and Lydus present similar accounts of the origin of chariot races and the symbolism of the hippodrome, in the latter case pointing toward Constantinople.[56] In reading these notices, we cannot help but think that fuller, earlier versions lie behind them. Were they in the original text of Hesychius? In Eustathius of Epiphania? Be that as it may, it is significant that the source of these materials has been lost, superseded by the sixth-century texts. The establishment of Constantinople at the heart of historical geography acted as a filter for the (partial) survival of its own material and the eventual loss of its own sources. Malalas, containing an Antiochene *Patria*, may have survived because of his subsequent move to Constantinople and Constantinopolitan addendum.[57]

The most perplexing historian of the foundation of Constantinople, in the same pagan constellation as Hesychius and John Lydus, is Zosimus. We cannot date him precisely, but we pretend to know that he wrote around 500 (a date that can possibly be moved decades in each direction). Zosimus was openly both a republican and a proponent of Roman paganism and enemy of Christianity. It is likely that the political and the religious are connected here too, as they probably were also in Lydus. That is, by 500 pagan intellectuals may have come to blame the imperial system for the gradual destruction of their ancient beliefs and practices. What we are interested in specifically is the role of Constantinople in Zosimus's history. Zosimus was, of course, hostile to Constantine, but at the same time he is perceived as having failed to combine his different sources into a coherent picture. For all his moral condemnation of the first Christian emperor, Zosimus presents a heroic account of his war against Licinius, drawn likely from one of the panegyrical biographies of Constantine.[58] And for all that he presents the decision to found Constantinople as the outcome of Constantine's crimes, the narrative of the foundation seems to reflect pride in the City. This *may* be our first extant account of the foundation after the vague one in Eusebius's *Life of Constantine*. Unlike Eusebius, Zosimus offers specific topographical information.[59] Whereas Eusebius tried hard to make the City appear as Christian a foundation as possible, and therefore had to suppress or distort most of what he knew about it (such as the statue of Apollo-Constantine in the forum), Zosimus, in violation of the narrative of Constantine's career that he has given so far, makes Constantinople a pagan foundation with

---

[56] Malalas, *Chronicle* 7.3–6; Lydus, *On the Months* 1.12, 4.30 (a more overtly pagan version).
[57] Paul Magdalino (personal communication).   [58] Krallis 2014.
[59] Zosimus, *New History* 2.30–1; cf. Eusebius, *Life of Constantine* 3.48–9, 3.54, 4.58–60.

Constantine absurdly trying to undermine the pagan aspects even as he was setting them up. Late pagans had a problem explaining the success of Constantinople. As we saw, they tried to paganize it and thereby normalize it against its own founder's Christian reputation. Zosimus reflected on the problem openly, and concluded that the City's success had been predicted by an ancient oracle.[60] At any rate, the *New History* is generally not a Constantinopolitano-centric work. It touches on Constantinople only as an aspect of Constantine's reign, of his biography even, as does Eusebius's *Life of Constantine* (only with the reverse interpretive axis).

The emergence of a historical tradition centered on Constantinople was a product of the period following the demise of the western empire and was likely stimulated by it. The reign of Justinian, who tried to reverse that demise, intensified this process. In recent decades, a school of thought has attempted to downsize the significance of the "fall" of the western empire, even, at an extreme, to deny that it even happened. Certainly, the individual steps taken along that path might not have caused existential anguish among the Romans of the east, but its end result did not escape their attention. Proponents of the "transformation" school, who have pushed back against the "decline and fall" school, like to point out that the first text that claims that the western empire "fell" in 476 is the chronicle of Marcellinus, written at the court of Justinian. Specifically, when he notes the deposition of Romulus Augustulus by Odoacer in 476, Marcellinus comments that this event ended the western empire whose history had begun with Augustus 709 years after the foundation of Rome, i.e., in 44/3 BC. This was, he says, the 522nd (and final) year of the western empire.[61] Yet whether or not the date is "artificial," it proves that Romans in the east could see history in those terms. Constantinopolitano-centric histories of Rome and eastern attempts to reclaim the west with armies happened at the same time.

Finally, a Constantinopolitano-centric view of history may have also stemmed from developments internal to the politics of the east, above and beyond the passing of the mantle of empire from the west to the east. This can only be touched on here, as the framework on which it rests requires more work. Still, the survival of the eastern empire between the late fourth and the late fifth centuries was marked by shifts in the distribution of real and symbolic power that tended to reinforce the role of the populace (or *populus*) of the City and create a closer relationship between it and the court. Specifically, it was during this

---

[60] Kaegi 1968: 136–9. [61] See n. 14 for Marcellinus; cf. Croke 1983; Bowersock 1996: 29–43.

period that the ceremonies of acclamation of new emperors shifted from being primarily military events – as under the itinerant military emperors of the third and fourth century – to primarily civilian, held in the hippodrome of Constantinople. The "republican" culmination of this process can be observed in the accession of Anastasius in 491, which was effected by the assembled masses, for whose benefit the emperor promises to work hard, as if he were an elected official.[62]

Another development, parallel to the previous one and probably linked to it, was the gradual emancipation of the political authorities of Constantinople from their quasibarbarian military "handlers," in other words, precisely what did *not* take place in the west, where the generals took over and eventually terminated the imperial authority. This divergence between the two halves of the empire is known,[63] but the people of Constantinople may have played a more important role than is realized, even if only by providing a civilian constituency to which the court could appeal for legitimacy in times of strife.[64] They may have intervened in more practical ways, too, by helping the court solve its Gothic problem in 400 through an uprising and mass slaughter;[65] they proved receptive to the redefinition of imperial virtue as piety rather than generalship proposed by the regime of Theodosius II (408–450);[66] they blocked the general Aspar's efforts to completely dominate Leo I and seem to have then endorsed and supported his murder;[67] and they called for a true "Roman" emperor in 491 to replace the Isaurian Zeno (and Anastasius would in fact wage a long internal war to suppress the Isaurian element in the imperial armies).[68] While much has been made of the consolidation of the imperial order through the public performance of religious processions in the fifth century, it is likely that the partnership extended to politics. The court may have had an interest in endowing the growing populace of Constantinople with the "constitutional" role of a Roman *populus*. This may have provided a domestic political imperative for reviving the modes and orders of ancient

---

[62] Accessions: Christophilopoulou 1956: 10–46; "republican" reading of 491: Kaldellis 2015b: 106–10.

[63] E.g., Liebeschuetz 1990: 94–5.

[64] Pfeilschifter 2013: 294–354, documents in detail the emerging relationship between the court and the people, within the overall context of an Akzeptanz theory of imperial power (Pfeilschifter considers, in turn, the relations between the throne and other pressure-groups, including the soldiers, the priesthood, and the aristocracy).

[65] Ibid. 111–25.   [66] Addressed by a number of chapters in Kelly 2013.

[67] Malalas, *Chronicle* 14.40; and, apparently from a different source, Constantine VII, *Excerpta historica iussu imp. Constantini Porphyrogeniti confecta*, v. 3: *de insidiis*, ed. de Boor 1905: 160: τοῦ δὲ δήμου ἐνστάντος καὶ τῶν μοναχῶν καὶ τῶν κληρικῶν. The event is discussed in detail by Croke 2005a: 147–203, who wants to minimize the ethnic dimension.

[68] Constantine VII, *Book of Ceremonies* 1.92; ed. Reiske 1829–30: 419–20.

Rome in Constantinople, marking the birth of what I have called the Byzantine Republic.[69]

Conclusion

In the fourth century, Constantinople is barely recognized by secular historians. Toward the end of the fifth, its archaic name experimentally becomes a rubric – *Byzantiaka* – that encompasses the entire eastern empire, as a quasiautonomous parallel to the western empire. Finally, in the sixth century, Constantinople moves to the center of both history and historiography, is endowed with many of the narrative attributes of Elder Rome and becomes the main bearer of the Roman imperial-republican tradition. Constantinople becomes a Greek version of Rome, and there was no need for it to have a different name: *Byzantium* as the name of the eastern empire fell out of use for more than a thousand years, and *Romanía* – "Romanland" – took its place. The beating heart of Romanía was New Rome, and time and space were both henceforth organized around it.

[69] Kaldellis 2015b.

CHAPTER 2

Beside the Rim of the Ocean
The Edges of the World in Fifth- and Sixth-Century Historiography

Peter Van Nuffelen

In his panegyrical description of Hagia Sophia, delivered between 24 December 562 and 6 January 563, Paul the Silentiary praises Justinian for having domesticated seas and rivers. 'These things', he continues, 'together with Western, Libyan, and Eastern triumphs, honour your power beside the rim of the Ocean'.[1] This is reminiscent of the praise of Pseudo-Themistius for an emperor tentatively identified with Justinian.[2] Such statements are topical, for imperial power was inherently universal: the claim to dominate the entire world is the spatial expression of the Roman Empire.[3] As C. Nicolet has shown for Augustus, claims of world domination go hand in hand with claims to knowledge about that world.[4] Yet the edges of the world mark the limits of power and knowledge. In a view of the world that identifies civilisation with centrality, the centre needs the periphery to affirm its own claim to civilisation. Precisely this was a function of ancient ethnographic accounts, even when they depicted barbarian nations as bulwarks of virtues that had been lost in Rome, as Tacitus did in the *Germania*.[5] Nevertheless, the periphery always escaped the firm grasp of the centre. Much less information was available on

---

[1] Paul the Silentiary, *Description of Hagia Sophia* 935–37. Tr. Bell 2009: 208. On the ideologically charged symbolism of rivers, in particular in Ammianus, see Vergin 2013: 277–83.

[2] Van Hoof and Van Nuffelen 2011: 423: 'But what it is possible to grasp and say for a human being, is that you are worthy, Emperor, to reign not only the Romans or the neighbouring Agarenoi, Iberians, Persians, Alans, the Scythian peoples, but the entire world, all land, inhabited or uninhabited, the whole sea, navigable or unnavigable, the islands of the Ocean and beyond. May you govern and rule these and expand Roman dominion to Cadiz and the pillars of Heracles'. See also Agathias, *Greek Anthology* 4.4.

[3] Symmachus, *Oration* 1.2; Ennodius, *Panegyric for Theoderic* 2.9.

[4] Nicolet 1991. For a similar approach to the collection of knowledge in the ancient world, see König and Woolf 2013.

[5] See most recently Woolf 2011; Almagor and Skinner 2013; Kaldellis 2013; Vergin 2013; Berzon 2016. Merrills 2004 argues that Christian depictions of monks drew on representations of alterity ultimately derived from the classical tradition.

regions farther away, and the edges of the earth had been an object of fascination, speculation and storytelling ever since Homer, as J. Romm has charted.[6] The exploration of the edges of the world is as much a study of the centre's self-representation as one of its awareness of its own limits. The edge of the earth is the crack in the armour of empire.

Late antique political history is characterised by fragmentation, most visibly in the West, but centrifugal tendencies can be observed in the East too. In the Danube region, several groups achieved virtual autonomy, and Isauria proved difficult to control until the end of the fifth century. If language is a proxy for culture, the source material suggests a greater degree of cultural diversity than previously, with substantial literature in Armenian, Syriac, Coptic and Georgian. Christianity introduced new traditions and stories to the social imagination and created new symbolic centres, such as Jerusalem. This finds expression in repeated doubts about whether the centre, Rome, will remain the centre – even though that doubt rarely develops into a rejection of the centre.[7] Furthermore, Rome was challenged and reduplicated in Constantinople.[8] If the centre is shaken, one expects the edges to move too.[9] Indeed, Félix Racine has argued for the sixth century that we see 'a new geographical discourse on exotic lands and people which emerged over the course of the fifth and sixth centuries in texts that could ignore or bypass the classical literary tradition', that is, hagiography and apocryphal acts of apostles, such as those of Andrew, the legend of St. Christopher or the story of St. Zosimus and the Rechabites.[10] Historiography is a different and altogether more conservative type of text, rooted in a long literary tradition, and one that often was closely aligned with the perspective from the centre. Accordingly, this chapter is not interested in verifying Racine's claim and exploring the fantastic vistas obtained at the edge of the world. Rather, I am interested in the role the edges of the world, or more broadly the periphery, play in four works that date from the second half of the fifth and sixth centuries – works,

---

[6] Romm 1994. See also Arnaud 2014; Janković 2014; Natal 2018.

[7] Claudian, *On the War against Gildo* 1.17–128; Orosius, *Histories* 2.3.6, 3.20.10–13; *Gallic Chronicle of 452*, 61; Zosimus 1.57.1, 1.58.4, 2.7, 3.32.6, 4.21.3, 4.59.3; Jordanes, *Romana* 2; Agathias, *Histories* 5.14.1. Cf. Van Nuffelen 2012: 45–62; Harich-Schwarzbauer 2013; Van Nuffelen 2015: 325.

[8] See Chapter 1 by A. Kaldellis; Praet 2018.

[9] Merrills 2005: 20–34 emphasises the impact of Christianity, which led to changes in the world view. With a more intra-Christian focus, cf. Inglebert 2001; Schleicher 2014. See also Chapter 5 by H. Leppin.

[10] Racine 2007: 105. His remark qualifies the position taken by Reed 2009 that Greek and Latin authors remained wedded to a world view that was classically focused on the empire, in contrast to the wider perspectives found in Syriac literature. Cosmas Indicopleustes is usually adduced in this context, but I restrict myself to historiographical texts in this chapter.

moreover, that have a strong tendency to affirm the role of the centre. How do edges and centre dialectically shape one another? What meaning do stories about the edge of the world hold in these histories? And how do they relate to the destabilisation of the core hypothesised previously, if they do so? We shall see that the margins become important places in the narratives, subject to fascination and invention. Yet this dynamic remains embedded in a focus on the centre. While the political centre may seem threatened in late antiquity, it remains the heart of the spatial conceptions found in historiography.

Hydatius, or the Periphery Defended

In 469, the bishop of Aquae Flaviae (Chaves) in Gallaecia, Hydatius, published the chronicle of Jerome, adding his own continuation until 468.[11] His preface expresses the humility expected of a bishop by situating himself both spatially and temporally at the periphery. He was, so he states, 'as much at the end of the earth as at the end of my life'.[12] Scholars have echoed and expanded this self-localisation at the end of the earth, depicting Gallaecia as effectively a remote corner of the empire battered for decades by the Suebi. His is the prime example of a provincial perspective.[13] This may be true, but falls short of fully grasping all the connotations that Hydatius's self-positioning at the edge of the earth implies. At the end of his preface, he returns to the theme more extensively:

> From that point,[14] having been undeservedly elected to the office of bishop and not unknowing of all the calamities of this wretched age, I have subjoined [an account of] the frontiers, doomed to perish, of the Roman empire that is oppressed by troubles, and, what is more lamentable, [an account of events] within Gallaecia at the edge of the entire world: the state of ecclesiastical succession perverted by indiscriminate appointments, the demise of honourable freedom, and the downfall of virtually all religion based on divine instruction, all as a result of the domination of heretics confounded with the disruption of hostile [barbarian] tribes.[15]

---

[11] See Muhlberger 1981: 193–266; Burgess 1993; Cardelle de Hartman 1994.

[12] Hydatius, *Chronicon* pr.1: ... *ut extremus plage, ita extremus et vitae* ... Tr. Burgess 1993: 73.

[13] Muhlberger 1981: 193; Cardelle de Hartmann 1994: 65; Wickham 2009: 91; Börm 2014: 199; Humphries 2017: 13.

[14] The third year of Valentinian III, that is, 427.

[15] Hydatius, *Chronicon* pr.6: *Exim inmerito adlectus ad episcopatus officium, non ignarus omnium miserabilis temporis erumnarum, et conclusi in angustias imperii Romani metas subdidimus ruituras et, quod est luctuosius, intra extremam universi orbis Galleciam deformem ecclesiastici ordinis statum creationibus indiscretis, honestae libertatis interitum et universe propemodum in divina disciplina*

Hydatius indicates his double geographical focus, the empire and Gallaecia, which is grafted onto another distinction, that between secular and ecclesiastical.[16] Indeed, the 'more lamentable' afflictions in Gallaecia are all of an ecclesiastical nature. The troubles of the empire are expressed in geographical terms: its boundaries are to collapse (*metas ruituras*), and *conclusi in angustias*, translated here as 'oppressed by troubles', evokes a spatial dimension too.[17] The empire, as a circumscribed geographical entity, is under threat. Similarly, the repeated mention of Gallaecia's location at the end of the world links the moral decline of that region to its peripheral position, much as earlier that position was an indication of Hydatius's failure to live up to the historiographical standards set by Jerome. The spatial dimension of this literary inferiority is expressed in Hydatius's recollection of his pilgrimage to Jerome in Jerusalem,[18] which was mentioned slightly earlier in the preface and significantly is dated to the period when he was a little child (*infantulus*). Whatever age precisely this term may indicate, the sentence links young age, a visit to a symbolic Christian centre[19] and deference to literary authority. It is worth recalling that the edges of the world could be very negatively charged. The Huns, the most 'othered' enemy of the Romans in late antiquity, come *ex ultimis terris*, as Ammianus put it.[20] Beyond this there is nothing.[21] The biblical Gog-Magog tradition was easily drafted to support that view, with the mythical gates of Alexander keeping out the wild nations.[22] To locate oneself at the extremities of the earth was, then, not something lightly done. In that regard, the preface of Hydatius strongly emphasises the moral connotations of periphery and centre. His position at the periphery is not just a geographical fact but also a way of positioning himself in a literary and moral hierarchy.

---

religionis occasum ex furentium dominatione permixta iniquarum perturbatione nationum. Tr. Burgess 1993: 75, adapted.

[16] Börm 2014 emphasises Hydatius's interest in the empire and his commitment to its existence. Muhlberger (1981: 214) does not notice the division between secular and ecclesiastical.

[17] Witness the translation by R. Burgess as 'narrowly-confined'.

[18] Dated by Burgess (1993: 4) to 406–7 (cf. *Chronicon* 33 [40]).

[19] Jerusalem is important for Hydatius: *Chronicon* 58 [66], 97 [106].

[20] Ammianus 31.4.4. Cf. Dionysius Periegetes 728–30 (reading, with a later correction, *Hynnoi* instead of *Thynoi*); Claudian, *Against Rufinus* 1.323–31; Orosius, *Histories* 1.2.45. Cf. Schuster 1940; Tausend 1984; Kelly 2009; Rosen 2016: 29–34. For other 'dangerous' peoples at the edges, see, e.g., Jerome, *Letter* 69.3.6; Jordanes, *Romana* 130 (= Florus 1.13.5).

[21] Cf. *Expositio totius mundi* 59: *inde oceanum esse dicitur et huius partem quam nemo hominum narrare potest. Sed quid ibi esse potest? Est enim desertum et, sicut aiunt, est ibi finis mundi.*

[22] Donzel and Schmidt 2010; Zadeh 2011: 34.

Hydatius's chronicle bears out some of the preface's emphases. He admits to a lack of information, especially regarding episcopal succession in the major eastern sees.[23] The events reported relate mostly to Spain, even though events from farther away do find their way into the chronicle. The suggestion that ecclesiastical troubles are worse than the secular ones is reflected in their temporal priority in the chronicle: heresies and problems with ecclesiastical discipline are dealt with most prominently early in the chronicle.[24] Nevertheless, while the preface highlights its author's peripheral position, the chronicle pulls in the opposite direction and seeks to underscore the universal relevance of what Hydatius saw happening around him. The pessimistic assessment of the dire consequences of Spain's conquest by the Vandals and Suebi in 409 depicts Spain as a *pars pro toto* of the world: 'And thus with the four plagues of sword, famine, pestilence and wild beasts raging everywhere throughout the world, the annunciations foretold by the Lord through his prophets came to fulfilment'.[25] *In toto orbe* may be a rhetorical sleight of hand, but it is needed to support the apocalyptic reading Hydatius adopts.[26] While Hydatius lists many events from Gallaecia, he takes care to narrate some that occurred in Gaul or even farther away in Syria.[27] Explicit statements about the way news reached him, through merchants, reports, letters, pilgrims and other travellers, suggest that Gallaecia is still connected to the rest of the empire.[28] Universality also works in the opposite direction. The sack of Bracara in 456/457, for example, is said to be another instance of divine wrath modelled on the ones inflicted on Jerusalem by Babylonians and Romans.[29] Here, sacred history functions as a template giving meaning to local events. Indeed, in the chronicle the local gives meaning to the universal and, in turn, the universal to the local.

Hydatius is not the only historian to espouse a local or provincial perspective in late antiquity. Ecclesiastical historiography would be one example. Whatever the claims put in for the universal validity of the narrative, church histories rarely had the same concern for the imperial centre as secular historiography. As Philippe Blaudeau has shown, the fifth- and sixth-century

---

[23] Hydatius, *Chronicon* 33 [40], 97 [106].   [24] Ibid., 12, 16, 25 [31].   [25] Ibid., 40 [48].

[26] I follow Muhlberger's prudent reading of Hydatius not committing himself to a precise, millenarian interpretation (1981: 260–4), against such an interpretation as proposed by Burgess 1996 (cf. Rebenich 1994).

[27] Hydatius, *Chronicon* 141 [149], 209 [214], 210 [215], 213 [217a/214a], 238 [244], 247 [253].

[28] E.g., ibid. 170 [177], 58 [66], 97 [106], 100 [109]. Cf. Muhlberger 1981, 212–17 and Börm 2014 for emphasis on the imperial perspective of Hydatius.

[29] Hydatius, *Chronicon* 167 [174]. See also 49 [57] on the marriage of Athaulf and Galla Placidia, linked to the prophecies of Daniel.

historians each put forward their own regional centre (Alexandria, Antioch, Constantinople) as the locus of orthodoxy.[30] Even if it attempts to write history about the empire, the history of Eunapius (c. 400) reveals the limits of his provincial standpoint when he complains about his inability to access information about the court in Asia.[31] The historian Candidus wrote a history of the years 457 to 491 (the emperors Leo and Zeno) that sought to integrate the Isaurians into imperial history by including a long genealogy. They had a reputation as brigands, yet in Zeno had managed to put one of their own on the throne.[32] All these authors accept that it would be easier to write from the centre, so as to have better access to information, but none of them believe that meaningful history (i.e., history that is valid for the entire empire) cannot be written from a provincial perspective. Even if the standpoint is local, the perspective is imperial. Scholars have remarked upon the fact that Hydatius remains loyal to the empire, which can be explained both by the genre he espouses (the chronicle is inevitably structured by imperial reigns and Olympiads) and by the fact that Suebic rule did not seem final. In addition, the biblical reading of events Hydatius offers also gives his work universal validity, if not in subject matter, at least as far as the meaning of the events was concerned. Finally, Jerusalem is put on the map as the centre of Hydatius's spiritual and literary universe:[33] not only is it the destination of pilgrimage but it is also the place of residence of the man whose work he was continuing, Jerome.

In sum, Hydatius's self-positioning at the edge of the earth is many things at once: a confession of a provincial perspective, part of a strategy of deference that hints at the moral judgement of events to be narrated, but also a claim that the meaning of events is not determined by a viewpoint from the centre.

Jordanes, or from Periphery to Centre

In 551–552, Jordanes finished his history of the Goths, strongly based on a similar history composed by Cassiodorus about thirty years earlier. Cassiodorus had intended it to be a panegyrical history of the Amal dynasty to which Theoderic (493–526) belonged. While much of that tone remains, Jordanes concluded his reworked summary of Cassiodorus's history with Justinian's victory over the Ostrogothic king Vitigis (540). It has proven

[30] Blaudeau 2006.   [31] Eunapius, *History* F66.2 (Blockley).
[32] Candidus Fɪ l. 50–1 (Blockley), with Meier 2014. Note the emphasis on the imperial perspective in Brandt 2014.
[33] Cf. Elsner 2000.

impossible to identify which parts exactly of Jordanes's account stem from
Cassiodorus, and in the following I shall take Jordanes to be the author of
the whole of the *Getica*.[34]

In spatial terms, the *Getica* trace a journey from periphery to centre.[35]
The Goths originate in Scandza, migrate to Lake Maeotis, to Thrace and
back again to the Black Sea region.[36] From there, they will force their way
into Spain and Italy. The first fifty chapters of the *Getica*, which outline the
first three migrations, are therefore strongly geographical in nature.[37] The
work opens with a potted description of the ocean and its islands (*Getica*
4–9), in which Jordanes signals the ultimate ends of the world:

> The furthest, impenetrable bounds of the Ocean not only [no] one has
> attempted to describe, nor has anyone even been able to cross: because of the
> resisting sedge and the ceasing of the blowing of the winds, it is felt to be
> impenetrable and known to no one except to the one who created it [that is,
> God].[38]

In this world of water, two islands stand out, Britain (*Getica* 10–15) and
Scandza (16–25) – the latter being the Goths' place of origin. As is well
known, the identification of Scandza as the Goths' native island is unique
to Jordanes and has been explained as authentic Gothic memory or, more
likely, a deliberate creation by the author.[39] Indeed, the emphasis at the
start of the *Getica* on islands at the edge of the world is striking because it
was far from necessary to do so. In the sixth century, the Goths were
sometimes located around Lake Maeotis from where they migrated to
Thrace,[40] while earlier accounts situated a people called G(o)utones in
northern Germany.[41] Jordanes could perfectly well have let their history
start there. There would have been a good reason to do so: the history
concentrates on the Amal family, which according to Jordanes emerges
during the reign of Domitian, when the Goths were once again settled

---

[34] For a discussion of these issues and bibliography, see Van Hoof and Van Nuffelen 2017 and forthcoming.

[35] Dagron 1971: 299.   [36] Jordanes, *Getica* 38.   [37] Merrills 2005: 115–16.

[38] Jordanes, *Getica* 5: *Oceani vero intransmeabiles ulteriores fines non solum describere quis adgressus est, verum etiam nec cuiquam licuit transfretare, quia resistente ulva et ventorum spiramine quiescente inpermeabilis esse sentitur et nulli cognita nisi ei qui eam constituit.* Note the same trope in Avienus, *On the sea coast* 117, 210, 230, 380, 410. See Van Hoof 2019.

[39] Cf. Svennung 1967; Goffart 1988: 101; Lozovsky 2000: 80–2; Christensen 2002: 270–1; Merrills 2005: 142–55; Wolfram 2009: 326; Ghosh 2016: 49.

[40] Cf. Stephanus of Byzantium, *Ethnika* s.v. Γότθοι· ἔθνος πάλαι οἰκῆσαν ἐντὸς τῆς Μαιώτιδος. ὕστερον δὲ εἰς τὴν ἐκτὸς Θράκην μετανέστησαν, ὡς εἴρηταί μοι ἐν τοῖς Βυζαντιακοῖς; Procopius, *Wars* 8.5.5. Orosius, *Histories* 1.2.53 situates the Goths in Dacia. Cf. Goffart 1988: 89–96.

[41] Strabo, *Geography* 7.1.3; Pliny the Elder, *Natural History* 4.14.99. Procopius, *Wars* 3.2.6 locates them north of the Danube.

north of the Black Sea.[42] This panegyrical focus on the Amals did not necessitate a geographical starting point at the edge of the world. Even if Jordanes had intended to trace a journey from the margins of the empire to its centre, he could still have located the beginning of Gothic history at Lake Maeotis, which was a traditional border of the empire.[43] Instead, Jordanes has Gothic history start at the edge of the world.

While the choice to start Gothic history at the edge of the world is more remarkable than sometimes assumed, the identification of Scandza as their place of origin has been extensively discussed. Jordanes seems to have taken as his starting point a brief reference in Ptolemy to a group of islands called Scandiai,[44] which was then expanded with material of unknown origin. If the sudden importance accorded to Scandza is striking, it is achieved by way of contrast with earlier identifications of the edge of the world. The traditionally most northern island, Thule, is mentioned by Jordanes, with the proper Virgilian quotation (Virgil, *Georgics* 1.30), but the brevity of the reference marginalises the place:

> And it [the ocean] has, in its most western region, another island called Thule, about which the Mantuan says, among other things, 'Distant Thule will serve you'.[45]

Thule had entered the classical imagination through the *periplous* of Pytheas of Marseille (fourth c. BC).[46] Jordanes's treatment of Thule (or lack thereof) stands out on two accounts. First, Jordanes locates Thule in the west, obscuring its northerly position.[47] Second, he accords it little importance beyond its remoteness. The brevity of Jordanes, though deriving from the equally laconic mention in Orosius (1.2.79), is no accident. In fact, Jordanes ascribes the characteristics usually reserved for Thule to Scandza,[48] as we

---

[42] Jordanes, *Getica* 79.   [43] Cf. Dexippus F14 Martin.

[44] Jordanes, *Getica* 19, with reference to Ptolemy, *Geography* 2.11.35 (mentioning *Goutai*). Pliny the Elder, *Natural History* 5.14.104 also mentions the islands called *Scandias*. Cf. Merrills 2005: 144–5. Note that the Armenian geographical treatise *šxarhac'oyc'* (on which see the chapter by Greenwood) 2.4 locates the Goths on the island of Scandza, which it distinguishes from Thule and Britain (Soukry 1881: 10; Hewsen 1992: 45). Yet in 3.4, it locates the Goths in Germany. The treatise is from the seventh century, but uses the geographer Pappus (d. c. 350).

[45] Jordanes, *Getica* 9: *Habet et in ultimo plagae occidentalis aliam insulam nomine Thyle, de qua Mantuanus inter alia: 'tibi serviat ultima Thyle'*.

[46] Cf. Rubin 1952: 452–9; Cassidy 1963; Romm 1992: 121–70, 206–11; Cunliffe 2001: 116–33; Mund-Dopchie 2009. The history of Thule is too often written under the label of 'myth'. As we shall see, by this time, it is in fact a real place.

[47] Cf. Ptolemy, *Geography* 7.1, 7.16; *Ašxarhac'oyc'* 1.2 (Soukry 1881: 2; Hewsen 1992: 42); Solinus 22; Priscianus, Translation of Dionysius Periegetes 580–1. Cf. Romm 1992: 121, 159.

[48] Strabo, *Geography* 2.5.8, Pomponius Mela 3.57, Procopius, *Wars* 6.15.4–26.

shall see in the following text. Clearly there is only room for one island at the very northern edge of the world.

The other possible rival to Scandza was Britain. Jordanes includes an account of Britain in between his description of the islands in the ocean and that of Scandza.[49] It clearly serves as a contrasting build-up to the description of Scandza.[50] Indeed, traditional descriptions of Britain emphasised its large area and its position at the edge of the world.[51] Jordanes repeats the trope he found in Pomponius Mela, that Britain was only 'recently' opened up by Caesar[52] and thus acknowledges that it was located at the periphery of the world. He then offers a description of the island and its inhabitants that notes some remarkable practices (such as tattooing) but is mainly concerned with bringing Britain into the fold of humankind. The display of precise knowledge about Britain renders it ordinary, unable to serve as the edge of the world[53] and a clear contrast to the truly different world that is Scandza.

As underlined by A. Merrills, Jordanes stresses the unique amount of information he offers on Scandza, for example by noting that Ptolemy mentions only seven of the many nations that live there.[54] Yet this information serves to render Scandza a different world, a real edge of the world with all the strangeness that this entails.[55] Jordanes pays ample tribute to that tradition, as the following examples show. The smaller islands west of Scandza are so inhospitable that wolves lose their eyesight (18). The Adogit, who live above the pole circle, are the happiest and most unhappy people on the world, for in summer they have forty days of continuous sunlight and in winter they see no sun for the same period.[56] They symbolise, as it were, the ambiguous nature of living at the edges of the world. Other

[49] Jordanes, *Getica* 10–15.
[50] Dagron 1971: 297–8; Goffart 1988: 91. Merrills 2005: 137 argues that the display of knowledge about Britain serves to inspire faith in the more problematic account of Scandza. This may well be true, but it was also a feature of the edge of the world that it could only be partially known.
[51] Dexippus F14 Martin = F15 Mecella; Solinus 22.1 (note that Solinus was known to Jordanes); Priscian, Translation of Dionysius Periegetes 580–1; Procopius, *Wars* 8.20. Cf. Procopius, *Wars* 6.15.4, where Thule is said to be ten times bigger than Britain; Dionysius Periegetes 565–8; Ptolemy, *Geography* 7.1; *Expositio totius mundi* 67; Libanius, *Oration* 59.137. Cf. Romm 1992: 141–2; Natal 2018.
[52] Jordanes, *Getica* 10; Pomponius Mela 3.49; Tacitus, *Agricola* 10. See also Priscianus, *Translation of Dionysius* 578.
[53] Britain had been described as the edge of the world: Romm 1992: 141; Natal 2018.
[54] Jordanes, *Getica* 19; Lozovsky 2000: 84; Merrills 2005: 147.
[55] See, e.g., Ammianus 23.6.61–70.
[56] This feature was usually ascribed to Thule: Pomponius Mela 3.57; Solinus 22.11; Pliny the Elder, *Natural History* 2.186; Dionysius Periegetes 580–8; Procopius, *Wars* 6.15.1–10. Strabo, *Geography* 2.1.18 attributes it to Britain, an alternative also mentioned by Pliny.

nations in Scandza do not eat vegetable food and live in dug out rocks (21–22). The crossing to the mainland into Scythia is not without its dangers – including quaking bogs (27). The ethnographic description of the peoples living on Scandza concludes, tellingly, by stating that they 'fight with the ferocity of wild animals' (24). Even if the Goths are never described as different, they nevertheless come from a place that is recognisably so. This is enhanced by another element. Seen from the empire's perspective, migration was a characteristic of barbarian groups and something for which northern, Germanic groups in particular were singled out.[57] Strabo highlights this especially for the Getae,[58] one of the nations claimed by Jordanes as avatars of the Goths. In the *Getica*, the knowledge that this migration will continue always hangs over the story of Gothic settlements until they settle in Spain (Visigoths) and Italy (Ostrogoths). Significantly, stability is only achieved within the empire. By giving the Goths an origin at the edge of the world and a long history of migration, the *Getica* clearly do not seek to deny their difference from the peoples settled in the empire.

The *Getica* may suggest the inexorable march of a nation towards taking over two of the heartlands of the empire, Spain and especially Italy, before being overcome by an even stronger man, Justinian. The positive tone towards the Goths is unmistakably present and the suggestion of the greatness of Scandza, in comparison to Thule and Britain, may well reflect the panegyrical tendency towards the Goths. Yet none of this necessitates their origins at the edge of the world, on an island that has all the hallmarks of Thule, the traditional claimant to that role. Jordanes could have started his account in one of the traditional places of origin, such as northern Germania or Lake Maeotis. Even if we believe that Jordanes was correct, that Scandza really is our Scandinavia and that the Goths really originated there,[59] there was no need to depict it as the edge of the world. It could have been depicted as part of northern Germany.[60] Yet Jordanes felt such a need, as attested by his deliberate marginalisation, in different ways, of Thule and Britain. As we shall see in the next section, Jordanes's

---

[57] Strabo, *Geography* 7.1.3, 7.2.1, 7.2.2. Cf. Censorinus 4.11; Ammianus 15.9.3–7. See further Maas 2012; Brodka 2013.

[58] Strabo, *Geography* 7.3.13.

[59] The ninth-century Ravenna Cosmography cites what seem to be Ostrogothic geographers (Heldebald, Marcomir, Atalaricus), who provide information on northern regions. Staab 1967 provides an argument in support of their possible historicity. Dillemann (1997: 57–8) is sceptical. If they are authentic, the possibility that authentic information would have reached Jordanes increases.

[60] As does *Ašxarhac'oyc'*, cited in note 44.

contemporary Procopius introduces Thule to play a role somewhat similar to that of Scandza in his account of the Heruls. It points towards a transformation of these places in the late antique imaginary. In classical literature, Thule 'presents itself as a place which can be perceived but not approached'.[61] In Jordanes and Procopius, islands at the northern rim of the world have become the origins of contemporary peoples, origins that can be described and visited. This change is more easily described than explained, but it confirms my initial suggestion that the fragmentation within and of the empire went hand in hand with a rethinking of the margins of the world – precisely because the representation of the centre was dialectically related to that of the periphery. Even though Jordanes may seem at first to affirm the periphery over the centre, his account remains wedded to this dialectical relationship. As I have pointed out, the edge of the world is an ambivalent and different world and, reassuringly for someone reading the *Getica* from the centre, the text ends with the victory of Justinian and Belisarius over the Ostrogoths. For all the power and virtue that the edges bring to the centre, Justinian's victory symbolically reaffirms the victory of the centre over the periphery. Indeed, also in moral terms, Greco-Roman culture appears as the yardstick of civilisation by which the Goths are measured.[62] The *Getica* are, then, only seemingly a challenge to the power of the centre.

Procopius, or from Centre to Periphery

Procopius published his history of the wars of Justinian about the same time as Jordanes his *Getica* (books 1–7 in 550/551, followed by book 8 in 552/553).[63] The geographical organisation of the material by theatre of war (Persia, Africa, Italy) suggests a clear awareness of the spatial dimension of history. Indeed, in the later book 8 Procopius confesses abandoning this grouping of material according to its location. Yet, as if to make up for it, he opens the book with a long discussion of the geography of the Pontus region.[64] Thus book 8 aligns itself with the practice found in Orosius and Jordanes of opening a history with a long geographical exposé. Procopius mentions the edges of the world a few times in passing,[65] but they are paid extensive attention only on two occasions.

[61] Romm 1992: 157.   [62] Jordanes, *Getica* 40.

[63] Greatrex 1994 and 2003; Croke 2005b. A later date of 557 for book 8 is defended by Evans 1996; Greatrex 2016 allows for later reworking and updating. For a status quaestionis, see Greatrex 2014: 97–9.

[64] Procopius, *Wars* 8.1.1–2, 8.2–6.

[65] Ibid., 4.13.29, 8.5.32, 8.6.30–1. Cf. Wolska-Conus 1978: 197–9.

In book 6, he narrates the causes of a revolt by the Heruls, a smaller Germanic group that had been settled in the empire after the Lombards had destroyed their kingdom north of the Danube (between 494 and 508). They killed their king and, having repented, sent a party to Thule to fetch a new ruler. Indeed, after the Lombard defeat, part of the Heruls, apparently including members of the royal family, had refused to enter the empire and travelled to Thule. The first candidate died on the way from Thule but the second one, called Datius, arrived at Singedunum only to find that the Heruls had already asked Justinian to provide them with a new king. The emperor had sent Suartuas, a Herul who had long served in Constantinople. The Heruls quickly abandoned Suartuas in favour of Datius and, out of fear of Justinian, they submitted to the Gepids, who were enemies of Rome at this point.[66]

In many striking respects, Procopius's account of the migration of part of the Heruls to Thule is a mirror of Jordanes's story of the migration of the Goths from Scandza. To start with, there can be no doubt that Procopius's Thule is the same place as Jordanes's Scandza. Located at the edge of the world, Thule is fittingly only reached after crossing a barren tract of land. It is home to nations one also finds on Scandza, the Scritiphini, Gauti (called Gautigoths by Jordanes) and Heruls – even though Jordanes mentions many more names. The Danes, who Jordanes situates on Scandza, are the last nation before Thule in Procopius. Just like Jordanes, Procopius also dwells on the exceptional brevity and length of days there. He highlights Thule's remarkable size, setting it off, again, against Britain. He also mentions some strange customs of the nations living there, even though only the Scritiphini live like animals.[67] Much as for the Goths, migration appears to be a fundamental feature of the Heruls's non-Roman identity.

Such similarities serve to better bring out the important differences between the two accounts. The vector of migration goes in a single direction in Jordanes, away from Scandza towards Rome. The main direction of travel is the opposite in Procopius, namely towards Thule, and the envoys of the Roman Heruls go to the island twice to fetch a new king.[68] Whereas the Goths of Jordanes are autochthonous in Scandza, there is no hint in Procopius that the Heruls go back to Thule as it is their place of origin. The only motivation ascribed to them is that they dislike crossing the Danube into Illyricum. In other words, they do not like entering the Roman

---

[66] Procopius, *Wars* 6.14–15. On the Heruls, see Sarantis 2010; Steinacher 2010. On the Gepids, see Sarantis 2009. On the account of Procopius, see Revanoglou 2005: 234–6.

[67] Procopius, *Wars* 6.15.1–16, 22, 26; Jordanes, *Getica* 16, 19–20, 22–3. Cf. Revanoglou 2005: 237–40.

[68] Procopius, *Wars* 6.15.27–8.

Empire. Thus Thule fully plays its role as the 'other' to the empire. In Jordanes, the migration is a journey towards integration into the empire through settlement and attempts at coexistence: over the course of their journey, the Goths become more and more like Romans. The opposite direction of travel in Procopius generates a different meaning. The arrival of the new king of the Heruls from Scandza leads to a split among the Heruls, the end of their alliance with Constantinople, and their pact with the Gepids against the empire. Thule takes the Heruls out of the fold of the empire.

Whereas Jordanes describes the Goths and Romans as similar in terms of civilisation and, by association, morality, Procopius opens his digression on the Heruls with a strong emphasis on their lack of civilisation. Pagans, they practiced human sacrifice, '[a]nd they observed many customs which were not in accord with those of other men'.[69] Their conversion under Justinian marked progress:

> As a result of this they adopted a gentler manner of life and decided to submit themselves wholly to the laws of the Christians, and in keeping with the terms of their alliance they are generally arrayed with the Romans against their enemies.[70]

This praise is immediately qualified, however:

> They are still, however, faithless toward them, and since they are given to avarice, they are eager to do violence to their neighbours, feeling no shame at such conduct. And they mate in an unholy manner, especially men with asses, and they are the basest of all men and utterly abandoned rascals.[71]

While such condemnation is absent from the depiction of the way of life on Thule, Procopius does underline that its inhabitants are pagans and practice human sacrifice.[72] Even if the journey to Thule is not a return to a place of origin, it is a return to a way of life that is un-Christian and hence un-Roman. Readers will not be surprised to learn that the arrival of the king from Thule creates dissent within the Heruls and a rebellion against

[69] Ibid., 6.14.2: νόμοις δὲ πολλοῖς οὐ κατὰ ταὐτὰ τοῖς ἀνθρώπων ἑτέροις ἐχρῶντο. Tr. Dewing, LCL, 403.
[70] Procopius, Wars 6.14.34: διόπερ τὴν δίαιταν ἐπὶ τὸ ἡμερώτερον μεταβαλόντες τοῖς Χριστιανῶν νόμοις ἐπὶ πλεῖστον προσχωρεῖν ἔγνωσαν, καὶ Ῥωμαίοις κατὰ τὸ ξυμμαχικὸν τὰ πολλὰ ἐπὶ τοὺς πολεμίους ξυντάσσονται. Tr. Dewing, LCL 413.
[71] Ibid., 6.14.35–6: ἔτι μέντοι αὐτοῖς εἰσιν ἄπιστοι καὶ πλεονεξίᾳ ἐχόμενοι βιάζεσθαι τοὺς πέλας ἐν σπουδῇ ἔχουσιν, οὐ φέροντος αὐτοῖς αἰσχύνην τοῦ ἔργου. καὶ μίξεις οὐχ ὁσίας τελοῦσιν, ἄλλας τε καὶ ἀνδρῶν καὶ ὄνων, καὶ εἰσι πονηρότατοι ἀνθρώπων ἁπάντων καὶ κακοὶ κακῶς ἀπολούμενοι. Tr. Dewing, LCL 413.
[72] Ibid., 6.15.23–5.

Rome. Whereas Jordanes excepted the Goths from the moral distance that geographical distance entails, Procopius may well have let his Heruls travel to Thule to highlight moral difference through spatial distance.

One of the stranger episodes in the *Wars* is that of the war between the Varni and the Angli, two nations living in Germania, which Procopius dates to around 550.[73] Not only is the episode unrelated to anything that happens in the empire and the major theatres of war,[74] it has a number of remarkable – not to say peculiar – features.

The first is the location of the Angli. They are said to live, together with the Frissones and the Brittones, on an island named Brittia. It is located between Britain and Thule, just opposite the mouth of the Rhine. Brittia looks very much like Britain, with Procopius having some knowledge of a wall dividing the island.[75] Much energy has been spent on identifying Brittia, with scholars seeing it as a mere reduplication of Britain[76] or taking Procopius's Britannia to be Brittany in France and Brittia to be Britain.[77] Such efforts have been guided by a desire to save Procopius's reputation as a reliable historian, maybe somewhat misinformed by his witnesses. If we abandon that concern and espouse a different approach, one that looks for the meaning of the episode, we may get somewhat further. The place name Brittia is only attested in Procopius,[78] suggesting he coined it precisely for this episode. The idea may well derive from the description of the world of Dionysius the Periegete, who locates two British isles opposite the mouth of the Rhine and whose description is quickly followed by a reference to Thule – two features that occur in Procopius, too.[79] Dionysius was being read in Constantinople in the sixth century, witness the Latin translation by Priscianus earlier that century. A further link with Dionysius is more speculative: in between his mention of the British Isles and Thule, Dionysius mentions an island where women practice the cult of

---

[73] Ibid., 8.20.

[74] Except for *Wars* 8.20.10 where some Angli are said to have been sent to Byzantium by the king of the Franks.

[75] Procopius, *Wars* 8.20.42.

[76] Burn 1955. Jutland, Heligoland and Rügen have also been suggested: Revanoglou 2005: 106–7.

[77] Thompson 1980. His argument that Procopius does not call Brittania an island here and hence that it can refer to Brittany is specious. He is forced to admit that elsewhere Procopius does call Brittania an island (cf. *Wars* 3.2.31): 507: 'probably nothing more than an oversight'. Yet it would be very odd that in the whole of his works *Brittania* means Britain, except in 8.20, where it would be Brittany – in fact, it would be as odd as the oddity Thompson seeks to explain. Carlson 2017 argues that the story told by Procopius can likely be traced to Old English Poetry. Even so, the specific oddities that I highlight cannot derive from that source.

[78] Athanasius, *Historia Arianorum* 28.2 uses the term for the Italian province of Bruttium.

[79] Dionysius Periegetes l. 566 (δισσαὶ νῆσοι ἔασι Βρετανίδες, ἀντία Ῥήνου), 580–8.

Dionysus. The core of Procopius's account is made up of the war waged by a princess of the Angli against Radigis, the ruler of the Varni who had rejected their betrothal. In both cases, women show themselves to be stronger than men.[80]

If this influence from Dionysius suggests a possible origin for the invention of Brittia, the question arises why Procopius needed an island. Indeed, his desire to have one was strong enough to turn the Frisians and the Angli, whom classical geography had always located on the mainland, into island dwellers. If his purpose simply was to tell a story about barbarian conflict, the tale could as well have been located somewhere in Germany. Again, there seems to have been a desire to depict an island at the edge of the world. Just as Scandza, which Jordanes calls 'a workshop of peoples or rather like a scabbard of nations',[81] overflows with nations, Brittia has a population surplus that migrates to the mainland.[82] The military expedition by the rejected fiancée signals quite a different social life from that within the empire, while Brittia's inhabitants' lack of civilisation is signalled by the fact that they are unfamiliar with horses.[83] The wall that divides the island has mysterious qualities: on one side, the land and way of life are normal, but the other side is infested with snakes and wild animals and the air there is so bad that one would be able to survive at most half an hour. If man or animal crosses the wall, they die instantaneously.[84] The end of the chapter is strangest of all. Procopius narrates it with due disclaimers ('a story which bears very close resemblance to mythology') but at considerable length: the villagers living just opposite Brittia on the mainland are summoned at night to ferry dead souls to the island.[85] The story obviously is reminiscent of the crossing of the Acheron and Styx in the classical imagination: Brittia is assimilated with the underworld. The alterity of Brittia is thus underscored by appealing to traditional tools (reversal of gender roles, ignorance of key elements of civilisation, geographical hostility) and enhanced by the assimilation with the underworld.

We are now in a position to answer the question of why Procopius needed an island for his story about the Angli. As we have gathered from Jordanes, when located in the north or west, islands were symbols of

[80] Ibid., l. 570–1: ἦχι γυναῖκες ἀνδρῶν ἀντιπέρηθεν.
[81] Jordanes, Getica 25: quasi officina gentium aut certe velut vagina nationum. See the discussion of this passage in Merrills 2005: 149; and Van Hoof and Van Nuffelen, forthcoming.
[82] Procopius, Wars 8.20.8.   [83] Ibid., 8.20.29.
[84] Ibid., 8.20.42–6. Cf. Pliny the Elder, Natural History 37.77; Severus of Minorca, Letter 2–3.
[85] Procopius, Wars 8.20.47–58.

otherness. Indeed, as the ocean was the outer limit of the earth, islands located there were places on the cusp between inside and outside the *oikoumene*. By the sixth century, the northern islands – Scandza, Brittia and Thule – had developed from places beyond knowledge to places that could be known, yet still remained symbols of otherness. They generated nations that would approach the Roman Empire, might become assimilated by the empire, but never entirely lost the difference imprinted on them by their place of origin. This may be the function of chapter 8.20 in the *Wars*. Without any immediate link to any of the narrative threads, it comes after an account of Roman dealings with the Huns – as I have noted previously, one of the most 'alien' barbarian groups – and is followed by an account of the end of the war against the Goths in Italy. Significantly, chapters 8.21–22 dwell extensively on the great history of Rome, focalised through the buildings of the city, its statues and the ship of Aeneas.[86] We move from the edge of the world to the centre of empire in a mere couple of pages. The progress of the narrative thus strongly underscores centrality, civilisation, empire and (bearing the end of the Brittia episode in mind) life as features of Rome – in contrast with the margins of the world, which lack all these qualities.[87] Much like Jordanes's account of Scandza and Procopius's earlier one about Thule, this is a story that affirms the empire by attributing to it geographical, civilisational and moral centrality. It is a message worth inventing an island for.

Andronicus, or the Centre Affirmed

Andronicus was a Syriac or Greek chronicler active during the reign of Justinian.[88] Besides a chronicle, which remained a prominent source for Syriac historiography until the thirteenth century, an astrological treatise and an explanation of the signs of the zodiac, there also exists a small treatise entitled 'a discourse that sets out what there is at the edges in the four quarters of the world, away from the whole world inhabited by men, set out by the philosopher Andronicus'.[89] It exists in two versions, a longer

---

[86] Ibid., 8.21.11–17, 8.22.5–16. Note also the digression on the *Odyssey* in 8.22.18–29.

[87] Cf. Revanoglou 2005: 246 on the link between distance and lack of civilisation. She also notes that Procopius puts the Persians on a par with the Romans.

[88] Hilkens 2018: 191–228; Debié 2015: 515–20; Hilkens 2015. The chronicler is generally assumed to have written in Syriac because he is only attested in the Syriac tradition, but that cannot be a decisive argument.

[89] Extended version: Furlani 1927: 239 (Birmingham Mingana Syr. 183; Berlin, Königliche Bibliothek, Syr. 59 802); brief version: Nau 1917: 462–71 = *Descriptio populorum et plagarum* (Brooks 1907: 351–4 [London, British Library Add. 25 875]).

and a briefer one. As the title indicates, it explores the edges of the world in contrast with the *oikoumene*, the inhabited parts of the world. Indeed, in the briefer version held in the British Library, it is preceded and concluded by the traditional biblical table of nations, that is, the division of the world among the descendants of Noah.[90] Although we cannot be sure the opening section was originally part of Andronicus's treatise, the closing one may well have been.[91]

The link with the table of nations allows us to speculate whether the treatise originally was part of a chronicle by Andronicus, with some other treatises preserved under his name. One is an account of peoples who do not know God,[92] and a brief account of the names given to the zodiac by Greeks and Hebrews.[93] Not only is this material that would fit into a chronography,[94] but the treatise on the zodiac ascribes its account of the Hebrew months to a historian called Asaph, who is also attested in Michael the Syrian as a source of information on the history between the Flood and the Patriarchs.[95] This makes it likely that Andronicus was the source through which Asaph was mediated to Michael, even though there may have been other intermediaries between Andronicus and Michael. As argued by Andy Hilkens, Andronicus is likely to have divided his work into two parts, as Eusebius did: a first part with tables of rulers and narrative sections (i.e., a chronography) and a second one with a year-by-year account.[96] The material this section deals with would fit well into the first part, which may have included an account of the geography, as well as an account of the constitutive parts of the calendar.

As it exists now, the text espouses both a Ptolemaic and anti-Ptolemaic position. The basic assumption seems to be that the world is surrounded by the ocean, which was the most widespread view in late antiquity.[97] It goes against Ptolemy's idea that the edges of the world are stretches of unknown

[90] Cf. Witakowski 1993.
[91] This shows that Brock's suggestion (1969: 216) that the briefer version is a mere abbreviation of the other version is not correct: rather, both seem to be drawn from a lost original. Witakowski (1993: 650–1) argues that the briefer version is a combination of Andronicus's treatise (as found in the extended version) with an anonymous treatise that gave the table of nations. Yet the briefer version indicates that the table of nations was in Andronicus.
[92] As yet unedited: Debié 2015: 519. [93] Mingana 1917: 88–9.
[94] See the definition of Burgess and Kulikowski (2013: 61) for 'annotated chronographs'. The table of nations also appears in the *Chronicon Paschale* (pp. 44–64) and in the so-called *Alexandrian World Chronicle* (1.2–3), as well as in the so-called *Chronicle of 724*.
[95] Michael the Great, *Chronicle*, 2.3; 2.4; 2.5; 2.6; 2.7 (Chabot 1910: 11–15). On Asaph, see Van Nuffelen and Van Hoof, eds., *Clavis Historicorum Antiquitatis Posterioris*: www.late-antique-historiography.ugent.be/database/, s.v. Asaph.
[96] Hilkens 2018: 226–8.
[97] Wolska-Conus 1978: 184; Schleicher 2014: 132. Cf. Romm 1992: 41–4.

and deserted land. However, Andronicus does describe such empty spaces in the east and the north. There were defenders of the Ptolemaic position in the sixth century, like John Philoponus and the historian Pseudo-Zachariah, and it seems Andronicus sought somehow to reconcile both views.[98]

The treatise surveys the four cardinal points one after the other, first east and west and then north and south (in the briefer version: south and north), offering a wealth of detail. While it relies heavily on classical sources in situating strange men and animals in these regions, it is also broadly biblical in nature. It mentions the sons of Japheth in the east, the sons of Ham in the south and Gog and Magog in the north, and describes 'mankind' as Adamite. The narrative tends to note a decline in humanity the further one moves towards the edges. The east goes from dwellers in tents to naked dwellers in the open and then on to double-headed, four-footed, winged creatures; in the west live naked people in woods, who dive into the ocean to be protected from the sun; in the south there are one-eyed giants, human-headed and dog-headed snakes as well as centaurs; in the north, one finds small naked men who fight with cranes and headless men with their faces on their breasts. Many of these figures are inherited from classical geography, even though Andronicus does not always seem to respect their classical location.[99] Just as in classical geography but also according to the Bible,[100] the four corners of the world are the places where precious metals and stones are discovered: gold in east and west, precious stones such as beryls in the south. Equally traditional is the location of particular animals such as jackals and apes in the west, storks and snakes in

---

[98] Ptolemy, *Geography* 7.5.2; John Philoponus, *On the Creation of the World* 4.5; Pseudo-Zachariah, *Ecclesiastical History* 12.7.i.

[99] Headless men: Herodotus 4.191; Pomponius Mela 1.48. One-eyed men: the Arimaspoi in the north, cf. Herodotus 3.116, 4.13, 4.27; Pomponius Mela 2.2. Pygmies, the small men fighting with cranes: Pliny the Elder, *Natural History* 6.188; Pomponius Mela 3.81 (they are usually situated in the south, but see Pseudo-Zachariah, *Ecclesiastical History* 12.7.k.x (Greatrex, Phenix, Horn 2011: 451)). Kynokephaloi: Herodotus 4.191; Solinus 52.27 (in the east); Pliny the Elder, *Natural History* 6.30. Snakes: Diodorus of Sicily 3.54; Strabo, *Geography* 17.3.7; Herodotus 4.179. Snakes and stones: *Letter of Alexander to Aristotle* 20. Various wild animals: Diodorus of Sicily 2.51.2–4. For a sceptical take on such accounts, see *Ašxarhac'oyc'* 4.8 (Soukry 1881: 28–9; Hewsen 1992: 51: monsters in the south), 5.35, 38 (Soukry 1881: 58, 62; Hewsen 1992: 775–6: animals in the east and distant places inhabited by strange peoples, capped by the remark that the author does not really believe this). In general, there are clear similarities between the treatise of Andronicus and the *Ašxarhac'oyc'*, e.g., in reporting the types of stone that can be found at the margins, besides the Ptolemaic background. This indicates at least an origin in the same tradition.

[100] Gen 2.10–12; Herodotus 3.102–5; Diodorus of Sicily 3.45.5–7; Strabo, *Geography* 16.4.18; Pliny the Elder, *Natural History* 11.111; Pomponius Mela 3.62. Solinus takes an extensive interest in stones and the places they are found.

the south, and cranes in the north. These are patterns that can be matched easily with the geographical compendia of Pomponius Mela and Solinus, even if there is little overlap in details. In contrast to Herodotus, who seems to be the distant ancestor of many of the features, the peoples at the edges are judged negatively and do not represent ideal communities, as the Hyperboreans or Ethiopians do in classical accounts.[101]

For all its peculiarities, then, the treatise is well embedded in the classical geographical tradition, on the one hand, and in the table of nations developed from the Bible, on the other. Indeed, Andronicus ties all human races into the genealogies of the three sons of Noah. Semi-human beings are then described as conscious creations of God or as belonging to the animal kingdom. The little treatise thus is an affirmation of knowledge. It integrates biblical and classical knowledge and affirms that the edges are known, at least as far inhabitation is concerned. It is also an affirmation of the centre of the *oikoumene*: the edges are strange places with human communities at a lower level of development and with semi-human beings and animals. In the absence of the idealisation of frontier communities, as found in some classical authors, civilisation is claimed entirely for the centre.

Conclusions

The margins of the world are a remarkable presence in late-fifth- and sixth-century historiography, especially when compared to the 1992 study by James Romm, which does not cover much material from Roman historians.[102] They retain the ambivalent nature they had in classical antiquity, but it plays out in different ways. While they remain the location of many marvels, the margins seem remarkably well known in late antiquity and appear intimately connected to the empire. The proliferation of Thule-like islands in the northern sea (Brittia, Scandza and Thule) is striking, demonstrating the symbolic significance of northern islands as the edges of the world. This is probably a product of the widespread view that the ocean surrounds the world,[103] rendering such islands liminal places. As we have noticed, Andronicus's brief treatise is first and foremost an affirmation of the fact that the margins can be known and constitute an entity in their own right, described in a separate treatise or section, and are

---

[101] Romm 1992: 45–81. This kind of idealisation is also found in the *Expositio totius mundi* 4 for the Camarini.
[102] Ibid. 142–6 has some discussion of Tacitus.   [103] Arnaud 2014.

not just an element of a larger description of the world. As the margins become better known, they also come closer to the centre. Procopius has the Heruls travel to Thule twice in his own time, and he claims to have had plans to do so as well.[104] Brittia is just off the mouth of the Rhine. In turn, Jordanes presumes that travellers are able to get close to Scandza in his own day.[105] Proximity does not mean that the edges of the world are characterised positively. The islands at the northern rim bring forth valiant nations, but such a distant origin renders these nations less civilised than and hostile to the inhabitants of the empire. Geographical distance is moral distance. While the Goths of Jordanes up to a point escape this negative characterisation by physically approaching the empire, the idea is strongly present in Procopius. Hydatius's self-marginalisation in Gallaecia plays with the same negative moral charge that a marginal position brings. His self-marginalisation is predicated on the acceptance of the imperial centre, balanced with a focus on the spiritual centre of Jerusalem. Indeed, all accounts of the edges of the world we have surveyed presuppose or defend the centrality of the empire. Even Hydatius only made a claim for the universal significance of his provincial standpoint and did not go as far as John of Biclaro, Isidore of Seville and the Venerable Bede, who turned Spain and Britain, respectively, into the centre of the world after the empire had disappeared in the west.[106]

How are we to explain this interest in the edges of the world? One explanation could be that Christian historiography is traditionally said to be universal in scope, also in geographical terms. The geographical introduction to Orosius's *Histories* and the chroniclers' claim to cover the whole world would be two illustrations. This development may have been driven by the urge to demonstrate the expansion of Christianity to the ends of the world and its salutary effects on mankind, which is indeed the explicit aim of the expansion of Ptolemy's description of the world found in Pseudo-Zachariah's church history.[107] I am mildly sceptical about the degree to which there is real universality in late ancient historiography,[108] but more important is the fact that only one of my case studies would fit this pattern, namely Andronicus – if my suggestion to include the treatise on the edges of the world in the chronicle is justified. In the three other cases, the edges play a role in a context where the concern with the empire is explicit. This

---

[104] Procopius, *Wars* 6.15.8. Claudian, *Panegyric for the Third Consulship of Honorius* 1.53 still states that Thule cannot be reached (cf. Orosius, *Histories* 1.2.79). Yet in his *Panegyric for the Consulship of Stilicho* (3.154–7) Thule has become easy to reach – as a symbol of the stability Stilicho brings.

[105] Jordanes, *Getica* 25, 27.   [106] Lozovsky 2000: 65–6; see Chapter 4 by M. Humphries.

[107] Pseudo-Zachariah, *Ecclesiastical History* 12.7.j.   [108] Van Nuffelen 2010, 2012: 170–85.

is most strongly the case in Procopius, where the edges serve to 'other' Germanic groups, but it is also the main dynamic in Jordanes and Hydatius. This brings us back to my initial assumption: periphery and centre are closely intertwined and when the centre is shaken, the margins are reimagined too. While chronicling how the empire is shaken and fragmented, the histories discussed in this chapter depict the edges of the world as places that can be known and described – and that thus, for all their destructive potential, can be controlled. They obey, then, the same logic that underpins the panegyrical topos with which I opened this chapter: the empire rules the world.

CHAPTER 3

Armenian Space in Late Antiquity

Tim Greenwood

In late antiquity, there was no single conception of Armenian space. Instead, there were different notions of what constituted Armenia, each contingent on date, context and perspective. For authors operating within an Armenian cultural milieu, Armenian space was automatically defined in terms of the land occupied by an imagined community because the standard expression for the land of Armenia was *ašxarh/erkir Hayocʻ*, the homeland of the descendants of Hayk, the eponymous ancestor of the Armenian people.[1] This social construction, therefore, created Armenian space wherever those who identified as Armenians were settled. It was not tied to a specific territory with fixed boundaries. At the same time, however, Armenian space was understood in terms of a political landscape, albeit a historic one, comprising the lands of the Arsacid kingdom before its demise in 428 AD. The idea of a land first settled by the progenitor of all Armenians was, therefore, reinforced by the historic experience of an independent kingdom of Armenia, although the overlap between them was imperfect. Finally, Armenian space could be conceptualised in geo-ecclesiological terms, as the network of episcopal sees and religious houses under the spiritual authority of the Catholicos.[2] This third space was also fluid, repeatedly renegotiated as political and confessional circumstances changed.

The extent to which these three projections of Armenian space were recognised at the time is impossible to determine, although it is highly likely that some sense of a mythic origin, a tradition of kingship and a clerical hierarchy would have been familiar to many. Yet these three singular expressions were confronted by a fragmented reality, a world of rival local lordships, of different expressions of Christian doctrine, practice

---

[1] Anderson 2006: 6–7, 11–22; Miles 1999; Pohl 2013. Although accepted in Armenian literary tradition, the etymology of Haykʻ, Armenians, from Hayk is impossible.
[2] Hewsen 1997.

and cult, overlaying a range of preexisting religious beliefs and traditions, even of different versions of the past and different dialects of Armenian.[3] This fluid, shifting experience produced regional and local constructions of space, some persistent, others ephemeral, traces of which can sometimes be discerned in the Armenian literary tradition.[4]

This is not the only perspective from which Armenian space was fashioned in late antiquity. Following the eclipse of Arsacid Armenia, every district of the former kingdom was under the notional control of one or other of the 'great powers' of Rome and Persia and incorporated into their provincial networks. The number, location and disposition of these provinces did not stay the same. They underwent significant revision between the fourth and the seventh centuries on both sides of the frontier, sometimes as a result of internal administrative reorganisation, sometimes as a result of conflict or negotiation between the two powers. Crucially, there was no gap between these imperial powers into which an independent Armenia might be squeezed. Authors writing outside the Armenian cultural milieu generally recognised this lack of autonomy, unlike Armenian authors, who usually sought to generate separate Armenian space, even when this contradicted the realities of provincial administration.

This study explores different conceptions of Armenian space. It examines how it was understood from the perspective of the two great powers, first Persia and then Rome, and then how it could be constructed by Armenian authors. Particular attention will be given to a much cited but little studied Armenian geographical composition titled *Ašxarhacʻoycʻ* and attributed historically to Movsēs Xorenacʻi, and more recently, to Anania Širakacʻi (Anania of Širak). Although its description of Armenia is well known, the universal dimensions of this composition, derived ultimately from Ptolemy's *Geography*, have not been fully appreciated. Armenian space received significant coverage in the composition but it was recognised as one of many lands that made up the geography of the world as conceptualised from a second-century Greco-Roman perspective and situated in that context. The spatial horizons of this composition were not confined to Armenia.

---

[3] Stepʻanos Siwnecʻi identified dialects from the districts of Korčaykʻ, Taykʻ, Xoytʻ, Fourth Armenia, Sper, Siwnikʻ and Arcax: Adontz 1970: 187.

[4] By way of illustration, the *History* of Łazar Pʻarpecʻi opens with a long eulogy to the land of Ayrarat. It is imagined as a rural paradise, overflowing with domesticated and wild animals, fish and birds, in which nobles and their sons can indulge their passion for hunting. Indeed it is the exploitation of the natural resources for enjoyment and pleasure, primarily through hunting, which dominates the account. Ayrarat is thus both idealised and exclusive space, the preserve of the elite, from which the rest of the population has been displaced: Łazar, *History of the Armenians* 1.7; tr. Thomson 1991: 42–4.

Armenia from a Persian Perspective

The scarcity of surviving written records from within Sasanian Persia presents an immediate challenge to anyone wishing to study the institutions of that state or relations between centre and periphery. In these circumstances, one might be tempted to doubt whether it is possible to obtain any sense of how Armenian space was configured from a Persian perspective. Yet although a complete solution to this question is always going to be out of reach, the evidence from inscriptions and seals confirms that the notion of Armin – a term that was derived from Old Persian Armina and first used in the trilingual Behistun inscription of the late sixth century BC – held meaning for contemporaries.[5]

The primary question is whether Armenia was included in the definition of Ērānšahr, the homeland of Zoroaster in the *Avesta* and the locus of divinely sanctioned, legitimate political authority.[6] If so, then its people – or at least some of them – were conceived as allies of Ohrmazd in the cosmic struggle against Ahreman and so were members of the community of Ērān, those of the Good Religion. If, however, Armenia was situated outside the boundaries of Ērānšahr, its people were categorised alongside others who were not of the Good Religion, Anērān. As Garsoïan judiciously observed, this cannot be answered categorically. The relationship between Armenia and Ērānšahr was ambiguous.[7] The famous trilingual inscription of the third-century *šahanšah* Šāpuhr I at Naqš-e Rostam states that he was king of Ērān and Anērān and includes Armenia in its definition of the former.[8] This is less surprising than it might seem because Šāpuhr had followed earlier Parthian tradition when installing his son, Ohrmazd-Ardašir, as the 'great king of Armenia'. Conversely the late-third-century inscription of the high priest Kerdīr, on the eastern face of the Ka'ba-ye Zardošt at the same site, stipulates that Armenia was part of Anērān, while acknowledging that it was under Sasanian control.[9] The Paikuli inscription from the end of the third century similarly distinguished Armenia from Ērānšahr, noting that Narseh, the son of Šāpuhr I, had been 'king of Armenia' before succeeding his brother Ohrmazd I as *šahanšah* in 293 AD: 'May the King of kings graciously move from Armenia hither to Ērānšahr.... We moved from Armenia towards Ērānšahr'.[10] This epigraphic sequence reveals that the privileged position Armenia had enjoyed

---

[5] Garsoïan 1981: 30.
[6] Payne 2015: 23–38. See also Wiesehöfer and Huyse 2006 and Shaked 2008.
[7] Garsoïan 1981: 29–31.   [8] Huyse 1999: ŠKZ §2/1/3, in Middle Persian/Parthian/Greek.
[9] Gignoux 1991: 71.   [10] Skjærvø and Humbach 1983: 28, 32, 45.

in the Parthian empire persisted in the first decades of Sasanian rule, although its relationship to Ērānšahr could be represented in different ways.

The dearth of contemporary literature makes it impossible to determine the subsequent development of this relationship. The Armenian historical tradition, however, indicates that it was still unresolved, at least from an Armenian perspective, two centuries later. In the third and final book of Łazar P'arpec'i's *History*, composed at the very start of the sixth century, the leader of the Armenian rebels in 485, Vahan Mamikonean, repeatedly identifies the Sasanian *šahanšah* as *tēr Areac'*, usually translated as lord of the Aryans, but more usefully rendered as lord of Ērān.[11] Łazar, therefore, represented Sasanian rulership in legal, genealogical and religious terms, for *tēr* denoted the head of a princely family, in whom title to the inalienable property of the family was vested, while the meaning of Ērān, those of the Good Religion, has already been considered.[12] The narrative also refers regularly to *Areac' ašxarh*, an Armenian calque on the Middle Persian Ērānšahr, the land of Ērān, and describes Persian armies as comprising *bazmut'eamb Areōk' ew Anareōk'*, a multitude of those of Ērān and Anērān.[13] These terms were employed by Łazar to stress the otherness of Armenia and those Armenians under Vahan's leadership. At one point, Vahan asks 'You who are of Ērān, withdraw your support and leave this country of Armenia, *zašxarhs Hayoc'*, to us and them', the latter being those Armenians who had sided with the Persians.[14]

At the start of the sixth century, therefore, Łazar left his audience in no doubt that Armenia was not part of Ērānšahr. Yet his insistence can be interpreted as evidence of an anxiety on his part, that many of the elite were untroubled by the prospect of operating within the institutional framework of Sasanian Persia and had compromised, or were at risk of compromising, their distinctive Christian Armenian identity. In the context of the relationship between Armenia and Sasanian Persia in late antiquity, we should remember that outright rebellion was exceptional.[15] The normal state of affairs after the demise of the Arsacid kingdom in 428 was for Armenia and Armenians to be integrated into the world of Ērānšahr, participating in the affairs of state as loyal subjects of the Sasanian

---

[11] This title occurs thirty-one times in book 3; by comparison it is used on just four occasions across books 1 and 2.

[12] Greenwood 2017: 211–12.

[13] The phrase *Areac' ašxarh* occurs twenty-five times in the composition. The quotation: Łazar III.85; tr. Thomson 1991: 215.

[14] Łazar, *History of the Armenians* 3.92; tr. Thomson 1991: 229.   [15] McDonough 2006.

šahanšah. It is striking that Vardan Mamikonean, the Armenian hero of Łazar's narrative who was killed on the battlefield at Awarayr in 451, is also described in the text as 'a man of courage, who assisted the lord of Ērān; the memory of his greatest actions persists in the land of Ērān and many military commanders and others of Ērān with whom he fought also remember, and even the lord who is like a god [i.e. the *šahanšah*] had seen with his own eyes at Marviṙot his love of valour'.[16] This assertion of prior loyal service on the part of Vardan to the *šahanšah* on the eastern frontier at Marviṙot/Marwrūd, southwest of Bahl/Balkh, sits uncomfortably with the primary focus of the narrative, namely conflict between Armenians and Persians. Armenian space may not have been as 'other' as Łazar maintains, his stress on the spiritual heroism of its lay and clerical protagonists in the face of impious oppressors designed to remind his audience of a faith lived out by their ancestors, its beliefs and traditions integral to who they were.[17] The martyrdoms of leading nobles sanctioned the actions of Vardan Mamikonean and his supporters in what could otherwise have been interpreted as a failed uprising. The self-sacrifice of leading clerics – including the Catholicos Yovsēp' – served to legitimise the present authority of the Armenian Church under the headship of the Catholicos, Babgēn I. It is significant that the last two decades of the fifth century were a time of sustained sectarian conflict within the Christian communities of Sasanian Persia.[18] The documentary records relating to the first Council of Dvin in 505/6 confirm that Armenia was not excluded from this turmoil.[19] Łazar's *History*, therefore, was composed in the context of ecclesiological and political tensions and its construction of Armenian space offers one response to them.

The description of Ērānšahr preserved in the Long Recension (LR) of the *Ašxarhac'oyc'* articulates an alternative conception of Armenia.[20] It records that K'ust-i-, the region of the Caucasus mountains, comprised thirteen *ašxarhs*, lands: 'Atrapatakan, Armn which is Hayk', Varǰan which is Virk', Ṙan which is Ałuank', Balasakan, Sisakan, Aṙē, Gełan, Šančan, Dlmunk', Dmbawand, Taprēstan, Ṙuan, Aml'. The three short glosses identifying Armenia, Iberia and Albania confirm that the description was

---

[16] Łazar, *History of the Armenians* 2.44; tr. Thomson 1991: 124.
[17] All the nobles were killed on the battlefield; all the priests were martyred outside the city of Niwšapuh in the eastern province of Aparšahr.
[18] Gero 1981: 97–119; Garsoïan 1999a: 168–88; Wood 2013: 93–9, 106–8.
[19] *Girk' T'ł'oc'* I: 41–7; *Girk' T'ł'oc'* II: 147–56; tr. Garsoïan 1999a: 438–46; Greenwood 2015a: 509–16.
[20] *Ašxarhac'oyc'* (LR) 40; 2157; tr. Hewsen 1992: 72.

composed in Middle Persian but transliterated into Armenian at some point and then incorporated into this composition. If one accepts that this passage offers a conception of the Persian world from a Persian perspective, albeit preserved in Armenian, it confirms that Armenia could be viewed as fully incorporated into Ērānšahr at the end of the Sasanian era.

The identification of a distinct Armenian space for Sasanian administrative purposes is confirmed through an analysis of the sigillographic evidence. Almost thirty years ago, Gyselen acknowledged the possibility that 'l'Arménie ait fait de l'administration provinciale sassanide aux époques où l'influence sassanide y était très forte, bien qu'on puisse limiter cette intégration aux seules administrations civiles et militaires'.[21] The situation changed in 2002 when she published bullae from the Ahmad Saeedi collection. These included four groups of bullae belonging to officials whose authority extended over Armin.[22] One parcel of forty-six bullae identifies the *āmārgar* of Armin and Šahr-pādār-Pērōz; a second parcel of nineteen bullae refers to the *āmārgar* of Bāzāhā ud Armin Šahr-ī-Mūgān ud Kust-ī-Ādurbādagān; the third parcel of three bullae identifies the *gund-ī-kadag-xwadāyagan-framādār* of Armin; and the final parcel of four bullae refers to the *zarrbed* of Armin ud Ardān ud Wirōzān ud Sīsagān ud Marz-ī-nēsawān. These parcels permit Gyselen's earlier conjecture in relation to civil and military functions to be developed, for the *āmārgar* was a senior official in the public Treasury, the *zarrbed* was in charge of the management of gold mines and the *gund-ī-kadag-xwadāyagan-framādār* may have held a general command over the military contingents raised from the Armenian noble families. None of these bullae can be dated with any confidence but collectively they support the proposition that Sasanian provincial government comprised distinct administrative structures that were configured individually rather than uniformly. From an institutional perspective, Armin defined the limits of a territory that could exist and operate as an individual jurisdiction, as the *gund-ī-kadag-xwadāyagan-fram ādār* attests, but that could also be combined with different territories. Furthermore it is clear that the jurisdiction of the *āmārgar* charged with responsibility for Armin changed at least once, although we cannot be sure of the sequence, nor when the change occurred, beyond noting the invocation in the toponym Šahr-pādār-Pērōz, 'Pērōz protector of the

---

[21] Gyselen 1989: 80.
[22] Gyselen 2002: 43, 55–6 for the *āmārgar* of Armin and Šahr-pādār-Pērōz; 40, 51 for the *āmārgar* of Bāzāhā ud Armin Šahr-ī-Mūgān ud Kust-ī-Ādurbādagān; 60–1 for the *gund-ī-kadag-xwadāyagan-framādār* of Armin; and 78–9 for the *zarrbed* of Armin ud Ardān ud Wirōzān ud Sīsagān ud Marz-ī-nēsawān.

šahr, almost certainly implies a date between 459 and 484 because it is hard to envisage such a name being retained for any length of time after his ignominious death in battle against the Hephthalites. One suspects that further sigillographic evidence will come to light, which will help to extend our knowledge of the institutions of the Sasanian state operating over Armenia.[23] For the present, perhaps the biggest surprise is that no seal identifying the *marzbān* of Armin has yet been discovered, for a number of different holders of this office, of Armenian and non-Armenian background, feature prominently in the Armenian literary tradition.

What is less certain is the extent to which the administrative status and territorial definition of Armin changed over time. Gyselen suggested that Armin may have come to comprise no more than the region of Ayrarat, 'le cœur de l'Arménie', although she also acknowledged that it might equally have retained a much broader definition.[24] Establishing the status and boundaries of Armin from a Persian perspective is always going to be problematic but Armenian literary tradition confirms that they were subject to alteration. The mid-seventh-century Armenian *History* attributed to Sebēos records that at some point before 572, Vahan prince of Siwnik' asked Khusro I that the *diwan* of the country of Siwnik' be transferred from the city of Dvin to the city of P'aytakaran and that he should allocate the city to the *šahrmar*, 'land-measuring', of Atrpatakan, 'so that they would not be called Armenian'.[25] The narrative reports that Khusro I complied with his request. This notice contemplates two administrative changes, the movement of the *diwan* and then the reallocation of the city of P'aytakaran, implying that both were needed to ensure separation. It also indicates that Armenia held a higher administrative status than Siwnik' at this time because the second change could be interpreted as evidence for a separate land-measuring of Armenia, equal to but separate from that of Atrpatakan. Intriguingly this notice also reveals that members of the regional elite could petition for administrative reform; evidently not every change was imposed from above or motivated by the interests of efficiency or good government. We shall return to the complex relationship between Siwnik' and Armenia.

Although the evidence for Persian perceptions of Armenian space is extremely limited, the material outlined previously demonstrates that Armin had political and administrative significance for the Sasanian state

---

[23] For the latest survey, see Garsoïan 2009.

[24] Gyselen 2002: 29–30. The territory around Dvin was called Ostan Hayoc' and there are several references to *ostaniks*, inhabitants of the Ostan, in Łazar's *History*.

[25] Sebēos, *History* 67–8; tr. Thomson and Howard-Johnston 1999: 6.

throughout late antiquity. It remains unclear, however, whether there was any awareness of Armenian space beyond the bounds of Ērānšahr. This is one of the ways in which Roman attitudes towards Armenia differed. Not only were there numbered provinces of Armenia within the Roman Empire but there was also recognition of Armenian space outside the empire under Persian control through the use of the term *Persarmenia*. It is to the Roman perspective that we now turn.

Armenian Provinces of the Roman Empire

The evolution of the network of Roman provinces of Armenia has been studied by others and can only be sketched in barest outline here, starting with the creation of Lesser Armenia/*Armenia Minor* and the formal recognition of the five Satrapies (the *Gentes* or *Ethne*) as *civitates foederatae liberae et immunes* in the reign of Diocletian; then the division of Lesser Armenia into First and Second Armenia and the agglomeration of several other districts as Inner Armenia/*Armenia Interior* under Theodosius I; then the wholesale reorganisation of all the territories of Roman Armenia into four numbered provinces during the reign of Justinian I in 536, first, and brilliantly, analysed by Adontz; and finally, the further reorganisation and expansion eastwards of Roman Armenia in 591 after substantial territorial concessions made by Khusro II to Maurice by treaty, requiring the creation of three new provinces: a second, and entirely separate, Inner Armenia/*Armenia Interior*, together with the newly devised Lower Armenia/*Armenia Inferior* and Deep Armenia/*Armenia Profunda*.[26] No attempt will be made to outline the complicated sequence of Roman territorial gains and losses across the districts of Armenia, and their administrative implications, in the course of the seventh century.

Eschewing description allows a number of more general observations to be advanced. The preceding summary confirms that Roman Armenia was disaggregated, always split into two or more provinces or territories. It was never administered as a singular or unitary space. Moreover, it underwent at least three major restructurings, under Theodosius I, Justinian I and Maurice, each of which generated new subdivisions. While those of Theodosius I and Maurice were in response to major political realignments along the frontier, the provincial reorganisation undertaken by Justinian was driven by different concerns. The legislation brought an end to the quasi-autonomous Satrapies and incorporated them in the new province of

---

[26] Adontz 1970: 25–154; Hewsen 1992: 17–27.

Fourth Armenia. It revised the boundaries of the existing provinces and asserted that Roman law would in future operate across all four provinces, with the intention of subverting the customary inheritance practices that had evidently preserved the landed wealth of the elite intact.[27] It seems likely that this reorganisation also had fiscal consequences. Procopius reports that in 538 the *anthypatos* Acacius, newly appointed governor of First Armenia, ordered his subjects to pay an unprecedented sum of four hundred pounds of gold in tax and was killed by them in response.[28] Sittas, the newly appointed *magister militum per Armeniam*, was also killed shortly afterwards, attesting local opposition once more.[29] The long-term aims of this legislation – to undermine entrenched interests and assert the military, judicial and fiscal authority of the Roman state – seem to have been realised. Although the provinces continued to carry the name of Armenia, many of the features that distinguished Armenian society and civilisation in late antiquity – including, but not limited to, an entrenched landowning elite, vernacular literary and oral culture and an autonomous Church – were progressively displaced. The vast majority of the Armenians who populate late Roman narratives are recorded as coming from outside the Roman Empire, not from one of the provinces of Roman Armenia.

The violent response to Justinian's restructuring of provincial govern-ment and administration, in which senior representatives of the state were targeted and killed, was repeated following the provincial reforms of Maurice in 591. The *History* attributed to Sebēos records that members of the Vahewuni house rebelled and planned to kill an unnamed Roman *curator* while he was staying at a spa outside the city of Theodosiopolis.[30] As *curators* were responsible for managing imperial estates, his presence in this part of Armenia implies that the recent reorganisation had also involved the transfer of property to the imperial domain. Unlike Acacius and Sittas, the *curator* survived the assassination attempt and the revolt was brutally suppressed, with several public executions in Theodosiopolis. Arguably, therefore, the dimensions of Armenian space within the Roman Empire expanded in late antiquity but were transformed in the process.

No Armenian literature survives from the provinces of Roman Armenia in late antiquity. Even the Armenian history to which Procopius claims to have had access records the actions of Armenians in the context of their historic dealings with Persia rather than the deeds of anyone from Roman

---

[27] Adontz 1970: 127–54; Greenwood 2017: 200–7. [28] Procopius, *Wars* 2.3.5–7.
[29] Ibid., 2.3.8–27. [30] Sebēos, *History* 89–90; tr. Thomson and Howard-Johnston 1999: 34–5.

Armenia.[31] This makes it all but impossible to discern how those affected
by the changes reacted to them, other than the local uprisings noted
previously. Quite why this should be so is unclear, but two solutions
may be advanced, albeit tentatively. A letter from the bishops of Second
Armenia to Leo I in 458 confirms that their province was demographically
and linguistically Armenian, but it is less clear whether this was the case
a century later.[32] It could, therefore, be that the dearth of Armenian
literature from Roman Armenia reflects a linguistic shift, from Armenian
to Greek. It is also possible that the mechanisms for preserving
Armenian literature were insufficient or nonexistent. We know that
bishops from Roman Armenia regularly attended Ecumenical Church
Councils from Nicaea onwards.[33] John of Sebasteia, the metropolitan of
First Armenia, signed the solemn definition of faith at the sixth session of
the Council of Chalcedon on 25 October 451, together with three of his
suffragan bishops, as did Constantine of Melitene, metropolitan of Second
Armenia, with six of his suffragans, or their proxies.[34] Their attendance at
Chalcedon, however, reminds us that they were loyal, orthodox representatives of the imperial church who wrote, and worshipped the liturgy, in
Greek, not Armenian. With regret, none of their archives have been
preserved but it would seem less likely that they preserved Armenian
literature. Similarly it is not possible to prove that any Armenian literature
was retained in monastic collections in late antique Roman Armenia.

There is, however, some evidence that points in a different direction.
The account of the conversion of Armenia by St Grigor the Illuminator at
the start of the fourth century attributed to Agat'angełos is unusual among
Armenian compositions in that it exists in different versions and different
languages.[35] Two main stems of the tradition have been identified, the
A recension, comprising the extant Armenian version, and its derivatives,
and the V recension, representing a lost Armenian version that was preserved in Greek, and its derivatives, which offer great variation in content
and exist in several languages, including Karshuni, Arabic and Syriac. No
trace of the V recension survives in Armenian although Armenian historical
texts contain versions of the conversion narrative that do not correspond to
the A cycle, indicating that there were also different stories in circulation in
Armenian. The Syriac witness of the V cycle (Vs) diverges in many respects,
introducing new elements and incorporating new locations. No other

---

[31] Procopius, Wars 1.5.9–40.
[32] Garsoïan 1983: 152–3 and n. 37; Garsoïan 1988: 257 and n. 34, 283 and n. 141.   [33] Garsoïan 1988.
[34] ACO II, I (1), 56 and 60; Garsoïan 1988: 268–9.
[35] For a helpful introduction, see Thomson 2010: 8–13.

version records that when the holy women Gayianē and Hṙipʻsimē fled
from their convent in Rome to the land of Armenia, they were accompanied by seventy-seven virgins, nor that on their arrival, they divided into
two groups, with forty of them going to live in a ruined wine press opposite
the city of Dvin and the remainder going to Awan where they settled in
a cave on a mountain.[36] This revision may appear inconsequential, but it
was only in the aftermath of the dramatic Roman expansion eastwards
under the emperor Maurice following the settlement agreed in 591 with
Khusro II that these two locations became significant at the same time.
This decade saw the emergence of two rival leaders of the Armenian
Church, Movsēs II of Eḷivard, based at Dvin in the Persian sector, and
Yovhan of Bagaran, based at Awan in the Roman sector, where he constructed a church.[37] This suggests that the foundational narrative preserved
in *Vs* was reimagined at this time to reflect the new political and confessional situation, when Awan emerged as a rival to Dvin as a legitimate site
of spiritual authority, prepared and sanctified through the earlier presence
of the holy women. Further revisions were made in connection with the
activities of Grigor, altering the Christian landscape of Armenia to the
advantage of places under Roman control and the oversight of the imperial
church. *Vs* records that Grigor retreated to the cave of Manē in the district
of Daranaḷi, where he lived for thirty years. Much later on, in the time of
Zeno, his body was rediscovered and transferred to Tʻordan in the adjacent
district of Ekeḷeacʻ.[38] Evidently even the traditional centres of early
Armenian Christianity were capable of transposition; the contours of the
past could be reshaped to suit the circumstances of the present. So it could
be that, in terms of literary production and historical memory, Roman
Armenia was not a silent space but a silenced space, its late antique
traditions preserved but in Greek and Syriac, rather than Armenian.

Armenian Space in Armenian Historiography

The mass of surviving late antique Armenian literature derives from Persian
Armenia. These compositions contain important reflections on the extent and
character of Armenian space as well as its complex relationship with Ērānšahr.
Armenian authors tend to stress its separate, autonomous character and
nowhere is this more apparent than in a story from the *Buzandaran*,

[36] Agatʻangeḷos *Syriac Vs* 77–8; tr. Thomson 2010: 222–3.   [37] Garitte 1952: 246–54.
[38] Agatʻangeḷos *Syriac Vs* 287–300; tr. Thomson 2010: 496–8. It is significant that the final notice in *Vs*
records the emperor Heraclius capturing the city of Tʻordan and building a splendid church over St
Grigor's remains. This supports the proposed early-seventh-century date.

a collection of epic traditions pertaining to the era of the Arsacid kingdom of Armenia in fourth century but assembled in the third quarter of the fifth century.[39] The narrative presents the Persian *šahanšah* Šāpuhr II in a quandary, as one who was eager to make peace with king Aršak II of Armenia after thirty years of warfare but mindful of his past duplicity. He therefore sought counsel from the soothsayers and astrologers at court. They advised Šāpuhr to send envoys to the land of Armenia to collect two loads of soil and a jar of water and to spread the Armenian soil over half the floor of his tent, pouring the water over it, leaving the other half composed of soil from his own land. Once the soil and water had been brought – by Arabian camels apparently – and the floor of his tent prepared as instructed, Šāpuhr then invited Aršak to discuss terms.[40] When standing on Persian soil, Aršak acknowledged that as one of Šāpuhr's servants, he was guilty and deserved to die. However, when standing on the imported Armenian soil, Aršak spoke imperiously – 'Get away from me, malign servant!' – and promised to take vengeance from Šāpuhr and his family for his own ancestors and the death of king Artawan, the last Parthian king. Šāpuhr escorted Aršak back and forth and observed how his attitude switched accordingly. He realised that Aršak was dissembling when he spoke on Persian soil and expressing his true opinion of Sasanian hegemony when back on Armenian soil. Aršak repeated his threats during a banquet that evening, when he had been relegated from his usual position and placed once again on the Armenian soil. Consequently, he was imprisoned for life in the fortress of Andmēš, also called Anuš, the Castle of Oblivion. This narrative contains several surprising features, not least the complete success of the plan suggested by the soothsayers and astrologers and the perfidy of Aršak II. For the purposes of this study, however, its principal significance is the absolute distinction made between Armenian and Persian soil, a distinction that held meaning in the middle of the fourth century but that evidently still resonated in Armenia in the third quarter of the fifth century when the *Buzandaran* was assembled.

With the exception of the *Ašxarhac'oyc'*, Armenian compositions do not supply precise definitions of Armenian space. Nevertheless, it is clear that it could be constructed in different ways and shifted over time. By way of illustration, in the *Buzandaran*, the city of Ganjak in Atrpatakan is repeatedly described as being situated at the borders of Armenia.[41] This should be

[39] *Epic histories* 4.54; tr. Garsoïan 1989: 170–3.
[40] Arabian camels: *tačik ułtuk'*: *Epic histories* 4.54; tr. Garsoïan 1989: 171.
[41] Garsoïan 2009: 93, n. 14 for the five references that include *i Ganjak sahmans Atrpatakan*, to Ganjak, the border of Atrpatakan, and *minčew i bun i sahmansn i Ganjak Atrpatakani*, up to the border, at Ganjak of Atrpatakan.

interpreted primarily in political terms because the kingdom of Armenia subsisted throughout the fourth century, but it is important to note that Ganjak was close to one of the principal Zoroastrian fire temples, dedicated to Ādur Gušnasp, and so may have evoked an alternative spiritual landscape. The use of the city to denote liminality is also revealing because it is uncommon for Armenian sources to configure space in such terms.

Łazar Pʻarpecʻiʼs *History* considers the same sector in its long account of the negotiations between the Armenian leader, Vahan Mamikonean, and the representative of the Persian king Vałarš, Nixor Všnaspdat, in 485.[42] The narrative records that Nixor came to the country of Armenia but did not presume to move forward into the Armenian positions, rather he stopped in the district of Her, at the village of Nuarsak, and sent a negotiating team on ahead.[43] Her was located northwest of Lake Urmia, 150 miles northwest of Ganjak. Evidently the border at Ganjak described in the *Buzandaran* held no meaning in the changed circumstances of Vahan's rebellion. Vahan Mamikonean, in turn, was persuaded to advance to the village of Ełind in the adjoining district of Artaz, from where he later travelled to Nixor in Nuarsak for face-to-face discussions.[44] In this episode, therefore, it seems that a temporary, neutral space was established between the representatives of the Persian *šahanšah* on one side, accompanied by the cavalry contingents of Atrpatakan and the districts of Her and Zarewand, all billeted in the village of Nuarsak, and the Armenian rebels and their contingents on the other side, under the command of Vahan Mamikonean, located in the village of Ełind. This neutral zone was created in order that negotiations could begin with sufficient distance between the respective armed forces, reducing the likelihood of accidental clashes. The movement of envoys and hostages back and forth also gave time for both leaders to consult with their advisors and supporters. Moreover, each successful exchange encouraged trust in the process of reconciliation and settlement.

The long-term impact of these events on the construction of Armenian space is impossible to determine. There seems to be little doubt that the autonomous Armenia briefly created by Vahan Mamikonean's rebellion was a fraction of the former kingdom. There is no sense that it persisted after the settlement had been reached. Instead it appears that Armenia was reintegrated into the institutions of the Sasanian state on the same terms, and in the same form, that it had been incorporated previously. Even

---

[42] Łazar, *History of the Armenians* 3.89–94; tr. Thomson 1991: 220–33.
[43] Ibid., 3.89; tr. Thomson 1991: 220.   [44] Ibid., 3.91; tr. Thomson 1991: 224.

before the final, public reconciliation at the court of Vałarš, Łazar records that Vahan had agreed with Nixor to assemble and equip the native cavalry of Armenia for service against Zareh, son of Peroz, who had rebelled.[45] Vahan placed the force under the command of one Vrēn Vanandacʻi and it fought with distinction and success. Shortly after the reconciliation, and on the recommendation of the *marzbān* of Armenia, Andekan, Vahan was appointed as his successor.[46] The promotion of a member of the Armenian elite to this position was unusual and almost certainly attests the contemporary fragility of the Sasanian regime. The *History* attributed to Sebēos, compiled in the middle of the seventh century, indicates that this was a temporary state of affairs, with Persians being appointed to this office once more following the end of Vard Mamikonean's tenure as *marzbān* in circa 510.[47]

Thus far, the construction of Armenian space by Armenian authors has primarily been analysed in terms of its relationship to Ērānšahr. As Łazar's *History* reveals, Armenia could be projected as autonomous and integrated at the same time. This reflects the gap between the purposes of the author and the lived and remembered experiences of the elite. Armenian space could also be constructed from within, as the sum of its constituent elements. This is illustrated most clearly in the complex, contested relationship between Armenia and the isolated, eastern region of Siwnikʻ. This can be traced in several ways through the extant sources although none of them offer a pro-Siwnian perspective on that relationship. Princes of Siwnikʻ are regularly cast as unreliable, deceitful and impious. By way of example, Łazar associates the origins of Vardan Mamikonean's rebellion with the machinations of one Varazvałan, a prince of Siwnikʻ, against his father-in-law, Vasak, prince of Siwnikʻ and *marzbān* of Armenia at the time.[48] Furthermore at the height of the rebellion, Vasak betrayed Vardan's plans to the *hazarapet* of Ērān, Mihrnerseh, and worked actively to destabilise the coalition assembled by Vardan.[49] Łazar observes with satisfaction that Vasak did not profit from his treachery and was deprived of his rank as lord of Siwnikʻ, which was transferred to his estranged son-in-law Varazvałan.[50] And while thirty years later the brave Babgēn of Siwnikʻ sided with Vahan Mamikonean and was seriously wounded in an

[45] Ibid., 3.94; tr. Thomson 1991: 232–3.   [46] Ibid., 3.98–9; tr. Thomson 1991: 239–40.
[47] For confirmation that Vard did indeed become *marzbān*, see *Girkʻ Tʻłtʻocʻ* I: 48; *Girkʻ Tʻłtʻocʻ* II: 157; Garsoïan 1999a: 446–7. For the statement that he was succeeded by Persian *marzbāns*: Sebēos, *History* 67; tr. Thomson and Howard-Johnston 1999: 6.
[48] Łazar, *History of the Armenians* 2.20–1; tr. Thomson 1991: 75–80.
[49] Ibid., 2.34; tr. Thomson 1991: 106.   [50] Ibid., 2.46; tr. Thomson 1991: 130–2.

engagement, proving his loyalty, Łazar reveals that the impious and inso-lent Gdihon, lord of Siwnikʿ fought on the opposite side under the Persian *marzbān* of Armenia, Šapuh, and was killed in combat.[51]

Tension with Siwnikʿ can be observed in other ways. Garsoïan analysed the evidence for rupture between the Catholicos of Armenia and the see of Siwnikʿ in the second half of the sixth century and considered it to be unpersuasive.[52] Nevertheless, the Catholicos Yovhannēs II Gabełean (c. 558–74) found it necessary to write to Vrtʿanēs bishop of Siwnikʿ and Mihr-Artašir, lord of Siwnikʿ, to express concern at the number of 'Nestorians' living in their country and urged that measures be taken to counter their influence.[53] This sense of Siwnian liminality is reinforced by a short passage in the *Chronicle* of pseudo-Zachariah Rhetor that asserts that there are four languages in the Caucasus: Armenian, Iberian, Albanian and Siwnian.[54] Furthermore, the administrative separation of Siwnikʿ from Armenia outlined previously is echoed in the *History* attributed to Sebēos whose final notices refer consistently to the princes of Armenia, Iberia, Albania and Siwnikʿ, implying that this fourfold division was a present reality.[55] In sum, there is sufficient evidence across a range of registers to show that at times Siwnikʿ was deemed to be autonomous from Armenia. Armenian space was, therefore, susceptible to internal fragmentation as well as external reconfiguration.

The Armenian historical sources of the fifth and sixth centuries are focused overwhelmingly on Armenia's relationship with Ērānšahr and offered little commentary on the world of the east Roman Empire. The *History* attributed to Sebēos, a work compiled a century and a half after Łazar's composition, attests a very different construction of historical space. Through a series of extracts lifted from a composition titled 'Royal History', it records Sasanian dynastic history and interactions with Armenia and Armenians, but predominantly from the perspective of the *šahanšah* rather than individual Armenians.[56]

---

[51] The brave, *law*, Babgēn: Łazar, *History of the Armenians* 3.69; tr. Thomson 1991: 180. The impious, *anōrēn*, Gdihon: Łazar, *History of the Armenians* 3.76; tr. Thomson 1991: 198.

[52] Garsoïan 1999a: 296–302.

[53] *Girkʿ Tʿłtʿocʿ* I: 79, at; *Girkʿ Tʿłtʿocʿ* II: 207; Garsoïan 1999a: 485.

[54] Pseudo-Zachariah, *Chronicle* xii.7k (i)–(iv), entries for Armenia, Gurzan, Arran and Sisakan; ed. Greatrex; tr. Phenix and Horn 2011: 446–7 and nn. 197–200. Compare the seal of the *zarrbed*; see note 22.

[55] Sebēos, *History* 166, 169, 174–5; tr. Thomson and Howard-Johnston 1999: 138–9, 143, 150, 153. A distinction is also made between the three thousand soldiers under Mušeł Mamikonean and the thousand troops under Grigor lord of Siwnikʿ who fought under the Persian commander Ṙostom at the battle of al-Qādisiyya in January 638: ibid., 137; tr. Thomson and Howard-Johnston 1999: 98–9.

[56] A heading reads *Matean žamanakean*, Chronological Composition, and *Patmutʿiwn tʿagaworakan*, Royal History: Sebēos, *History* 72; tr. Thomson and Howard-Johnston 1999: 13 and n. 89. For analysis of this dimension, see Greenwood 2002: 327–47; Howard-Johnston 2010: 74–6, 82–3.

Only the long and highly successful career of Smbat Bagratuni, in first Roman and then Sasanian service, is given extended treatment, reflecting recourse to a heroic biography recording his deeds and rewards.[57] Yet this *History* also addresses the reigns of Roman emperors, Maurice, Heraclius and Constans II, again predominantly from their perspective, although again reporting their interactions with Armenia and Armenians. Historians have long been aware of the particular value of this composition for studying the decades of conflict between the two great powers, the emergence of Islam and the conquests that followed. Its remarkable broadening in terms of geographical scope and spatial range has been less appreciated.[58] No other late antique Armenian history possesses such a supra-Armenian dimension, nor extends so far beyond the traditional parameters of Armenian space. By way of illustration, the *History* contains a description of Jerusalem shortly after its capture in 638 and the appropriation of sacred space on the Temple Mount by first Jews and then Muslims.[59] Although Armenians had been travelling to Jerusalem for instruction, worship and pilgrimage for at least three centuries, the focus on Jerusalem within an Armenian historical composition is rare.[60] The absence of any Armenian involvement in the narrative makes it unique.

This expansion of historical vision is connected with the compiler's eschatological apprehension, his conviction of the imminence of the Second Coming. He explicitly cites Daniel 7 and other biblical prophecies and these possess a universal dimension.[61] But this unprecedented scope also attests a changed political and cultural context, one in which the Roman Empire is afforded much greater prominence than previously. This reflects the sustained engagement of successive emperors with Armenia from Maurice onwards. It is, therefore, less surprising to discover that the composition displays a much greater awareness of political intrigue in Constantinople from the 630s onwards, the product, one suspects, of the involvement of members of the Armenian elite in these affairs. By way of comparison, in Łazar's *History*, Armenians are represented operating in Armenian and Persian, but not Roman, space. Vardan's unanswered appeal to the emperor illustrates the sense of separation established by Łazar.[62]

---

[57] Greenwood 2002: 347–52; Howard-Johnston 2010: 84–5.
[58] See now Howard-Johnston 2010: 78–9, who stresses this aspect.
[59] Sebēos, *History* 139–40; tr. Thomson and Howard-Johnston 1999: 102–3.
[60] Renoux 1989, 1999; Terian 2008.   [61] Greenwood 2002: 375–88.
[62] Łazar, *History of the Armenians* 2.33; tr. Thomson 1991: 104–5.

A Geographical Treatise: The *Ašxarhac'oyc'*

A universal perspective is also a feature of the *Ašxarhac'oyc'*. As observed previously, this geographical composition is frequently cited for individual notices but has been little studied as a whole. Key features, including its date of compilation, authorship and purposes, remain unresolved. To compound these uncertainties, the work survives in two recensions. The LR is preserved in one manuscript at San Lazzaro in Venice (V1245), dated 1605; the Short Recension (SR) is preserved in at least fifty-three manuscripts, of which the oldest is preserved in the monastery at Bzommar (BZ204), dated 1178, and the best, according to Hewsen, in the Matenadaran in Yerevan (M1267 and M3160), copied in the fifteenth century and mid-seventeenth century, respectively.[63] A modern edition of SR remains a desideratum because it is unclear whether all fifty-three preserve the same recension. Twenty-five years ago, Hewsen published an important survey of past scholarship and his own analysis of the work, alongside an annotated English translation of both recensions, and this remains the most recent study. Although a comprehensive reassessment cannot be supplied here, the significance of the *Ašxarhac'oyc'* for the construction of Armenian space in late antiquity is such that a brief analysis of the work as a whole is required.

The *Ašxarhac'oyc'* in its present form is the product of an extremely complicated process of transmission. Ultimately it is related to Ptolemy's *Cosmographia*, but indirectly rather than directly, almost certainly through the lost *Geography* of Pappus of Alexandria, or an abridgement thereof.[64] It is also possible that an otherwise unknown work, the *Christian Topography* of Constantine of Antioch, also had some part to play in the transmission of the work.[65] Soukry's contention that this work is the same as the Christian Topography of pseudo-Cosmas Indicopleustes is unpersuasive. The *Ašxarhac'oyc'* reflects the contribution of at least three Armenian

---

[63] Hewsen 1992: 3.

[64] 'Now let us begin according to the *Geography* [*Erkragrut'ean*] of Pappus of Alexandria who, according to the dimensions of the original circuit of the *Cosmographia* [*Tiezeragrut'eanc'*] of Claudius Ptolemy, began with the double Torrid zone to the north and south': *Ašxarhac'oyc'* (LR) 9; 2139; *Ašxarhac'oyc'* (SR) 339; 2178; tr. Hewsen 1992: 44, 44A. See also Pseudo-Zachariah, *Chronicle* xii.7a–j; ed. Greatrex; tr. Phenix and Horn 2011: 431–45 and nn. 27–195, which also draws on Ptolemy's *Cosmographia* or an epitome thereof. His version, however, does not mention Pappus of Alexandria and identifies Ptolemy Philometor as responsible for commissioning the work. Pseudo-Zachariah's abridgement is given a specifically Caucasian coda, at xii.7k (i)–(iv); cf. note 54. Its content does not overlap with either of the Armenian recensions, but the decision to include such material is a surprising coincidence.

[65] *Kostandianos Antiok'ac'i i K'ristoneakan Telagrut'ean: Ašxarhac'oyc'* (LR) 7; 2138; *Ašxarhac'oyc'* (SR) 338; 2178; tr. Hewsen 1992: 43, 43A. cf. Soukry 1881.

scholars, one of whom was responsible for the initial translation and adaptation of the underlying Greek work, also lost, and two others who created, independently of one another, their own versions of that text, which survive as the two recensions, LR and SR. This convoluted sequence of transitions and transformations, coupled with the loss of two of the four principal works in the sequence – the *Geography* of Pappus and its Armenian translation – makes it extremely challenging to establish 'authorship' or 'date of composition' with any degree of confidence. By way of illustration, when a passage preserved only in SR states that 'Pappus of Alexandria derived an abbreviated *Geography* from the original circuit of [Ptolemy's] *Cosmographia*, from which we also made an abridgement and copied down only the greatest and most significant', does the first-person 'we' denote an intermediate scholar working in Greek or could it be the voice of the Armenian translator?[66] The reworking of the material by successive scholars makes it very difficult to disentangle the various accretions and determine what was added and when.

How should this amalgam of material be approached? Rather than attempting to reconstruct the missing composition from which the two recensions derive, as Eremyan valiantly sought to do, this brief assessment will analyse the two recensions as separate texts with their own purposes and contexts before working backwards to offer some thoughts on the lost work common to both.[67]

The use of long and short to describe the two recensions is so embedded in the literature that it would be futile to suggest alternative titles. While this distinction is correct on the basis of their overall length relative to one another, it does not follow that every notice in LR is more substantial than the equivalent notice in SR. If, for example, we examine the introduction, we find that SR offers a short description of the scope of Ptolemy's work which is missing from LR.[68] Or again, in its description of Italy, SR describes the island of Sardinia in much greater detail than LR, but LR

---

[66] *Ašxarhac'oyc'* (SR) 338, 2177; tr. Hewsen 1992: 43A. Linguistically this is proximate to the citation in note 64.

[67] Hewsen 1992: 7.

[68] *Ašxarhac'oyc'* (SR) 337–8, 2177; tr. Hewsen 1992: 42A. 'But a deopatta is needed for measuring land, with which Claudius Ptolemy measured in *stadia* the whole of human settlement in length [longitude] making a beginning in the west, which is the Unknown sea Ovkianos/Ocean, from the tip of the country of Spain to the east, to the edge of the country of China, to the unknown land, one hundred and eighty degrees. Likewise for breadth [latitude], he made a beginning at the Torrid Zone and measured to the unknown sea and land in the north, seventeen degrees, as the entirety of latitude is eighty degrees. And the part beyond that, no-one has seen or comprehended the edge of the world as Ptolemy says, but it is called unknown land and ocean'.

refers to 'Greater Greece, next to which is the delightful Campania', omitted in SR.[69] And on a broader scale, SR identifies forty-four countries of Asia, all of which are present, whereas LR only records thirty-eight countries in its survey of Asia. It is well known that the description of the four quarters of Ērānšahr, referred to previously, appears only in LR;[70] less well known is the observation that LR is missing the Roman provinces of Honorias, Pamphylia, Second Cappadocia, Third Armenia, First Armenia and Cappadocian Pontus, all of which obtain brief entries in SR.[71] There are instances, therefore, when SR contains entries, or details within entries, missing from LR.

Comparing the two recensions indicates that their respective authors approached the underlying text in different ways. Although both acknowledge their debt to the *Geography* of Pappus of Alexandria, and his dependence in turn on the *Cosmographia* of Claudius Ptolemy, and both also refer to the *Christian Topography* of Constantine of Antioch, it is striking that the compiler of LR was more open to naming authorities than the compiler of SR. He cites Hipparchus for his calculations of where cities are located as well as for his description of a lunar eclipse at Arbela and at Carthage.[72] In the next sentence, he commends Marinus of Tyre for his astronomical measurements. Both Hipparchus and Marinus influenced Ptolemy's work and so these references must derive ultimately from this. The compiler of LR also disparages the views of the pagan authors Dionysius and Apollo who maintain that the Ocean surrounds everything.[73] More intriguingly, in one instance, he cites 'our illuminator', that is St Grigor, as an authority and the short extract that follows is found verbatim in the *A* recension of Agat'angełos.[74] He follows this with quotations from St Basil of Caesarea and 'the Theologian', St Gregory Nazianzus; a later passage cites Eusebius.[75] In terms of approach, therefore, the compiler of LR reveals a willingness to cite pagan, patristic and

---

[69] Sardinia's shape is described as having a longer side from north to south; it has five rivers, rugged mountains and strong places, as well as nine cities and twenty districts: *Ašxarhac'oyc'* (SR) 342, 2181; tr. Hewsen 1992: 48A. For the description of Greater Greece, see *Ašxarhac'oyc'* (LR) 15, 2143; tr. Hewsen 1992: 46.

[70] *Ašxarhac'oyc'* (LR) 40, 2157; tr. Hewsen 1992: 72.

[71] *Ašxarhac'oyc'* (SR) 346–7, 2184–5; tr. Hewsen 1992: 52A, 54A, 55A.

[72] *Ašxarhac'oyc'* (LR) 6, 2137; tr. Hewsen 1992: 43: *Iparḱ'os; Maṙin tiwṙesac'i.*

[73] Ibid., 8, 2138; tr. Hewsen 1992: 43: *Dionesios ew Apołon.*

[74] Ibid., 9, 2139; tr. Hewsen 1992: 44: *i veray oč'ěnč'i kaṙuc'eal zerkir.* Agat'angełos *A* §259.

[75] Basil of Caesarea, *Hexaemeron*, 1.9, cites the same verse, Psalm 23:2 and develops the argument attributed to him; tr. Thomson 2012: 70–1. The source of the Eusebian citation is unknown: *Ašxarhac'oyc'* (LR) 13, 2142; tr. Hewsen 1992: 46 and n. 216.

Armenian authorities, unlike the compiler of SR who was reluctant to cite scholarly proofs.

The compiler of LR also reveals more about the circumstances in which he was writing. In his description of Thrace, he notes that on one of the islands in the Danube called Piwki, 'Asparhruk, the son of Xubraat' was living, who had fled from the Khazars, from the mountain of the Bulgars and had come and expelled the Avar people westwards and had settled there'.[76] In a second, separate passage, defining the country of the Sarmatians, LR again records that 'the son of Xudbadra' had fled from the Hippic mountain'.[77] The figures of both Koubrat and Asparuch are attested in the early-ninth-century *Short History* (*Breviarium*) of Nicephorus and *Chronographia* of Theophanes.[78] They both report that Koubrat, the leader of the Bulgars, died during the reign of Constans II and that shortly afterwards his five sons scattered in different directions. His third son Asparuch settled close to the river Danube, at a site called Onglos, which was marshy and encircled by rivers. Following this, the Khazars conquered all the former territories of Koubrat. The evidence of LR complements and clarifies the information preserved in these later Greek works, asserting that Asparuch fled from the Khazars, which seems far more likely, and that he settled on the island of Peuke in the Danube delta. The displacement of the Bulgars by the Khazars took place in the late 660s. LR also records Bulgar settlement on the Danube at the expense of the Avars rather than the Romans. This passage, therefore, appears to predate the major campaign undertaken by Constantine IV against Asparuch in 680 or 681.[79] This resulted in a heavy Roman defeat, a peace treaty involving the payment of an annual tribute and formal recognition of Bulgar expansion south of the Danube. Hewsen dismissed the first passage as 'probably an interpolation into the original text' and did not comment on the second.[80] Yet while they may indeed represent interpolations into the underlying text, they also indicate that LR was completed in the 670s, when Asparuch had only recently arrived in the Danube delta, before his conflict with Constantine IV and the Bulgar expansion into Roman territory.

This dating obtains support from two other brief notices in LR. The description of Mauretania in the section on Libya concludes with the

---

[76] *Ašxarhac'oyc'* (LR) 17, 2144; tr. Hewsen 1992: 48: *Aspar-hruk ordin Xubraat'ay.*
[77] Ibid., 25, 2149; tr. Hewsen 1992: 55: *ordin Xudbadray.*
[78] Nicephorus, *Short History* cc. 35; Theophanes, *Chronicle* 357–8; tr. Mango and Scott 1997: 498.
[79] Nicephorus, *Short History* cc. 36; Theophanes, *Chronicle* 358–9; tr. Mango and Scott 1997: 498–9.
[80] Hewsen 1992: 94, n. 98.

unexpected statement that 'three other [cities] were built, Tisoba, Idisia, Pondika, which the wise Nerseh Kamsarakan, *patrikios* and lord of Širak and Aršarunik' controlled'.[81] These sites are not known; they may be corrupt forms of cities mentioned by Ptolemy in the vicinity of Tripoli. There are several seventh-century figures named Nerseh Kamsarakan, lord of Širak and Aršarunik'. One appears in the foundation inscription at Mren, dated to the late 630s.[82] A second is eulogised in the colophon attached to the Armenian translation and adaptation of the *Ecclesiastical History* of Socrates undertaken by P'ilon Tirakac'i in Constantinople and dated 695/696.[83] P'ilon addresses this Nerseh as *apohypaton* and *patrikios*. An inscription records that this figure also founded the small church at T'alin.[84] Nothing is known about Nerseh's earlier career but it is conceivable that he held a command in Byzantine North Africa, prior to its fall to the Arabs in 698. It is impossible to prove that they are one and the same figure, but it is certainly suggestive. If so, this establishes a plausible intellectual context for the production of LR.

Support for a date of composition in the second half of the seventh century also occurs in LR's description of the country of Babylon. Having described several different branches of the river Euphrates, it observes that certain streams 'reunite and pass to the east of Akałałi, where the Arab army settled'.[85] This is the Syriac form of Kūfa, the first Arab encampment in Iraq, a new foundation in 638. The parallel entry in the SR, although of a very difference character, identifies the four districts of Babylonia as 'Akoła, Basra, Babelon and Tisbon'.[86] This knowledge of Kūfa may, therefore, have originated in the underlying text common to both recensions; if so, this would supply a *terminus post quem* for that text of 638.[87]

In sum, these entries indicate that the LR was compiled in the 670s by someone who was aware of the Bulgar arrival in the Danube delta and a prominent Kamsarakan appointment to an office in North Africa. Both have a Byzantine dimension to them. The retention of some literary and

[81] *Ašxarhac'oyc'* (LR) 18; 2145; tr. Hewsen 1992: 50.
[82] Greenwood 2004: 36, 66–7 and A.7; Greenwood 2015b: 73.
[83] Thomson 2001: 9–11, 35–40 and 229.   [84] Greenwood 2004: 67–8, 74 and A.12.
[85] *Ašxarhac'oyc'* (LR) 38, 2156; tr. Hewsen 1992: 71: *ork' yirears ekeal anc'anen yelic' Akałałi bnakeal banaki Tačkac'*.
[86] *Ašxarhac'oyc'* (SR) 351, 2189; tr. Hewsen 1992: 71A.
[87] There are several other references in LR that offer broad support for this dating. See, e.g., *Ašxarhac'oyc'* (LR) 37, 2155; tr. Hewsen 1992: 71: 'P'ałan which I think the Arabs call Mak'a'; *Ašxarhac'oyc'* (LR) 30, 2152; tr. Hewsen 1992: 59: 'the river K'ałirt which the Arabs call Šit'ma, which means 'Full of Blood'. This betrays a knowledge of Arabic, *dam*, pl. *dima*', blood. However, these do not supply specific dates.

patristic citations, coupled with the insertion of others, largely of an Armenian character, point to someone with scholarly interests and training. We have seen that P'ilon Tirakac'i was an Armenian scholar active in the second half of the seventh century who was commissioned by Nerseh Kamsarakan to translate the *Ecclesiastical History* of Socrates in Constantinople.[88] It has been argued elsewhere that he may also be responsible for the compilation of the *Anonymous Chronicle*, a miscellany assembled between 686 and 690.[89] Even if P'ilon Tirakac'i was not responsible, the LR bears the impress of an Armenian scholar with Byzantine and Kamsarakan connections.

Much less can be discerned about the identity of the compiler of the SR or its date of compilation. He reveals almost nothing about himself by way of interpolation. It is very difficult to work out if a particular feature should be credited to the compiler, the author of the underlying Armenian translation, Pappus of Alexandria or an intermediate scholar working in Greek. By way of example, the description of Spain at the start of the section on Europe in SR includes a coherent introduction that sets out the approach it will adopt thereafter. '[Spain] is divided into three small provinces which have many districts and cities, which we have considered an unprofitable exercise to list by name. And not just districts and cities but we have reckoned it [useful] to write only the names of mountains and major rivers and famous cities. And if [it has] any other notable features, we shall completely omit the numbers and measurements and detailed stories'.[90] With the notable exception of the description of Armenia, this statement of intent is fulfilled. By contrast, the entry in LR comments: 'But we write only the renowned rivers and famous cities, having left out those which are unremarkable'.[91] The coincidence in content and language suggests that these comments derive from one of the missing links in the sequence rather than the mind of either compiler. However, the compiler of SR recognised the importance of articulating general principles at the outset, whereas the compiler of LR included only a partial summary, thereby reducing its significance and meaning.

This more structured approach by the compiler of SR is also attested in its description of the Persian world. As noted previously, the singular account of the four quarters of Ērānšahr, originally in Middle Persian but transliterated into Armenian, appears only in LR. Its apparent

[88] See note 83.   [89] Greenwood 2008: 248–9.
[90] *Ašxarhac'oyc'* (SR) 341, 2180; tr. Hewsen 1992: 47A.
[91] *Ašxarhac'oyc'* (LR) 14, 2142; tr. Hewsen 1992: 47.

omission from SR has been used as a chronological marker, that SR must postdate the 'destruction' of the Persian Empire in 636.[92] Yet we should recognise that the last Sasanian *šahanšah*, Yazdgerd III, was killed fifteen years later, in 651/2, and it is only with the benefit of hindsight that the Arab campaigns of the mid-630s can be seen to have inaugurated momentous change. Furthermore, the dramatic transformation in the political landscape need not have been accompanied by a parallel, simultaneous administrative transformation. There is no reason to believe that this description of Ērānšahr became obsolete immediately. As a result, the traditional *terminus post quem* of 636 for SR should be set aside. In fact, careful examination of the description of the Persian world in SR reveals that its compiler was familiar with that famous freestanding account of Ērānšahr but elected to incorporate its information into his composition. The thirty-fifth *ašxarh*, Mark', 'which is called K'ust-i-K'apkox' is described as situated to the east of Armenia and on the shore of the Caspian Sea.[93] Of its ten named provinces, eight appear, in the same sequence, in the separate account preserved in LR. Tellingly, Armenia, Iberia, Albania and Sisakan have been removed from the list. Their omission should not be interpreted as incontrovertible evidence for their political or administrative separation; it could equally reflect the compiler's desire for literary coherence. The thirty-seventh *ašxarh*, Ełimac'ik', 'which is called K'ust-i-Xorasaran' (for which read Xorabaran), i.e., the Western Region, is subdivided into ten named provinces, all of which feature in the same sequence in LR, with the exception of Xužastan, which has been transferred from the following entry.[94] The thirty-eighth *ašxarh*, Parsk'en/Persia 'which is called K'ust-i-Nemeŕos', i.e., the Southern Region, is split into nineteen provinces, almost identical to the sequence found in LR. Finally, the thirty-ninth *ašxarh* in SR, Arik' 'which is called K'ust-i-Xorasan', i.e., the Eastern Region, contains twenty-four regions, as opposed to LR's twenty-six; again the sequence is identical. In other words, the compiler of SR elected to incorporate the freestanding description of Ērānšahr into the existing entries. This confirms that this description was part of the text underlying both recensions; it was not inserted by the compiler of LR. Evidently the compiler of SR recognised the duplication its inclusion generated and so consolidated the information into single entries. This reveals that he was prepared to edit the text in the interest of

---

[92] Hewsen 1992: 13, 33–4.   [93] *Ašxarhac'oyc'* (SR) 352, 2190; tr. Hewsen 1992: 72A.

[94] Ibid.; tr. Hewsen 1992: 74A. The other two entries are both found on these pages and so have not been given separate footnotes.

coherence. This contrasts with the compiler of LR who did insert additional material into his composition but was reluctant to undertake major restructuring. The two recensions, therefore, express different scholarly responses to the underlying text.

The composition from which both recensions derive cannot be analysed in any detail here. In any event, many of its characteristics are likely to remain hidden. Nevertheless, if we examine the proximate relationship between the two recensions, three of its features may be discerned. As noted in the preceding text, firstly, the references to Akoła/Kūfa and Basra in both recensions indicates that it was produced after 638. Secondly, it included both the freestanding description of Ērānšahr, discussed previously, and the detailed description of the fifteen *ašxarhs* of what is termed 'Greater Armenia', discussed in the following section. Although this afforded Armenia greater exposure than other regions, it was not prioritised within the structure of the work, nor was it treated differently in terms of content. And lastly, this underlying text possessed a universal dimension, defining and describing the world according to the tripartite division established by Ptolemy – Europe, Libya and Asia – and perpetuated by Pappus of Alexandria and other intermediaries. It did not attempt to revise this classical conception of the world to reflect the contemporary reconfiguration of the Middle East.

Armenia in the *Ašxarhac'oyc'*

How, then, was Armenian space conceptualised in the *Ašxarhac'oyc'*? Both recensions define the provinces of Roman Armenia separately from the fifteen *ašxarhs*, the lands or regions of Greater Armenia, although they do so in different ways. SR offers short entries for Third, First and Second Armenia, together with Cappadocian Pontus; LR lacks Third and First Armenia and Cappadocian Pontus but preserves a description of 'Second Armenia which today is called First Armenia'.[95] But both recensions also include Fourth Armenia as one of the lands of 'Greater Armenia' rather than as one of the Roman provinces.[96] There is no straightforward answer as to why Fourth Armenia, first established in 536 under Justinian I, was treated in this way, but it may reflect recent and possibly ongoing instability, when control of regions

---

[95] Ibid., 347, 2185; tr. Hewsen 1992: 54A–55A; although the title 'Third' Armenia is missing, this could be because the word 'Nineteenth', in Armenian *Innewtasnerord*, has virtually the same ending as the word for 'Third', *errord* and that an overzealous scribe, seeing apparent duplication, removed the latter in error. *Ašxarhac'oyc'* (LR) 24–5, 2148; tr. Hewsen 1992: 54–5.

[96] *Ašxarhac'oyc'* (LR) 30, 2151–2; *Ašxarhac'oyc'* (SR) 349, 2187; tr. Hewsen 1992: 59; 59A.

like Fourth Armenia changed hands repeatedly, enabling traditional designations to persist.

In addition to maintaining this distinction between Roman Armenia and Greater Armenia, LR attests change in the construction of Armenian space. Its description of Iberia records that the districts of Klarčk' and Artahan 'had been taken from Armenia' as well as three unnamed valleys all situated to the south of Tiflis (almost certainly Cobap'or, Kołbop'or and Jorop'or).[97] The city of Hnarakert and districts farther south and west of Tiflis, specifically Jawaxk', Tṙełk', Tašir and Gankark', are treated in exactly the same way, as formerly Armenian. Conversely LR's definition of the Armenian *ašxarh* of Gugark' lists these same nine districts but reports that 'now Iberia possesses, having taken from Armenia'.[98] This shows that whoever was responsible for these revisions had remembered to adjust the definitions of both Iberia and Armenia. A similar process can be seen in respect of Albania. Its description of Albania notes that all the border districts along the river Kur had been taken from Armenian control and the equivalent entry for the region of Arc'ax in Armenia names the same districts and records their transfer to Albania.[99]

The compiler of LR was aware, therefore, that Armenian space was susceptible to alteration. He was not, however, responsible for these revisions. Although the equivalent description of Iberia preserved in SR gives no indication of any transfer of Armenian territory, SR's description of Gugark' acknowledges that its nine districts are in the possession of Iberia. Moreover its description of Albania identifies districts that have been removed from Armenia.[100] SR's description of Armenia refers to Albania having possession of the twelve districts of Arc'ax and the seven districts of Utik'.[101] The appearance of these updating remarks in both LR and SR confirm that they must have been present in the underlying work. As a result, we can be confident that this substantial description of 'Greater Armenia' was already historic when it was incorporated into the underlying work.

---

[97] *Ašxarhac'oyc'* (LR) 28, 2150–1; tr. Hewsen 1992: 57: *i Hayoc' haneal ē*. I have translated this as 'Armenia' rather than 'the Armenians' because this is a text primarily concerned with physical not human geography.

[98] Ibid., 35, 2154; tr. Hewsen 1992: 65.

[99] Albania/Ałuank': *Ašxarhac'oyc'* (LR) 28–9, 2151; tr. Hewsen 1992: 57–9; Arc'ax: *Ašxarhac'oyc'* (LR) 33, 2153; tr. Hewsen 1992: 65.

[100] Gugark': *Ašxarhac'oyc'* (SR) 35, 2188; tr. Hewsen 1992: 65A; Albania: *Ašxarhac'oyc'* (SR) 348, 2186–7; tr. Hewsen 1992: 57A–59A.

[101] Arc'ax and Utik': *Ašxarhac'oyc'* (SR) 350, 2188; tr. Hewsen 1992: 65A.

According to both recensions, 'Greater Armenia' was divided into fifteen numbered *ašxarhs*, and these are listed in the same sequence in the opening description.[102] In LR, each *ašxarh* is situated by reference to territory adjacent to it, either Armenian or non-Armenian, or in relation to a river. By contrast, SR preserves a bare, unnumbered list but prefaces this with a description of the borders of Greater Armenia by neighbouring countries, rivers and mountains. The compiler of SR, therefore, placed Greater Armenia in its wider context. The compiler of LR situated the individual *ašxarhs* but displays less interest in the relative position of Greater Armenia as a whole. The two recensions, therefore, display different approaches to Armenian space.

Although both recensions list the fifteen *ašxarhs*, LR contains descriptions of only thirteen. It lacks the eleventh and twelfth, P'aytakaran and Utik'. Moreover, the description of the fifteenth region, Ayrarat, is situated between the tenth, Arc'ax, and thirteenth, Gugark'. As the introductory list of regions in LR includes both P'aytakaran and Utik', it seems highly likely that these were lost in the course of transmission. The transposition of Ayrarat is also likely to have taken place subsequently. It could be explained by a phrase attached to Ayrarat in the opening list in LR, *i mēj noc'a*, in the midst of them.[103] As noted previously, each *ašxarh* in the LR was accompanied by a short notice locating it in space and that is how this phrase should be interpreted. It is possible, however, that a copyist mistook this for an instruction to position the description of Ayrarat in the middle of the sequence and so transposed it.

This is not the occasion to give a comparative study of each *ašxarh* as depicted in the two recensions. Nevertheless, several features merit attention. Both recensions identify the districts in each *ašxarh* by name and delineate the mountains, rivers and natural resources – the animals and birds that can be hunted, the minerals and fruits – in each. Sometimes they also include specific cities and fortresses. The entry for Ayrarat refers to the cathedral and the martyria dedicated to the holy women – that is, St Hŕip'simē and St Gayianē – in the city of Vałaršapat, but this attention to the sacred landscape of Armenia is exceptional.[104] Although LR describes the *ašxarhs* in significantly more detail than SR, the overall content across both recensions is consistent with the rest of the composition. By way of illustration, Dalmatia is described in SR as being situated

---

[102] *Ašxarhac'oyc'* (LR) 29, 2151; *AŠX* (SR) 348–9; 2187 tr. Hewsen 1992: 59, 59A.
[103] Ibid., 29, 2151; tr. Hewsen 1992: 59.
[104] Ibid., 34, 2154; tr. Hewsen 1992: 70: *mayr ekelec'eac' kat'ołikē ew martirosuheac'n matrunk'n*. SR refers only to the mother of churches.

east of Gaul and next to Germany; in the east it extends to the sources of the river Danube and is bounded by the Danube to the north and east. It has six provinces and cities and many districts; six mountains, twenty rivers and five islands. It has a wild animal like a great ox, called a bonos, which hurls its excrement at hunters and burns them![105] In other words, the description of the fifteen *ašxarhs* of Armenia is consistent with those of other countries.

Yet the description of Armenia is also unique in the composition because it lists the individual districts of each *ašxarh* by name.[106] Moreover, LR takes this one level further. The individual districts in the regions of Fourth Armenia, Turuberan, Vaspurakan, Tayk' and Ayrarat, are given precise locations, either in relation to one another or in relation to specific topographical features. Where did this information come from? By what means were the names of the individual districts of all fifteen *ašxarhs* of Armenia preserved? In what circumstances was it deemed necessary to record not only the relative locations of the fifteen regions but also the districts within them? And how did Iberia and Albania obtain similar treatment, the names of their individual districts also being available for inclusion in this Armenian composition?

SR alone offers some insight into the process of composition of the description of Armenia which, as noted previously, must have been included in the underlying text from which both recensions derive. Having named the fifteen regions, it preserves the following comment: 'Now I intend to describe these in minute detail, if I shall labour a little in texts [*gir*] and records [*k'artez*]'.[107] This suggests that the author consulted an archive of documents belonging to an institution that spanned the whole of the country. As to the nature of that institution, two solutions may be advanced. It is possible that the writer turned to ecclesiastical records of some kind. In principle, a network of episcopal sees extended across the whole of Armenia, and Iberia and Albania as well. Yet there is no obvious relationship between the fifteen regions and the episcopal sees of the Armenian Church, either in name or definition. This lack of coincidence reduces the likelihood that records of this character were exploited, and one would also need to posit access to a similar source for the churches of Iberia and Albania, which were out of communion with the Armenian

---

[105] *Ašxarhac'oyc'* (SR) 342, 2180–1; tr. Hewsen 1992: 47A.

[106] Although both Iberia and Albania are subdivided into named districts, they are treated as single *ašxarhs* and not divided into named *ašxarhs* and districts, as Armenia. This is a significant difference in categorisation.

[107] *Ašxarhac'oyc'* (SR) 349, 2187; tr. Hewsen 1992: 59A.

Church for periods of the seventh century. In the alternative, the author may have had access to provincial administrative records. In support of this contention, the sequence of Armenian *ašxarhs* indicates a coherent structure, moving from west to east, rotating in an anti-clockwise motion, concluding with Ayrarat, the central *ašxarh* and the location of the provincial capital, Dvin, itself situated in a district that is termed the Ostan of Armenia. This is not conclusive evidence, but it is suggestive. An administrative origin could explain the attention paid to the relative positions of all fifteen regions as well as the priority afforded to Ayrarat. It would also justify the similar precision with which Iberia and Albania are described because these too had administrative definition. It may even explain quite what it meant for districts to be transferred from Armenia to Iberia or Albania, that this expressed administrative change rather than any political, ecclesiastical or social transformation. The *ašxarhs* of Gugarkʻ, Arcʻax and Utikʻ, may have lost their administrative designation as 'Armenian' but they were evidently remembered as once having been Armenian and may have still contained communities who thought of themselves and the settlements they occupied as Armenian.

As to the nature of these records, it seems less likely that were linked to military recruitment because this was structured around individual lordships rather than regions or districts.[108] Instead this knowledge of individual districts and their configuration within the fifteen *ašxarhs* could be related to land registers. No such register survives but we have already seen that in the middle of the sixth century, the *diwan* of Siwnikʻ was transferred from Armenia to the *šahrmar*, 'land-measuring' of Atrpatakan.[109] One of the final notices in the *History* attributed to Sebēos, dated to circa 654, observes that Albania and Siwnikʻ had previously been included in the *ašxarhagir*, 'land-book', of Atrpatakan until the destruction of the Persian kingdom.[110] These references confirm that such registers were a feature of Sasanian provincial administration in late antiquity and that the *ašxarh* was a meaningful unit, capable of transposition. If the meticulous description of Armenia preserved in the *Ašxarhacʻoycʻ* was based upon local provincial records, it is likely that these were produced and preserved in Dvin. This is not to suggest that either recension retains the form of those records. The description of each *ašxarh* is the product of complex processes of revision, interpolation and abridgement that may never be fully understood. Nevertheless, the proposition that both recensions of the *Ašxarhacʻoycʻ*

---

[108] See note 55.   [109] See note 25.
[110] Sebēos, *History* 175; tr. Thomson and Howard-Johnston 1999: 153.

preserve vestiges of Sasanian bureaucratic tradition offers a new perspective from which to view this composition. Its description of the fifteen lands not only imagines a singular Armenia stretched to its widest extent, all political, doctrinal and linguistic divisions set aside, but it also depended upon the resources of the provincial administration.

Conclusion

In conclusion, Armenian space was constructed in multiple ways in late antiquity. It was controlled by the empires of Rome and Persia through their provincial institutions, to the extent that after 428, there was no gap between them into which an autonomous Armenia might be fitted. Yet at the same time, Armenia was represented in the mass of literature generated in Persian Armenia as distinctive and autonomous. Within these literary works, however, it is possible to detect tensions, as clerical writers struggled to balance their ambitions and purposes with contemporary experience. Even the most familiar expression of Armenian space, the *Ašxarhac'oyc'*, offers a complex response, with Armenia situated in a universal context, its fifteen *ašxarhs* defining a stretched Armenia, yet reliant on provincial records to achieve that expression and seemingly already aware that its widest definition had passed. Constructed, reshaped, altered, contested, Armenian space offers a dynamic perspective from which to view the Middle East in late antiquity.

CHAPTER 4

Narrative and Space in Christian Chronography
John of Biclaro on East, West and Orthodoxy

Mark Humphries

If, from its beginnings, historical writing in the Graeco-Roman world was bound up with choices about which spaces to include, this was no less true of the Christian varieties of historiography that emerged in late antiquity.[1] Part of the challenge for Christian authors offering narratives of the intersections between the classical and the Christian pasts was deciding how to delineate the geographical spaces in which those histories took place. At the beginning of the fifth century, Paulus Orosius famously prefaced his *Seven Books of Histories Against the Pagans* with a description of the world based on Roman provinces – a choice that presented problems when he came to narrate the biblical past, at which point he was forced to offer various glosses to provide his readers with spatial orientation.[2]

Two of the most important historiographical innovations of the era are associated with Eusebius of Caesarea (d. 339): the *Ecclesiastical History* and the *Chronicle*. Both works provided models for numerous continuators and translators from the later fourth century onwards, and in both cases it is clear that Eusebius's followers found it challenging to define the spaces with which their works were defined. In the context of the Christian empire, it was attractive to determine that the space of ecclesiastical history was coterminous with that of the Roman state; this was particularly the case in the Greek East, where the empire remained robust. Thus one continuator of the *Ecclesiastical History*, Socrates Scholasticus, noted the sympathy between affairs of state and those in the Church as a justification for including so much imperial history in his account.[3] But other continuators could offer a view of Church affairs that went beyond the imperial frontiers: the Latin continuation by Rufinus famously includes details of Christian

---

[1] For an overview, see Inglebert 2001: 463–512.
[2] Merrills 2005: 64–97; Van Nuffelen 2012: 170–85; cf. Humphries 2007: 51–4.
[3] Socrates, *Ecclesiastical History* 5.pr.

missions to India and Ethiopia. [4] The prominence of imperial affairs in ecclesiastical historiography is not difficult to understand. Eusebius began his narrative with the Incarnation, when the Roman Empire dominated the *oikoumene*; and the different editions of his *History* were published in response to the shifting status of Christianity in the empire before and after the Diocletianic persecution.[5] To that extent, Eusebius regarded the empire as part of God's plan to foster the dissemination of the Gospel: this view receives more explicit treatment in his *Praeparatio Evangelica* and *Tricennial Orations* in honour of the emperor Constantine. [6]

A more universal approach to human history was taken by Eusebius's other major historical work, known conveniently as the *Chronicle*, but properly comprising two elements: a *Chronographia* that discussed the principles on which a universal history might be reconstructed, and the *Chronological Canons*, which tabulated the findings of that investigation. It was an apologetic enterprise, designed to argue for the priority of Christian belief (as represented by the Hebrews of the Old Testament) over Graeco-Roman paganism. [7] Thus it began with the Old Testament patriarch Abraham (before whom Eusebius did not feel it possible to reconstruct accurate dates), and therefore encompassed the histories of many more peoples than the Romans. This was explicit in its full title, as given by Eusebius elsewhere in his writings: Χρονικοὶ κανόνες καὶ ἐπιτομή παντοδαπῆς ἱστορίας Ἑλλήνων τε καὶ βαρβάρων ('Chronological Tables and an Epitome of Universal History of both Greeks and Barbarians').[8] Moreover, the wider view of the space in which human history took place was reflected in the layout of Eusebius's text, in which the histories of different peoples were set out in parallel columns, covering two facing pages of a manuscript codex.[9] This design was so complex that the work was considered much too cumbersome to reproduce as its originator had intended, with the result that by the sixth century it was no longer being copied (so that it no longer survives) and more straightforward layouts, based usually on one column of text encompassing the whole of history, came to predominate.

By the end of the fourth century, Eusebius's chronological tables (or, rather, a version of it that had been continued down to 350) had been translated into Latin by Jerome. [10] His Latin version offered a slightly

---

[4] Rufinus, *Ecclesiastical History* 10.9–10; cf. Humphries 2008: 159, with references to other work.
[5] Barnes 1981: 126–63. See now Cassin, Debié and Perrin 2012.   [6] Johnson 2006; Singh 2015.
[7] Burgess and Kulikowski 2013: 119–31.   [8] Ibid., 119 n. 79.   [9] Barnes 1981: 116–20.
[10] Burgess and Kulikowski 2013: 98, 184.

simpler layout for the text, which, unlike Eusebius's original, is preserved in numerous manuscripts.[11] From this, the apologetic conception of the chronicle is clear. Over time, the number of columns decreases, culminating with its reduction to a single column after the destruction of the Jerusalem temple in 70, after which the only history narrated is that focussing on the empire. As a Latin writer, Jerome was concerned to increase the space covered by the text to include details from Roman history and culture that Eusebius had omitted.[12]

Jerome's Latin version of the chronicle proved to be an enormous success. A chief reason for the work's popularity was that it could be added to and brought up to date by later redactors, and this was precisely what a number of individuals did in the course of the fifth and sixth centuries. Once more, questions of space and its representation in chronographic narrative loomed large in what Jerome's successors sought to do. Thus, for example, Prosper of Aquitaine produced no less than three revisions of his continuation taking the narrative down to 433, 445 and 455.[13] All of them were prefaced not by Jerome's original text, but rather by an epitome of it, which dispensed with Jerome's layout in parallel columns in favour of a single column that could fit on one manuscript page. But Prosper's version of Jerome also contained additions, notably of consular dates from the time of Christ's crucifixion (which Prosper located in the fifteenth regnal year of Tiberius).[14] Moreover, even if Prosper simplified Jerome's layout, he still sought to maintain something of the universal outlook of the chronicle format, occasionally mentioning events beyond the empire's frontiers such as the dispatch of Palladius as bishop to Irish Christians, or events in the Hunnic Empire beyond the Danube.[15] This contrasts markedly with the character of another fifth-century continuator, the Spanish bishop Hydatius of Lemica, whose narrative betrays a narrowing of his geographical horizons to events limited to the Iberian peninsula, as his sources for events further afield became more sparse.[16]

The aim of this chapter is to explore these connections between narrative and space in the late-sixth-century Spanish chronicler John of Biclaro. His

---

[11] In terms of the manuscript tradition, there is still much of use in the introduction to Fotheringham 1905. A particularly fine example, which shows the elegant arrangement of the text, is the late-fifteenth-century north-Italian copy preserved in Geneva as Bibliothèque de Genève, Ms. lat. 49, which may be read online in a photographic reproduction: www.e-codices.unifr.ch/en/list/one/bge/lat0049 (accessed 28 July 2017).

[12] Muhlberger 1981: 19–21.   [13] Burgess and Kulikowski 2013: 184 and n. 24.

[14] Muhlberger 1981: 65.

[15] Prosper, *Epitome chronicorum* 1307 (Palladius); 1353, 1364, 1367 and 1370 (Huns).

[16] Burgess 1996.

Chronicon provides a particularly striking example of how the representation of narrative and space in the ostensibly terse and arid chronographic format could be manipulated to convey a particular argument – namely that with the conversion of the Spanish Visigoths to Nicene Christianity at the Third Council of Toledo in 589, it was they, and not the Romans of the Eastern Empire, who became the chief custodians of Christian orthodoxy and, in effect, the people most favoured by God. Although scarcely treated in its own right by modern scholarship,[17] John's work stands at an important bridge between antiquity and the Middle Ages: his work is one of the last that self-consciously continues the enterprise begun by Eusebius and continued by Jerome; but it was also used as an important source for a new style of chronicle (which abandoned the concept of providing a continuation and instead offered a single narrative from Creation to the author's own day) begun in the seventh century by his fellow Spaniard Isidore of Seville.[18] After an overview of the text, its author and its composition, the chapter will examine how John's *Chronicon* intersects with the Latin chronographic tradition, and how this influences its presentation of narrative and space. Next it will explore how the *Chronicon* presents a particular geographical vision of the late antique world organised around the twin histories of the Eastern Roman Empire and the Visigothic Kingdom in Spain and southern Gaul.[19] Finally, it will demonstrate how the relationship between narrative and space in the *Chronicon* is deployed to present the Visigothic Kingdom, and not the Roman Empire, as the true torchbearer of Christian orthodoxy.

John of Biclaro and His Chronicle

John's *Chronicon* is not a long text by comparison with earlier exponents of the genre – only twenty-five pages in the most recent critical edition.[20] It

---

[17] Helpful studies of and commentaries on John are found in the editions of Campos 1960 and Cardelle de Hartmann 2001 (together with the historical commentary of Collins 2001), as well as in the translation of Wolf 1999. For his perspective on Gothic history and identity, Teillet 2011: 428–55 is important, while Álvarez García 1997 provides an overview of religious themes. On religious matters see further Ferreiro 1986 (with reservations noted in n. 58); also Ferreiro 1987 on his account of the Suevi. Most surveys of Visigothic history give John some consideration.

[18] Burgess and Kulikowski 2013: 187, 193; Wood 2012: 97–104.

[19] In what follows, *Spain* will be used as shorthand term for the full extent of the Visigothic Kingdom.

[20] I have chiefly used the edition of Cardelle de Hartmann (ed.) 2001: 57–83; but I have also consulted the older and widely used edition of Mommsen 1894: 211–20, as well as Campos 1960. (A rudimentary online edition of Campos's edition, giving the text only, is available at www .staff.uni-giessen.de/gloning/tx/chro-bi2.htm [accessed 13 July 2017].) The translation is taken, sometimes with minor adjustments, from Wolf 1999.

covers a correspondingly brief span of history, from the death of Justinian
and the accession of Justin II in 565 to the seal set on the conversion of the
Spanish Visigoths under the direction of their King Recarred (586–601)
from 'Arian' to 'Catholic' Christianity at the Third Council of Toledo in
589 – a span of more than twenty years. In spite of this brevity, John
manipulates the chronicle format to articulate a particular argument about
the histories of the Eastern Roman Empire and the Visigothic Kingdom in
the sixth century.

About John, we are reasonably well informed. While he is rather
reticent about himself in the *Chronicon* (only mentioning that he had
been an eyewitness to an outbreak of plague at Constantinople in the
early 570s),[21] some compensation is offered by a brief biography of him in
Isidore of Seville's *De uiris illustribus*. First and foremost, Isidore identifies John as bishop of Gerona in northeastern Spain: on the basis of
subscriptions by bishops of Gerona to Spanish church councils from this
period, and from a brief mention of John in the biography of his
successor Nonnitus in Ildefonsus of Toledo's *De uiris illustribus*, we can
deduce that John held the see from around 590 until his death sometime
in (probably) the 620s.[22] Among other important details that Isidore
provides are that John was born of Gothic stock (*natione Gothus*) in
Lusitania (western Iberia), that he spent a period studying Greek and
Latin at Constantinople,[23] before returning to Spain where he was
arrested and sent into internal exile at Barcelona for ten years during
the suppression of Catholic clergy by the Arian King Leovigild (569–586).
Isidore does not explain why John, in spite of his Gothic parentage, was
a Catholic rather than an Arian, given that, before Reccared, most Goths
were Arians; but, as will be argued in this chapter, this combined Catholic
and Gothic identity was important for the narrative of John's *Chronicon*.
At some point in his career, Isidore also informs us, John founded
a monastery 'which is now called Biclaro', for which he wrote
a monastic rule.[24] Isidore also singles out and celebrates the quality of
John's *Chronicon*, and describes accurately its beginning and end dates –
details he will have been well placed to know because he used John's

---

[21] John of Biclar, *Chronicle* 26: *In regia urbe mortalitas inguinalis plage exardescit, in qua multa milia
hominum uidimus defecisse.*

[22] Iledfonsus of Toledo, *On Illustrious Men*, 9. For discussion of conciliar subscriptions and their
relation to the chronology of John's episcopate, see Cardelle de Hartmann 2001: 128*.

[23] There is debate over the length of time of John's sojourn in the East: older printed editions of Isidore
gave a figure of seventeen years, but the most recent edition of the text suggests that he spent seven
years there instead: Mommsen 1894: 208; Cardelle de Hartmann 2001: 124*–5*.

[24] On the monastery and rule, see Cardelle de Hartmann 2001: 126*–8*.

narrative as a source for his own historical works.[25] He mentions further that John produced other writings, but that he did not have access to them.[26]

From this abbreviated biography, a number of important details emerge that will be relevant for the discussion here. First, that John was a Goth who was nevertheless a Catholic and suffered under Leovigild's suppression of Catholics has a bearing on the overall shape of his narrative and the place of Catholicism and the Goths in it. As we will see, his portrait of Leovigild is surprisingly favourable for an author who had been exiled by the king. Second, John's period of study at Constantinople hints at an individual with an outlook that encompasses not only Spain but also the wider Mediterranean world, and that could explain why his *Chronicon* includes detailed discussion of eastern affairs; indeed, it has been suggested that John acquired his copy of his predecessor Victor of Tunnuna's chronicle while at the imperial capital.[27] Even so, his account of eastern affairs is often summary or defective, and eastern history is ultimately subordinated to a narrative that lays greater emphasis on events in Spain.

Finally, there is the question of the date of the *Chronicon*. Opinion is divided on this. Although the narrative concludes with events in 589/90, all manuscripts of the chronicle contain two entries that look forward to events at the beginning of the seventh century: references to the lengths of the reign of Maurice (§ 63) and the pontificate of Gregory the Great (§ 81), which indicate knowledge of their deaths in 602 and 604, respectively. Most scholars have assumed that these are additions to John's text by a later redactor, and so have dated the chronicle to the immediate aftermath of the Third Council of Toledo in 589.[28] But Carmen Cardelle de Hartmann, the most recent editor of the text, suggests that these entries might be John's own, and that he wrote at the beginning of the seventh century. This was a volatile time for the Visigothic Kingdom: Reccared died in 601, and his successor, Liuva II was overthrown by Witteric in 603. Perhaps the final entry in the *Chronicon*, which offers a cautionary tale about rebellions against the king (see p. 96), was designed to advocate the benefits of a united, Catholic kingdom at a time when its stability was under threat.[29] Neither the

---

[25] Isidore of Seville, *On Illustrious Men*, 44: *ab anno primo Iustini iunioris principatus usque in annum octauum Mauricii principis Romanorum, et quartum Recharedi regis annum.*

[26] Ibid. *Et multa alia scriber dicitur, quae ad nostrum notitiam non peruenerunt.*

[27] Collins 2004: 51.

[28] Mommsen 1894: 208; Campos 1960: 53. This dating has been followed by the majority of scholars: e.g., Teillet 2011: 428.

[29] Cardelle de Hartmann 2001: 130*–1*; Collins 2004: 51.

argument for composition around 590 nor that for writing a decade later is without its problems.[30] Nor does it help much to look to Isidore of Seville, who shows detailed knowledge of the *Chronicon* in his *De uiris illistribus* (the date of which is also contested) for help in establishing an exact *terminus ante quem* for the work.[31] At best, we can locate composition of the *Chronicon* sometime in the period between 589 (the date of the Toledan council) and just after the death of Pope Gregory in 604. In spite of these uncertainties, one thing does seem to be clear: the observable cross-references and connections between different parts of the *Chronicon* (see pp. 95–6) suggest that it was no haphazard catalogue of events put together year after year, but rather that John put it together all at one point and selected material for inclusion quite deliberately.

Tradition, Time and Narrative: John's Chronological Frameworks

John's connection with the chronographic tradition is stated explicitly in his preface:

> Bishop Eusebius of the church of Caesarea; the priest Jerome, known throughout the entire world; Prosper, that most religious man; and Bishop Victor of the church of Tunnuna in Africa have woven together the history of practically all peoples with the greatest brevity and diligence, bringing the accumulation of years up to our own age, and passing on, for our understanding, those things that happened in the world. We, in turn, with the assistance of our Lord Jesus Christ and for the sake of informing those who will come after us, have taken pains to record, using a concise format, those events that have occurred in our own times. Some of those events we have witnessed faithfully with our own eyes, while others we have learned from the reports of trustworthy individuals.[32]

---

[30] Neither Mommsen nor Campos explain *why* the details of the reigns of Maurice and Gregory must be later additions, beyond the assumption that because the chronicle ends with the Council of Toledo, it must be written soon after that. Nor does Cardelle de Hartmann explain why John, if he was writing after Reccared's death in 601, gives no reference to the length of the king's reign at the time of his accession (§ 79) that corresponds to such entries for Maurice and Gregory; it should be noted that he does not offer a figure for the length of Leovigild's reign either (§ 10).

[31] Wood 2012: 75, supporting an early date for the *De uiris illustribus*.

[32] John of Biclar, *Chronicle* pr., trans. Wolf. Campos's edition (1960: 77) adds a 'praescriptio' from the thirteenth-century manuscript at the Complutense: *Huc usque Victor Tunnennensis ecclesiae episcopus Affricanae provinciae ordinem praecedentium digessit annorum; nos quae consecuta sunt adicere curavimus.* The manuscript continues further with a sentence that Campos relegates to his apparatus: *Ab hinc historiam ducit uenerabilis pater noster Iohannes abbas monasterii Biclarensis.* Similar statements are found in the Complutense manuscript at the points where Prosper takes over from Jerome, and Victor from Prosper: Cardelle de Hartmann 2001: 104*–5*.

The most important manuscript containing John's *Chronicon* – Madrid, Biblioteca General de la Universidad Complutense, Fondo Histórico, 134, dating to the thirteenth century – preserves this arrangement in its first twenty-five folios: it begins with an epitome of Eusebius-Jerome, continues with the 455 edition of Prosper of Aquitaine's *Epitoma Chronicon*, but only down to the year 444, after which comes Victor of Tunnuna's *Chronicon*, and then John's own narrative. The rest of the codex is filled with a wide variety of short historical works, including numerous other chronicles, episcopal lists and various theological treatises.[33]

This arrangement means that John's presentation of his materials was influenced to some extent by that adopted by his predecessors. Of particular importance was the presentation of material in Victor of Tunnuna's chronicle, from whom John inherited both his chronological framework and a focus on imperial affairs. Like his predecessor Prosper (whose narrative he effectively plagiarises for the first eleven years), Victor had used consular dating alongside the system of emperors' regnal years used in Jerome's version of Eusebius, but was forced to revert to regnal dating by the ending of the annual consulship after the appointment of Anicius Faustus Albinus Basilius in 541, although he continues to note twenty-three post-consulships of Basilius down to 563.[34] The reversion to dating by emperors reflects the centrality of the empire in Victor's worldview. While he certainly betrays a local bias by including in his chronicle African matters, especially the Vandal suppression of Catholics, his central reference point remains the Roman Empire.[35]

The effects of this inheritance on John's *Chroncion* are abundantly clear at the point where his narrative takes over from Victor's. After his review of his predecessors, John begins with a summary of the last events covered in Victor's narrative, which explicitly refers back to his predecessor: 'Thus, in the fifteenth indiction, as has been said [*sc.* by Victor], on the death of Justinian, his nephew the younger Justin was made emperor'.[36] In the next section, John – like not only Victor, but also Prosper and Jerome's version of Eusebius before him – states Justin's position in the imperial succession and the number of years he sat on the throne, before proceeding to an account of the first year of Justin's reign.[37] Two general points are worth

---

[33] For this codex, see Cardelle de Hartmann 2001: 27*–38*; also Cardelle de Hartmann 1999: 19–20.
[34] Bagnall, Cameron, Schwartz and Worp 1987: 7–12.   [35] See especially, Teillet 2011: 423–7.
[36] John of Biclar, *Chronicle* 1: *quinta decima ergo indictione, ut dictum est, Iustiniano mortuo Iustinus iunior nepos eius Romanorum efficitur imperator*; cf. Victor of Tunnunna, *Chronicle* 172: *Quadragesimo imperii sui anno Iustinianus uite suscept finem indictione XV.*
[37] John of Biclar, *Chronicle* 2: *Romanorum LIII regnat Iustinus iunior annis XI. Qui Iustinus anno primo regni.*

observing here. The first is that a variety of chronological systems is deployed to triangulate the date of Justin II's imperial succession. Unfortunately, however, John's chronology is profoundly muddled. From Victor he inherited the mistaken detail that Justinian died in the fifteenth year of the tax cycle (indiction), but that was 566, and not 565, the actual year of Justinian's death and Justin's succession; to compound the error, John described Justin's reign (incorrectly) as lasting eleven years rather than twelve.[38] The next two years are listed as the second and third regnal years of Justin; and the use of imperial regnal years continues down to the last year covered by the *Chronicon*, which was *anno VIII Mauricii imperatoris* (§ 91). The second general point worth noting is that the pattern of noting the sequence of emperors and the lengths of their reigns continues to be used later in the chronicle at the points when one emperor succeeds another (§§ 43–44 and 62–63).

But parallel to this imperial chronology is another that lists the regnal years of Visigothic kings. This does not commence with the beginning of the *Chronicon*, but only three years into it, when Leovigild's succession to Liuva is mentioned in § 10:

> in the third year of the emperor Justin, Leovigild, the brother of King Liuva, was appointed king of Hispania Citerior while his brother was still living. He received in marriage Gosuintha, the widow of Athanagild and wonderfully restored to its former boundaries the province of the Goths, which by that time had been diminished by the rebellions of various men.[39]

Leovigild's reign is reckoned from the third year of Justin's rule, so the next section begins with a formula that sets imperial and Visigothic regnal chronologies side by side: 'in the fourth year of the emperor Justin, which is the second year of king Leovigild'.[40] This formula of calibrating imperial and Visigothic regnal years continues for the rest of the *Chronicon*, and it neatly encapsulates the twin geographical poles around which his narrative is structured.[41]

---

[38] For the error in the length of Justin's reign, see Collins 2001: 110. For John's chronological weaknesses more broadly, see Cardelle de Hartmann 2001: 135*–9*. John's grasp of chronology is so insecure that in Mommsen's 1894 edition, every single *sub anno* date noted in the margin is attached to a question mark.

[39] John of Biclar, *Chronicle* 10: *Huius imperii anno tertio Leouegildus, germanus Liubani regis, superstite fratre in regnum citerioris Ispanie constituitur, Gosuintam relictam Atanaildi in coniugium accipit et prouinciam Gothorum, que iam pro rebellione diuersorum fuerat diminuta, mirabiliter ad pristinos reuocat terminos.*

[40] John of Biclar, *Chronicle* 11: *Anno IV Iustini imperatoris, qui est Leouigildi regis secundus annus.*

[41] One difference is worth noting: when John notes the deaths of Visigothic kings and the elevation of their successors (§§ 6, 10, 79), he does not give the lengths of their reigns.

Narrative and Geographical Space in John's Chronicle

John's preface hints at its aspiration to universal scope in the spirit of Eusebian chronography: his predecessors had 'woven together the history of practically all peoples (*omnium pene gentium*)' and 'pass[ed] on . . . those things which happened in the world (*acta sint in mundo*)'. John aims to continue in this tradition and, in his first entries, follows Victor of Tunnuna in demonstrating a particular interest in imperial history. The first five entries deal with the affairs of the East, noting Justin II's succession to Justinian (§ 1), his religious policy (§ 2), affairs on the eastern frontier and in the Caucasus (§ 3) and failed plots against Justin at Constantinople and Alexandria (§§ 4–5). Only then do we get our first Spanish entry (§ 6), noting succinctly the death of the Visigothic King Athanagild and the succession of Liuva I.

Another reflection of the imperial focus of the narrative can be seen in the only other sets of chronological markers that John offers in addition to the successions of emperors and Visigothic kings. First, John notes the papal succession: his entries are formulaic, noting how one bishop takes the place of his predecessor, and indicating how many years the new bishop was to reign as pope; by this stage of the discussion, it will occasion no surprise that they are uniformly inaccurate in terms of the dates they are attached to (in fact, Gregory I did not become pope until after the events narrated in the *Chronicon* came to an end).[42] John also notes the death of one Lombard king (Alboin) and the election of another (Authari).

All these entries belong to that part of John's narrative that focuses on imperial affairs. All the papal successions are embedded in accounts of imperial history, as might be expected given that the popes were effectively representatives of the emperor in Italy: Benedict I's succession to John III (§ 29) follows an account of a barbarian embassy to Constantinople (§ 28); that of Pelagius II (§ 42) falls between accounts of an Avar assault on Thrace (§ 41) and the succession of Tiberius to Justin II (§§ 43–44); and that of Gregory I (§ 81) comes after the emperor Maurice's elevation of his son Theodosius as Caesar (§ 80) and before notice of an imperial alliance with the Franks against the Lombards (§ 82). The Lombard succession also belongs to this imperial narrative: the death of Alboin at § 23 is followed by a notice that 'his treasure, along with the queen herself, came under the dominion of the Roman state';[43] similarly, the succession of Authari at § 58

---

[42] On John's errors, see Mommsen 1894: 210; cf. Collins 2001: 142 for a possible cause of the confusion.

[43] John of Biclar, *Chronicle* 23: *thesauri uero eius cum ipsa regina in rei puplice Romane ditionum obueniunt.*

is presented as a prelude to significant Lombard advances at imperial expense in Italy.[44] It should be noted, furthermore, that the very first mention of the Lombards comes with their defeat of the Gepids in the Balkans and the killing of the last Gepid king, Cunimund, after which Cunimund's nephew Reptila together with an Arian bishop presents the royal treasure to Justin at Constantinople (§ 19).

Further inspection of the *Chronicon* allows us to distinguish a number of thematic and geographical foci split between the empire and the Visigothic Kingdom. These are set out in Table 1, from which it is clear that there is a significant degree of coherence within and between the imperial and Spanish narratives of the *Chronicon*. Ecclesiastical affairs, and their place in the balance of power between the empire and Spain, will be discussed later (see pp. 103–105), but for now it is worth highlighting examples of some other themes and how the various elements of the chronicle connect with each other.

First, in both the imperial and Spanish narratives, there is a great deal of emphasis on dynastic succession and legitimacy. Thus, the first two mentions of Visigothic affairs at all concern the successions of Liuva and Leovigild (§§ 6 and 10). A substantial number of entries for the reigns of Leovigild and Reccared, moreover, concern their responses to challenges to their authority and their suppression of rebels and usurpers (see Table 1). This is so dominant a feature of John's view of history that his very last entry, on an attempt to overthrow Reccared by his retainer Agrimund, finishes with an explicit demonstration of the fate of traitors: the captive Agrimund, having been tonsured and with his right hand cut off, was paraded through Toledo on an ass, allowing John to comment that he was 'an example to all, teaching servants not to be presumptuous to their lords'.[45] If the *Chronicon* was indeed written in the febrile atmosphere following Witteric's bid for power in 603, that would give the conclusion of the narrative a striking contemporary resonance (see p. 91).

Moreover, this interest in succession and legitimacy perhaps also explains why John's narratives of the empire's relations with its neighbours often foreground the achievements of individuals who later came to the throne: thus the future Tiberius II is mentioned as the agent of imperial successes against the Avars (§ 13) and of treaty negotiations with the Saracens (§ 34); and the only references to conflict with Persia in

[44] John of Biclar, *Chronicle* 58: *Longobardi in Italiam regem sibi ex suo genere eligunt uocabulo Autharic, cuius tempore et milites Romani omnino sunt cesi et terminus Italie Longobardi sibi occupant.* Further Lombard successes are listed at § 78.
[45] John of Biclar, *Chronicle* 93: *exemplum omnibus ... dedit et docuit famulos dominis non esse superbos.*

Table 1. *Thematic and geographical distribution of entries in John of Biclaro,* Chronicon

Theme	Eastern/Imperial Narrative	Spanish/Visigothic Narrative
Political succession and legitimacy	Dynastic affairs at Constantinople: §§ 1 (accession of Justin II), 4–5 (plots against Justin), 25 (Justin's illness), 33 (Tiberius becomes Caesar), 43 (death of Justin II), 44 (succession of Tiberius), 61 (dynastic arrangements for the succession), 62–63 (death of Tiberius and succession of Maurice), 80 (dynastic arrangements), 88 (dynastic arrangements).	Dynastic policy and succession: §§ 6 (death of Athanagild; succession of Liuva); 10 (Leovigild co-ruler; married to Athanagild's widow Gosuintha), 24 (Leovigild sole ruler), 27 (elevation of Hermenegild and Reccared), 53 (marriage of Hermenegild and alliance with Franks), 74 (Reccared's successful Frankish war), 79 (Reccared succeeds Leovigild), 89 (death of Gosuintha). Success against rebels and usurpers: §§ 20, 50, 54 (revolt of Hermenegild), 64–66 (Leovigild besieges Hermenegild at Seville), 67 (defeat of Hermenegild), 73 (Hermenegild murdered by Sisibert), 75–76 (treatment of Galician usurpers Audeca and Malaric), 83 (death of Sisibert), 87 (pro-Arian rebellion by Sunna and Segga), 89 (pro-Arian revolt of Ildida), 93 (revolt of Agrimund).
Domestic affairs	Events at Constantinople: §§ 19 (embassy), 26 (plague), 33 (plague abates after Tiberius becomes Caesar), 34 (Persian triumph), 36 (embassy).	Urban foundations: §§ 50 (Reccopolis), 60 (Victoriacum), 66 (restoration of Italica).
Military history and foreign policy	(i) Military affairs in the Balkans: §§ 13 (Avars), 19 (Gepids), 40 (Sclaveni), 41 (Avars), 45 (Avars), 52 (Avars), 59 (Scalveni). (ii) Military affairs on the Persian frontier and the Caucasus: §§ 3, 15, 31, 34, 36	(i) Successes against the empire in coastal Spain: §§ 12, 17, 46. (ii) Affairs in the north and northwest (Sueves and Basque country): §§ 14 (accession of Miro), 21

Table 1. *(cont.)*

Theme	Eastern/Imperial Narrative	Spanish/Visigothic Narrative
	(incl. alliance with the Saracens), 38, 48, 56, 71, 92.	(Miro's wars), 27 (?),[46] 32 (Cantabria), 35 (near Galicia), 39 (invasion and treaty with Miro), 60 (Gothic expansion in Basque country), 65 (Miro supports Hermenegild; death of Miro, succession of Eboric), 67 (revolt of Audeca against Eboric), 72 (conquest of Galicia), 75–76 (treatment of Galician usurpers Audeca and Malaric), 84 (conversion of Suevi).
	(iii) Military affairs in Africa: §§ 7 (Garamantes), 8 (Moors), 9 (Maccuritae), 11 (Moors), 28 (Maccuritae), 47 (Moors).	(iii) Dealings with the Franks: §§ 53 (dynastic alliance), 74 (Franks invade Narbonensis at imperial urging), 85 (victory over the Franks), 90 (Frankish invasion of Narbonensis repelled).
	(iv) Military conflict with the Lombards in Italy: §§ 37, 49, 58, 69 (Franks attack Lombards at Maurice's behest), 78 (Lombard successes at imperial expense), 82 (Romano-Frankish alliance).	
Religious affairs	(i) Religious history: §§ 2 (restoration of Chalcedonian orthodoxy), 92 (conversion of Persian king).	(i) Religious history: §§ 57 (Arian synod at Toledo), 84 (conversion of Reccared and other Visigoths; also Suevi), 86 (restoration of church property; patronage), 91 (council of Toledo).
	(ii) Papal successions at Rome: §§ 29 (Benedict I), 42 (Pelagius II), 81 (Gregory I).	(ii) Important churchmen in the kingdom (incl. Narbonensis): §§ 18, 22, 51, 55, 70, 77.

[46] Much depends on the location of the toponym *Sabaria* in this chapter: for the suggestion that indicates a location close to Salamanca, see Collins 2001: 119–20.

Tiberius's reign single out the role played by the future emperor Maurice (§§ 48 and 56) and pave the way for the achievement of peace when Maurice had ascended the throne (§ 92).

Secondly, there are noticeable clusters of entries dealing with particular geographical regions. In terms of the empire, four major foci can be identified: the Balkans, the eastern frontier in the Caucasus and with Persia, Africa and the frontier with the Lombards in Italy. As the chronicle proceeds, the majority of the entries about conflicts in these regions come to stress the difficulties experienced by imperial forces, repeatedly presenting the empire as on the defensive. The clusters visible for the Visigothic narrative are, by contrast, more positive, telling of the kingdom's consolidation and expansion under Leovigild in particular. There are three major theatres of conflict: against the empire in southern and eastern Spain (although imperial control of these regions is never specifically mentioned); against the encroachment of the Franks (sometimes in alliance with the empire) in Gallia Narbonensis; and against the Suevi in the mountainous terrain of Galicia. John's account of the Suevi is one of the most detailed accounts of this people to survive from late antiquity – but it is wholly subservient to the theme of Leovigild's achievement of Iberian unity under Visigothic rule and, as such, instructive of John's aims in marshalling information to tell a particular story.[47]

Thirdly, we can deduce that the narratives of events in these various theatres were no random accumulation of facts but rather made up a cogent, connected narrative. John's account of imperial relations with the Moors under Justin refers to the successive deaths of a number of imperial officials, respectively Theodore, prefect of Africa (§ 8), Theoctistus, the *magister militum* (§ 11), and a further *magister militum* Amabilis (§ 16). The connections between these separate events are demonstrated by John's account of the resolution of the conflict after a decade of war:

> Gennadius, the *magister militum* in Africa, ravaged the Moors. He defeated in battle that most powerful king, Garmul, who had already killed the three previously named commanders of the Roman army, and killed him with the sword.[48]

The explicit reference to the *tres duces superius nominatos* makes it clear that § 47 completes a narrative begun in § 8. This is not the only cross-reference in

---

[47] Noted by Ferreiro 1987: 201–3.
[48] John of Biclar, *Chronicle* 47: *Gennadius magister militum in Affrica Mauros uastat, Garmulem fortissimum regem, qui iam tres duces superius nominatos Romani exercitus interfecerat, bello superat, et ipsum regem gladio interficit.*

the text. We have already seen how the *Chronicon*'s narrative begins with a reference back to Victor of Tunnuna's chronicle (see p. 92). Elsewhere, John's account of Tiberius's elevation to the rank of Caesar notes that this individual had previously been mentioned with the title of *comes excubitorum*; similarly, the entry on Maurice elevating his son Theodosius as co-emperor refers to an earlier mention of the son when he had been made Caesar.[49]

At other times, it is probably safe to assume that John intended readers to make connections even when he did not include specific cross-references and that such connections within the chronicle reflect his selection of material when he came to write the chronicle. Thus his reference in § 70 to Eutropius, abbot of Servitanum, as having been a disciple of the previous abbot Donatus is designed to encourage the reader to recall that Donatus had been mentioned as abbot at § 18. Similarly, his account in § 28 of an embassy coming to Constantinople from the Maccuritae, during which gifts of elephant ivory and a giraffe were presented to Justin, is surely to be understood as a diplomatic sequel to their conversion mentioned in § 9.

Finally, another way in which John ties the narrative together is to use entries for individual years to summarise events that, in actuality, extended over several years. The very first entry under Justin II encapsulates this approach. It offers a reasonably discursive account (by the standards of the chronicle format) of Justin's championing of the orthodoxy of the councils of Constantinople (381) and Chalcedon (451), and these are listed as happening 'in the first year of his reign'; but this notice describes policies enacted not just in Justin's first year, but over the course of several years, and therefore stands as a summary of Justin's early religious policy more generally.[50] A similar character can be ascribed to those entries that describe the good fortune of Leovigild's reign in general terms (§§ 10 and 50; see p. 106). Into this category may fall references to Spanish churchmen: there are several of these scattered across the *Chronicon*, and they follow a formulaic pattern found in his models Prosper and Victor, simply stating that a given ecclesiastic was held in high esteem (*clarus habetur*).[51] While some of these entries may be tied to clerical successions,[52] the entry on bishop Leander of Seville (§ 77) demonstrably is not: in terms

---

[49] Tiberius: John of Biclar, *Chronicle* 33 (*Tiberium, quem superius scubitorum comitem diximus*), referring back to § 13 Theodosius: § 88 (*Theodosium filium, quem supra Caesarem diximus*), referring back to § 80.

[50] John of Biclar, *Chronicle* 2; cf. Collins 2001 110.

[51] For the formula, see Lançon 2004: 197–200.

[52] As is perhaps the case with the mention of successive abbots of Servitanum at §§ 18 and 70.

of John's chronology, it is mentioned under the year 584/5, which year was neither the beginning nor end of Leander's episcopate.[53]

Between Romans and Visigoths: Manipulating Space for Narrative Ends

While the chronicle is certainly wide-ranging in terms of the events and regions it covers, it is also clear that John has manipulated his narrative to articulate a story of Visigothic exceptionalism. The *Chronicon* culminates with the Third Council of Toledo in 589 and the events in its immediate aftermath: as such, the chronicle narrates a story that would have had particular appeal to John as a Catholic Goth, that of his people's progress from heresy to orthodoxy. But it is possible to read the text as aiming at rather more than this, and that the balancing of imperial and Spanish narratives throughout the chronicle was carefully crafted to present the Visigoths as a people specially favoured by God.[54]

It has already been seen that the first few entries of the chronicle contain only minimal information on the history of the Visigothic Kingdom, with notices restricted to details of the royal succession. But gradually the Visigothic material occupies more of the narrative. While imperial regnal years continue to be used as an essential component of John's chronological framework, the proportion of the chronicle given over to imperial affairs gradually diminishes, as can be seen in the graph and chart set out in Figure 1, showing how the amount of coverage of imperial and Visigothic affairs changes over time, and Figure 2, which shows the different proportions of each year's entries dedicated to imperial and Spanish events. They show an unmistakeable swing in favour of Spanish material in the last years covered in the *Chronicon*.

In general, a division is apparent in the entries before and after the early 580s.[55] Before that, imperial history either shares equal footing with Spanish events, or it predominates (most notably in the years 566/7–567/8, 572/3–575/6 and 580/1). But from 582/3 onwards, the narrative is dominated by Spanish material, to the extent that in several years Spanish material accounts for more than two-thirds of the narrative, that in two years (582/3 and 588/9) there are

---

[53] Collins 2001: 141. Jamie Wood (pers. comm.) suggests that the date is perhaps connected with the end of Hermenegild's rebellion, and Leander's return from exile in Constantinople.

[54] For this theme in Isidore, see Wood 2013.

[55] In what follows, and in the figures, I have given the years in the form 566/7 to account for John's chronological imposition. The earlier date is that given by Cardelle de Hartmann in her edition; the latter is the one found in, e.g., Mommsen, Campos and Wolf.

Figure 1. Geographical distribution of the contents of John of Biclaro, *Chronicon*,
based on numbers of lines in the Cantelle de Hartmann edition.

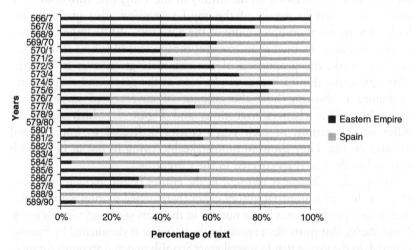

Figure 2. Percentage of coverage of Imperial and Spanish affairs in John of Biclaro,
Chronicon, based on numbers of lines in the Cantelle de Hartmann edition.

no imperial events listed at all beyond the regnal year of the emperor and that
in a further two years (584/5 and 589/90) Spanish affairs account for more
than 90 percent of the material recorded. It has been suggested that part of
the reason for the decreasing importance of eastern affairs in John's narrative

is that it reflects his own access to eastern information: up until the 570s, when John was resident at Constantinople, he was able to recount events such as outbreaks of plague that he had witnessed; but after his return to Spain, John had less access to eastern information, and so his account of events in the empire was restricted only to the succession and major wars.[56] Without denying that this was likely a factor in John's coverage of eastern material, it does not satisfactorily explain all aspects of the preponderance of entries on Visigothic affairs in the second half of the chronicle.

Another indication of the westward drift of John's perspective can be seen in his entries on ecclesiastical history. As noted previously, John lists papal successions at Rome as a chronological marker (albeit one he consistently gets wrong) alongside the successions of Roman emperors and Visigothic kings. In singling out Roman bishops, John's chronicle takes a narrower view of ecclesiastical affairs than did his immediate predecessor Victor of Tunnuna, who had listed episcopal successions not just at Rome but also at the other ancient apostolic sees of Alexandria, Antioch and Jerusalem, as well as at Constantinople and, on occasion, Carthage. However, Victor often grouped several successions into a single entry, and in that respect is often no more chronologically precise than John.[57] In terms of the western chronographic tradition, however, John's narrower perspective is not unprecedented: an exclusive concentration on Roman episcopal successions had been a feature of Prosper's continuation of Jerome, even while Prosper's epitome of Jerome followed both Eusebius and Jerome in noting successions also at Jerusalem, Antioch and Alexandria.[58]

As well as the more western focus demonstrated by notices of the papal succession, John's narrative also emphasises an ecclesiastical history that

[56] Cardelle de Hartmann 2001: 140*.
[57] Episcopal successions noted by Victor: Constantinople §§ 9, 38 (with Rome, Antioch, Jerusalem), 99 (with Antioch), 108 (with Rome, Alexandria, Antioch and Jerusalem), 121; Alexandria §§ 11, 23, 69 (with Rome, Antioch, Jerusalem), 73, 77 (with Antioch), 99 (with Constantinople), 108 (with Rome, Antioch, Jerusalem and Constantinople), 123 (schism after the death of Timothy III), 128 (with Rome); Carthage §§ 26 (amalgamates a number of successions), 119 (with Jerusalem); Antioch §§ 29 (with Jerusalem), 38 (with Constantinople, Rome and Jerusalem), 49 (with Jerusalem), 69 (with Alexandria, Jerusalem and Rome), 77 (with Alexandria), 108 (with Rome, Constantinople, Alexandria and Jerusalem), 127, 138, 154; Jerusalem §§ 29 (with Antioch), 38 (with Antioch, Constantinople and Rome), 49 (with Antioch), 69 (with Alexandria, Antioch and Rome), 108 (with Rome, Constantinople, Alexandria and Antioch), 119 (with Carthage), 133, 146; Rome §§ 34, 38 (with Antioch, Constantinople and Jerusalem), 69 (with Alexandria, Antioch and Jerusalem), 76, 108 (with Constantinople, Alexandria, Antioch and Jerusalem), 122, 128 (with Alexandria), 130 (amid a much broader narrative relating to the Three Chapters controversy), 157 (exile of Vigilius), 159, 167.
[58] Muhlberger 1981: 80.

concentrates on the Visigothic Kingdom by mentioning throughout a number of important clergy as distinguished in the life of the Church there.[59] In part this echoes the practice of Victor of Tunnuna, whose account mentions distinguished African churchmen.[60] That said, the Spanish churchmen whom John lists with approval (i.e., with the comment *clarus habetur*) in his *Chronicon* are exclusively representatives of Catholic orthodoxy.[61] As such, they fit neatly with a narrative that culminates with the council of 589, not least because two of the clergy mentioned, bishop Leander of Seville and abbot Eutropius of Servitanum, later appear as the leading figures in John's account of the council.[62]

This emphasis on Catholic Christianity within the Visigothic Kingdom, alongside the increasing concentration on Visigothic political affairs, fits neatly with the importance attached in the *Chronicon* to the Third Council of Toledo as the climax of the narrative. But this enterprise involved John in a surprisingly positive account of the reign of Leovigild, the king who, according to Isidore, had exiled him to Barcelona as part of an anti-Catholic campaign.[63] As a number of scholars have noted, John's account of Leovigild's reign is significantly different, even to the point of distortion, from that found in other sixth- and seventh-century authors, and presents a picture of Arian-Catholic relations under him that is strikingly harmonious given known religious tensions in his reign. Most famously, John's account of the rebellion of Hermenegild says nothing at all about his conversion to Catholicism, which not only seems to have been instrumental in the

---

[59] The selection of clerics has been sensibly examined by Ferreiro 1986: 145–50, but I disagree with his exclusion (at 149 n. 11) of Domninus of Helna (modern Elne, south of Narbonne), mentioned by John at § 22; because Gallia Narbonensis was still under Visigothic control (as, indeed, is made clear at § 24), this makes Domninus a cleric within the kingdom.

[60] Victor, *Chronicle* §§ 26, 79, 135, 143, 145, 149, 153, 155 and 165; cf. §§ 30, 50–1, 78 and 106 on Vandal persecution of African Catholics.

[61] The connection of orthodoxy with fame is explicit in the account of Masona of Merida: *Mausona Emeritensis ecclesie espiscopus in nostro dogmate clarus habetur* (John of Biclar, *Chronicle* 30). In that respect Ferreiro ('Omission of St Martin of Braga', 146) is mistaken in listing the Arian bishop Sunna (John of Biclar, *Chronicle* 87) alongside the others: he is not glossed with the formula *clarus habetur*, and instead should be categorised alongside Uldida (inexplicably designated 'non-Iberian' by Ferreiro at 1986: 149 n. 11) at § 89 as part of the lingering Arian opposition to Reccared's pro-Catholic policies.

[62] John of Biclar, *Chronicle* 91: *summa tamen synodalis negocii penes sanctum Leandrum Ispalensis ecclesie episcopum et beatissimum Eutropium monasterii Sirbitani abbatem fuit*. The earlier notices of Leander and Eutropius are at §§ 70 and 77, respectively. Cf. how Isidore's *de uiris illustribus* listed Spanish Nicene bishops in an effort to accord the Iberian Church a resolutely Catholic pedigree: Wood 2012: 228–9.

[63] Isidore, *On illustrious men* 33: *Hunc supradictus rex, cum ad nefandae haeresis crudelitatem compelleret, et hic omnino resisteret, exsilio trusus, et Barcinonem relegatus, per decem annos multas insidias, et persecutiones ab Arianis perpessus est.*

deteriorating relations between father and son, but also predated that of Reccared by several years and had allowed other authors, including no less a figure than Pope Gregory the Great, to present Hermenegild as a martyr and his father as a persecutor.[64] Certainly, Spanish authors writing after John were much less reticent about presenting Leovigild as an oppressor: Isidore of Seville, while acknowledging Leovigild's political successes, nevertheless noted that 'the error of his impiety tarnished the glory his great success'.[65] Similarly, the anonymous author of the *Lives of the Fathers of Merida*, in his account of the episcopate of Masona (a figure celebrated also in John's chronicle: § 30), condemns Leovigild for his cruelty, savagery and tyranny.[66]

The closest John gets to a critical account of Leovigild's religious policies is in his account of the Arian synod at Toledo in 579 (§ 57). This synod had sought to make it easier for Catholics to convert to Arianism by dispensing with the requirement to undergo a second baptism, making do instead with, as John states, a laying on of hands by an Arian cleric (*per manus impositionem*), the taking of communion and uttering an Arian creedal formula. John's account remarks that while many Catholics did convert, they were driven more by greed (presumably for royal reward) than by compulsion, which seems to shift the blame from the king to the Spanish Catholics.[67] Finally, John's account shifts discussion of some aspects of pro-Arian policy under Leovigild to the reign of his successor, where they can be commented upon without requiring explicit criticism of the king. Thus, he remarks that one of Reccared's first acts on becoming a Catholic was to restore property that had previously been stripped from the Church, but he makes no reference to the alienation of such property under Leovigild (§ 86). His accounts of Arian plots against Reccared include one mounted by an Arian *Sunna episcopus* (§ 87); but there is no indication that he was a partisan of Leovigild, who had appointed him bishop of Merida in opposition to the Catholic Masona, a figure whom John singled out for praise.[68]

---

[64] Gregory the Great, *Dialogues* 3.31. For Hermenegild's posthumous reputation: Fuller 2009: 898–901.

[65] Isidore of Seville, *History of the Goths* 49: *sed offuscavit in eo error impietatis gloriam tantae virtutis.*

[66] *Lives of the Fathers of Emerita* 5.4.2: *unde accidit ut haec opinio saevissimi atque crudelissimi Wisigothorum Leovigildi regis penetraret auditum.* It is striking, however, that the *Vitae* is silent on Hermenegild's rebellion and its religious dimension, even though Merida was a stronghold of the revolt: Fear 1997: xx–xxi.

[67] John of Biclar, *Chronicle* 57: *plurimi nostrorum cupiditate pocius quam impulsione in arrianum dogma declinant.* It is worth noting also that the verb is active and the Catholics are the subject of it, which further distances the king from culpability. See further Stocking 2000: 53–4.

[68] *Lives of the Fathers of Emerita* 5.5.2ff.

This positive depiction of Leovigild is consonant with the wider portrait of him in the *Chronicon* as energetically uniting Spain and Narbonensis under Visigothic rule, defeating usurpers and rebellions within the kingdom and expelling foreign invaders. A number of passages have about them the whiff of panegyric,[69] a tendency that is abundantly clear in the very first entry about him:

> In the third year of this emperor [sc. Justin], Leovigild, the brother of king Liuva, was appointed to the kingdom of Hispania Citerior while his brother was still living; he received in marriage Athanagild's widow Gosuintha, and the province of the Goths, which by that time had been diminished by the rebellions of various men, he wonderfully restored (*mirabiliter ... reuocat*) to its former limits.[70]

Midway through the reign, in Leovigild's eleventh regnal year, we are told that 'King Leovigild, having destroyed tyrants on all sides and overcome Spain's invaders, had peace to reside with his own people'.[71] Even the domestic disturbance caused by the rebellion of the king's son Hermenegild is set against a background of an otherwise peaceful and stable rule, free from foreign incursions.[72] Finally, when Leovigild died, the fact that his son Reccared was able to accede to the throne *cum tranquillitate* was a testament to his father's achievements.[73] To underscore the good fortune of the kingdom under its new ruler, the chronological marker for the first year of Reccared's reign describes it as his *primus feliciter annus*.[74] The positive tenor of John's entries on this succession are made all the more clearer when we compare them with the account of Leovigild's death in the *Lives of the Fathers of Merida*, which summarises Leovigild's achievements with damning words.[75]

---

[69] For the possibility that John was familiar with imperial panegyric, and used it as a source for his account of Tiberius, see Collins 2001: 122.

[70] John of Biclar, *Chronicle* 10: *Huius imperii anno tertio, Leouegildus, germanus Liubani regis, superstite fratre in regnum citerioris Ispanie constituitur, Gosuintam relictam Atanaildi in coniugium accipit et prouinciam Gothorum, que iam pro rebellione diuersorum fuerat diminuta, mirabiliter ad pristinos reuocat terminos.*

[71] John of Biclar, *Chronicle* 50: *Leouegildus rex, extinctis undique tyrannis et peruasoribus Ispanie superatis, sortitus requiem propriam cum plebe resedit.*

[72] John of Biclar, *Chronicle* 54: *Leouegildo ergo quieta pace regnante, aduersariorum securitatem domestica rixa conturbat.*

[73] John of Biclar, *Chronicle* 79: *Hoc anno Leouegildus rex diem clausit extremum et filius eius Reccaredus cum tranquillitate regni eius sumit sceptra.*

[74] John of Biclar, *Chronicle* 80: *Anno V Mauricii prinicpis Romanorum, qui est Reccaredi regis primus feliciter annus.*

[75] *Lives of the Fathers of Emerita* 5.9.1: *magis perderet quam regeret Leovigildus Hispaniam.*

This portrait of Visigothic success contrasted with Roman misfortune is underscored by the oscillation between imperial and Iberian space throughout John's narrative. One of its striking features is how the story of imperial success declines just as that of Visigothic good fortune increases. Entries on the empire in the first decade covered by the *Chronicon*, with only a few exceptions, stress imperial success, with the conversion of peoples like the Garamantes and Maccuritae (§§ 7, 9); military successes against the Avars (§ 13, 52), Persians (§§15, 34) and, after some reverses, the Moors (§ 47); and diplomatic interactions (recognising imperial supremacy) with the Maccuritae (§ 28), Saracens (§ 36) and Caucasian Suani (§ 38). Even the defeat of the Gepids by the Lombards redounds to the empire's benefit because the fugitive remnants of the Gepid court seek refuge at Constantinople (§ 19). While some imperial successes, notably with regard to Persia (§§ 56 and 92), are noted in the second decade covered by the *Chronicon*, John's account of imperial matters tends, instead, to stress imperial failure, with a particular emphasis on reverses inflicted by the Lombards on imperial forces in Italy (§§ 58 and 78) and by the Scalveni in Illyricum (§ 59); forebodings of imperial failure had been hinted at already in the first ten years of the narrative with mentions of imperial retreats in the face of Lombards (§§ 37, 49) and Avars (§§ 40–41, 45).

But rather more than this, the successes of Leovigild and Reccared are juxtaposed with this account of imperial failure. Thus, entries for 573/4 present the reader first with a breakdown of peace on the empire's Persian frontier as a result of which Roman control is lost over the city of Dara, with great loss of imperial troops (§ 31), and then with Visigothic expansion into Cantabria (§ 32). For the year 576/7, a brief notice of an Avar advance to the Long Walls in Thrace, from which a blockade of Constantinople was mounted, is contrasted with a lengthier entry recounting Leovigild's submission of regions near Cartagena to Visigothic control (§§ 45–46). Under 577/8, imperial success against the Moors (after numerous reverses: § 47) is tempered by disastrous conflict (*lacrimabile bellum*) against the Lombards in Italy (§ 49), while in Spain Leovigild's good fortune reaches something of a climax, on which a seal is set by the foundation of Reccopolis in honour of Reccared (§ 50). To be sure, the following year sees the eruption of troubles for the Visigoths with Hermenegild's rebellion, but it is not long before the Visigothic star is again in the ascendant: by 580/1, while the empire suffers serious reverses in Italy and the Balkans (§§ 58–9), Leovigild scores major advances into the Basque country and is once again founding a city, Victoriacum, in celebration of his achievement (§ 60). By the time

Reccared succeeds his father, imperial fortunes are in precipitate decline: the notice of Reccared's succession *cum tranquillitate* (§ 79) follows immediately upon an account of serious disasters for imperial forces in Italy and a considerable expansion there of Lombard power (§ 78). A partial Roman recovery in Italy listed under 586/7 is achieved only in alliance with the Franks (§ 82); but the same year's entries note also that when other Frankish forces engaged those of Reccared, they were defeated by the Goths and their general and many of their troops were slain (§ 86).

From East to West: The Third Council of Toledo and the Climax of History

Alongside this narrative of imperial decline and Visigothic vigour is one that shows how the religious profile of the respective states has undergone a significant transformation. By the last entries of John's *Chronicon*, the Visigoths are ruled by an impeccably Catholic king in the form of Reccared. Indeed, the victory over the Franks just mentioned (§ 86) is sandwiched between entries that stress Reccared's orthodox devotion: § 85 describes the king's personal conversion from Arianism to Catholicism and his encouragement of his subjects to follow suit, while § 87 records Reccared's restoration to the Catholic Church of properties previous taken from it by his Arian predecessors (*a precessoribus*). The stage is now set for John's account of the Third Council of Toledo, which dominates John's account of Reccared's reign. By now, Visigothic history dominates the narrative, with only a very few lines given over to imperial affairs; hand in hand with this is an affirmation that it is Visigothic Spain, and no longer the empire, that is the true guarantor of Christian orthodoxy.

Much of this is achieved through the presentation of Reccared. He is portrayed as an ideal Christian ruler (§ 91: *Christianissimus Reccaredus*), reaching the decision that he should convert to Catholicism and seeking to persuade his subjects to come with him (§ 84), acting as a generous patron of the Church (§ 86) and convening the Toledan council and taking an active role in its deliberations (§ 91). The benefits for Reccared of his conversion to Catholicism are abundantly clear: attempts at rebellion by Arian opponents are repeatedly foiled (§§ 87, 89, 93) and Reccared's armies score significant victories against the Franks in southern Gaul (§§ 85, 90). That these successes are the result of Reccared's adherence to orthodoxy is sometimes implied by the juxtaposition of events, such as when Reccared's personal conversion (§ 84) is immediately followed by a defeat of Frankish forces (§ 85). At other moments, John is quite explicit on the matter, ascribing Reccared's conversion, a victory over the Franks at Carcassonne, the success of the council and the destruction of Arianism to God's action in the world.[76] That these factors are connected is underscored by John's evocation of biblical parallels for Reccared's successes. The victory of his forces over the numerically superior Frankish forces at Carcassonne paralleled the success of Gideon and his three hundred troops against the seemingly overwhelming forces of the Midianites.[77] John also gives the number of bishops who had attended the council of Nicaea as 318, a number pregnant with symbolic capital because, as Ambrose of Milan had noted long before, it was both the number of those who had assisted Abraham in his struggles against the five kings who had captured Lot and, in Greek numerals, was written as TIH, which could be seen as representing both the Cross (T) and the first two letters of Jesus's name (IH).[78] These passages encourage recognition of Reccared as God's agent in worldly affairs, a conclusion suggested also by the very last entry on imperial history. This details the conversion of the Persian King Khusro I to Christianity and his treaty with the emperor Maurice, which is described as a consequence of the work of God already manifest in the extinction of heresy: in the context, this can only mean the Visigothic conversion and Reccared's role in it.[79]

This presentation of Visigoths enacting God's will on Earth is all the more remarkable when it is contrasted with the depiction of the Romans at the beginning of the *Chronicon*. After describing Justin II's succession to Justinian, John related how the new emperor sought to undo his predecessor's controversial innovations in Trinitarian matters at the Council of Constantinople in 553, and to restore the creed approved at the council of Constantinople in 381 and ratified at Chalcedon in 451.[80] At that point, it was Justin and the Romans who were the custodians of Christian orthodoxy, and they were suitably rewarded for this: the next entry recorded how Christians in Armenia and the Caucasus, on coming under attack from Persia, looked to imperial leadership (§ 3); similarly, other nations that convert to Christianity seek alliances with Constantinople.[81] The

---

[76] John of Biclar, *Chronicle* 84 (the king's conversion happens *deo iuuante*), 90 (victory is granted *Deo nostro*), 91 (Catholicism prevails *fauente Deo*).

[77] Judges 7:8 and 8:4.

[78] Genesis 14:14; with exegesis in Ambrose of Milan, *On faith* 1 pr.3 and 1.18.121.

[79] John of Biclar, *Chronicle* 92: *In his ergo temporibus, quibus omnipotens Deus prostrato ueternose heresis ueneno pacem sue restituit eccliesie, imperator Persarum Christi suscepit fidem et pacem cum Mauritio imperatore firmauit.*

[80] John of Biclar, *Chronicle* 2.

[81] John of Biclar, *Chronicle* 7 (Garamantes), 9 and 28 (Maccuritae).

statement of Justin's piety is followed also by descriptions of how those plotting against him were confounded (§§ 4–5), an indication of the good store he had built up. But later in his reign, Justin had fallen ill owing to mental incapacity, which John describes as having been ascribed by some to demonic possession.[82] Immediately, the fortunes of the empire suffered a blow, with an outbreak of plague that John had witnessed (§ 26). It was only when Tiberius was elevated ruler in Justin's stead that the plague abated[83] – but imperial fortunes never quite recover in the rest of the chronicle, and stories of success instead concentrate on the Visigoths.

The transition from imperial to Gothic success is mirrored in John's narrative by a spatial translation of the home of orthodoxy from the empire under Justin to the Visigothic Kingdom under Reccared. The account of the Council of Toledo encourages this view of the Visigoths as inheriting the mantle of orthodoxy from the Romans: Reccared's presence at the council is described as

> reviving in our own times the image of the ruler Constantine the Great, whose presence illumined the holy synod of Nicaea, or that of the most Christian emperor Marcian, in whose presence the decrees of the Council of Chalcedon were established.[84]

These evocations of imperial presence at church councils are wholly John's contribution to the narrative, and are not culled by him from the acts of Toledo – unlike the detail of the 318 bishops at Nicaea, which *was* mentioned in the debates in 589.[85] Such details, however, serve to connect the narrative that John has written with that found in the predecessors whose chronicles he explicitly continued: indeed, he finishes his account of the Council of Toledo by noting that 280 years had elapsed between the emergence of Arianism under Constantine and its defeat under Reccared, and by remarking that the reassertion of orthodoxy had been granted by divine will (*fauente Domino*). The idea that Reccared was bringing to completion a task begun by Christian Roman emperors could hardly be more explicit.

John's insistence on Visigothic Spain taking up the mantle of the Roman Empire neatly reflects shifting ideological balances in his lifetime. The second half of the sixth century had seen a notable upsurge in the

---

[82] John of Biclar, *Chronicle* 25: *ab aliis demonum uexatio putabatur.*

[83] John of Biclar, *Chronicle* 33: *Huius Tiberii Cesaris die prima in regia urbe inguinalis plaga sedata est.*

[84] John of Biclar, *Chronicle* 91: *memoratus vero Recharedus rex, ut diximus, sancto intererat concilio, renouans temporibus nostris antiquum principem Constantinum magnum sanctam sinodum Nichenam sua illustrasse presencia, nec non et Marcianum christianissimum imperatorem, cuius instancia Calcidonensis sinodi decreta firmata sunt.*

[85] Text in Martínez Díez and Rodríguez 1992: 61–2.

Visigothic kings' deployment of ideology inspired by imperial models – a factor likely to be explained by the confrontation between Visigothic and imperial forces in southern and eastern Spain.[86] This was a period of crisis for Visigothic rulers, not only because of the military challenge from the empire on Iberian territory but also because of the extinction of the Balth dynasty, from which all Visigothic rulers had hitherto claimed descent.[87] In the resulting contest for legitimacy, new claimants to the kingdom looked to imperial models to buttress their claims, using new coin types directly inspired by east Roman models, but that they made wholly their own. A similar strategy can be detected in John's narrative: he reports a number of incidents that must surely belong to the context of Leovigild's conflict with the empire in Spain. But in contrast to his enumeration of Leovigild's enemies among the Suevi, Franks and even his own people, John never explicitly mentions that the conflicts in eastern and southern Iberia were with the empire (in contrast to the later account of Isidore of Seville[88]), nor does he make clear that the revolt of Hermenegild was likely influenced by imperial and Gothic rivalries in Spain, only remarking that after the rebellion failed Hermenegild fled to imperial territory.[89] On the contrary, Spain is a space in which the empire never has a foothold, and which is first and foremost the location of Visigothic suzerainty.

Conclusions

Both in its own terms, but even more especially as part of a composite history of the world from Creation down to the fourth year of Reccared, John of Biclaro's *Chronicon* presents a tale of God's agency in human history that reaches its climax in the Visigothic Kingdom. In important ways, therefore, John's narrative anticipates the praises of Visigothic religious preeminence found in the work of Isidore of Seville. [90] It has been argued here that John's arrangement of his narrative results in Spain being the space in which the history of orthodoxy, and of God's intervention in human affairs, reaches its culmination. In that respect, John was a worthy inheritor of the traditions of Christian chronography in the Latin West. As has been noted, the chronicles of his predecessors Eusebius, Jerome, Prosper and Victor of Tunnuna used various means to stress the centrality of the Roman Empire in God's plan for humankind. But John's final

---

[86] Hillgarth 1966.   [87] Collins 2004: 45.   [88] Reydellet 1970.

[89] John of Biclar, *Chronicle* 68: *ad rem publicam conmigrante*. For imperial involvement in such rebellions, see Wood 2010: 310–11.

[90] For this aspect of Isidore's treatment, see Wood 2012: 191–232.

iteration of the narrative significantly shifted the spatial focus of the narrative away from the empire to Visigothic Spain. This westward drift was not, however, a result of a poverty of sources, such as had led the earlier Spanish chronicler, Hydatius of Lemica, to give his narrative a particularly Iberian focus. Instead, the spatial shift in John's chronicle from imperial east to Visigothic west was part of a deliberate narrative strategy, in which the true representation of God's will on earth, once to be found among the Israelites and later to be found among the Romans, was now unequivocally located in the Kingdom of the Catholic Visigoths. [91]

[91] I am grateful to Peter Van Nuffelen for his invitation to contribute to this volume and his help (not to mention his exemplary patience) as an editor. Earlier versions of this chapter were delivered at seminars in Swansea and Durham, and I am grateful to Ian Repath and Helen Foxhall-Forbes for facilitating those events, as well as to the audiences on each occasion for helpful insights. Earlier drafts were read by Juan Strisino and Jamie Wood, who saved me from a great deal of error and inelegance.

CHAPTER 5

The Roman Empire in John of Ephesus's Church History

Being Roman, Writing Syriac

Hartmut Leppin

Although time is crucial for historiography, space is another important dimension of historical writing. The kind of space that is relevant to authors and becomes visible in their works depends on their respective contexts and approaches. As regards church historiography, one major issue is the relationship between ecclesiastical and political space, which ideally should coincide, but never does. This becomes even more palpable in works that stem from the periphery of the empire. One case in point is the ecclesiastical history of John of Ephesus.

John of Ephesus was an influential Syriac Christian church politician of the sixth century. For most of his life he was persecuted by Roman emperors for not embracing the Chalcedonian creed. He was also a prolific author, writing about the lives of holy men and women. In addition, he composed a *Church History*, which I would like to examine in this chapter. My main questions are quite simple: What did it mean to produce a church history in an empire that the author experienced as a persecuting power – a church history written in Syriac, which was not the language of power? Can we here discern one of the subaltern voices that are missing so starkly from antiquity? To what degree does John assume the position of a cultural broker? And how does this relate to his construction of ecclesiastical and political space? I must confess that my findings will be much less spectacular than could be expected. In my opinion, John of Ephesus was in fact not so different from other church historians. He has much in common with the established Eastern tradition of church histor-iography, even in regard to the established view of political and

I am grateful to Chris Rands, Philip Wood, Peter Van Nuffelen, Philip Forness, and David Wierzejski for their substantial help and to my audiences in Ghent, Oxford and Sheffield for discussions on the topic of this article.

ecclesiastical space in the Roman Empire. However, he had a clear message: his *Church History* demonstrated that the persecution of his co-religionists damaged the whole empire and argued that cooperation with his co-religionists in the Roman Empire might be extremely useful. Although writing in Syriac, he adopted a pronouncedly Roman stance.

I will start by highlighting some aspects of the construction of space(s) in Christian Greek historiography. After some remarks regarding John's life and work, I will analyse John's description of political and ecclesiastical spaces both inside and outside the Roman Empire and follow this with some brief comments on his *Lives of the Eastern Saints*.

Construction of Space(s) in Christian Greek Historiography

John's historiography needs to be seen in the context of the development of Christian historiography in Greek, which he was familiar with at least to a degree. From its beginnings, Christian historiography was not only about Christian agents and institutions but also about the Roman Empire. And necessarily so. Christian history unfolded within the Roman Empire, yet Christianity also transcended Roman borders. Thus, Christian historiography always has two layers of space: political space and Christian space, which develops into ecclesiastical space over time. While the political space of the Roman Empire is restricted by its borders,[1] the Christian space remains borderless. The Great Commission in Matthew (28:19 f.) states that Jesus's disciples should spread his teachings to all the nations of the world. The two spaces must be distinguished heuristically, although they overlap often.

The *Acts of the Apostles* mark the beginning of Christian historiography, even if the genre of church historiography developed later. They illustrate the birth and development of a Christian space while dealing primarily with the spread of Christianity in various parts of the Eastern Roman Empire. While the apostles typically began their work in political or economic centres, smaller villages such as Derbe or Lystra are mentioned also. The structures of the communities were still unstable and often dependent on the apostles' personal presence.

The authorial perspective is uneven: the main focus lies on Palestine, Syria, Asia and Greece. However, the *Acts* are not restricted to the Roman

---

[1] But see Chapter 2 by Van Nuffelen regarding how concepts of empire influence the perception of the edges of the world.

world. A famous passage narrates how the apostle Philip baptised an Ethiopian eunuch. The eunuch is introduced as a foreigner, a man from Ethiopia who observed Jewish traditions. After his baptism he returns to Ethiopia, the end of the inhabited world in the eyes of contemporaries.[2] Besides, as is well known, the account of Pentecost in the second chapter of *Acts* includes peoples from both inside and outside the empire. The borders between the Roman Empire and the rest of the world are not perceived as strong barriers. Consequently, Christian space is not identical to the space of the Roman Empire.

This obviously does not mean that political space is superseded by Christian space. The empire is taken for granted and its power structures accepted. Encounters with Roman authorities may be unpleasant, but the Jews are depicted as the principle opponents. Thus, in regard to space and empire, the *Acts* offer three basic features of Greek Christian historiography: a focus on the East, a universal Christian claim and the unquestioned acceptance of Roman power structures.

Let us now leap forward in time to discuss a second example: Eusebius's *Church History*, the last version of which was finished under Constantine the Great. It is a time when the Roman Empire might appear to be identical to the Christian church. Emperor Constantine seems to fulfil God's plans. The structures of the church are much more stable by now: Eusebius is able to name incumbents of the most important episcopal sees on a regular basis. They are usually cited as a kind of chronological framework and attest to the apostolic succession of certain sees of the orthodox churches. At the same time, the repeated mention of certain ecclesiastical centres underlines their importance for the geographical structure of the church and their hierarchical status in it. Because Rome is undoubtedly one of the main sees, Eusebius's *Church History* refers to it consistently, thus reaffirming its importance. In certain contexts, he also names western cities and regions.[3] Nevertheless, his main focus continues to lie on the East.

Although developments outside the empire are noted only rarely, the universal claim is upheld. At the beginning of the third book, Eusebius comments on the missionary areas that were assigned to the apostles:

> Meanwhile the holy apostles and disciples of our Saviour were dispersed throughout the world. Parthia according to tradition, was allotted to Thomas as his field of labour, Scythia to Andrew, and Asia to John, who,

---

[2] Acts 8:26–39, see Hengel 1983: 164–5.
[3] E.g., Eusebius, *Ecclesiastical History* 5.1.3, 6.43.3, 8.6.10.

after he had lived some time there, died at Ephesus. Peter appears to have preached in Pontus, Galatia, Bithynia, Cappadocia, and Asia to the Jews of the dispersion. And at last, having come to Rome, he was crucified head-downwards. . ... What do we need to say concerning Paul, who preached the Gospel of Christ from Jerusalem to Illyricum, and afterwards suffered martyrdom in Rome under Nero?[4]

Once more, Christianity transcends Roman borders, even though Eusebius is so enthusiastic about the soteriological importance of the Roman Empire, which seems to represent Christianity.

Christians were soon to make the infuriating experience that Christian emperors could embrace the wrong beliefs. This is reflected in the pre-Chalcedonian Nicene Greek church historians of the Theodosian age: Socrates, Sozomen and Theodoret.[5] They have much to say about conflicts between bishops, whom they regard as orthodox, and emperors, who are dismissed as heretics. Yet they never doubt the legitimacy of any Roman emperor nor condemn the Roman Empire as such. All three of them have a clear regional focus on the East, or rather, on certain parts of the East. Socrates and, to a lesser degree, Sozomen are centred on Constantinople, whereas Theodoret has a Syrian perspective focused on Antioch. While Socrates takes an interest in the West, Sozomen – and Theodoret even more so – mentions this half of the empire only rarely. Theodoret even ignores the sack of Rome in 410.[6] Nevertheless, all three embrace a universal perspective. They spend much time on accounts of the Christianisation of nations outside the Roman Empire, enacted by missionaries connected with Rome. Again, ideally, every nation should be at least part of a Roman commonwealth.[7]

John's Life and Work

John of Ephesus obviously had some knowledge of the genre of Greek church historiography. Perhaps he made use of a synopsis of the

[4] Eusebius, *Ecclesiastical History* 3.1 (tr. Kevin Knight). The remarks on Peter go back to the first letter of Peter (1:1) and are based on the names of provinces in contrast to the first paragraph.
[5] Leppin 2003.
[6] I am here unable to discuss the relationship between John and Zachariah of Mytilene, whose work can be partially reconstructed on the basis of Pseudo-Zachariah who was a near-contemporary of John's and probably also wrote a work, mostly referred to as a *Chronicle*, which, however, might have been a *Church History*. It seems a consensus has emerged that those works were probably based on a common source, but were composed independently of each other, see Greatrex et al. 2011: 37–9, who argue convincingly that Ps.-Zachariah and John drew on common (Amidene) sources; cf. Minov 2010: 68–9.
[7] Leppin 1996: 30–2; Van Nuffelen 2004: 105–24, 128–30; Wood 2010: 30–7.

Theodosian church historians.[8] Nevertheless, his approach was special as he decided to use Syriac as his literary language and because his Miaphysite church was restricted almost solely to the eastern part of the Roman Empire and adjoining regions.[9] Moreover, his church was barely established and existed under constant pressure. It was not easy to uphold continuity under circumstances such as these.

In the following I will mostly deal with part three of the *Church History*, which comprises the time from about 571 to 588.[10] Nevertheless, I will allow myself some side glances at other parts of John's works.[11] The main reason for focusing on the last part of the *Church History* is that it has been preserved more or less completely and transmitted to posterity directly. By contrast, part one has been lost almost entirely, while some passages of part two of the *Church History* seem to survive in other sources. By far the most important among them is the third part of the *Chronicle of Zuqnin*, which also drew on other sources, however.[12] It should be used very carefully when it comes to analysing John's position.

Despite its direct transmission, the third part of the *Church History* displays many imperfections and does not give the impression of having received a final revision. In addition, John did not write it all at once, but obviously worked on it successively[13] so that we cannot assume perfect consistency.

Allow me to make a few very brief remarks on John's life. While these are mainly deduced from his own writings, there is no reason to cast doubt on their fundamental reliability:[14] John was born in Ingila, in the north of Amida (what is today Diyarbakır), in about 507 and was destined to become a monk from his childhood. He grew up in a world where Miaphysitism (to use this contested term) had begun to establish a church of its own, but under difficult circumstances.[15] The monks of

---

[8] Van Ginkel 1995: 52–44.

[9] On the Greek background of Syriac historiography, see Debié 2009: 11–31.

[10] Van Ginkel 1995: 70–85.

[11] Brooks 1935–6. An English translation has been produced by Payne Smith 1860, a German one by Schönfelder 1862; both of them are not without shortcomings, see Honigmann 1939: 615–25.

[12] Van Ginkel 1995: 55; Witakowski 1987, 1991, 1990: 299, 303–6. Text: Chabot 1927–33. Translations: Witakowski 1996; Harrak 1999.

[13] Van Ginkel 1995: 73–7.

[14] On his life, see ibid., 27–37; Ashbrook Harvey and Brakmann 1998: 553–64, 553–5; Richter 2002: 29–41; Bruns 2006: 65–72; and, extremely rich in material, Destephen 2008: 494–519, cf. Allen 1979: 251–4. More recently Debié 2015: 137–9.

[15] Hainthaler 1990; Menze 2008: 145–93. Alois Grillmeier's *Christ in Christian Tradition* is still a fundamental source on all the Christological controversies (Grillmeier and Hainthaler 1986–2002). For the political context, see Maraval 1998: 458–81.

the community he belonged to were forced into exile from 521/2 to 530. On his travels, he met several admirable ascetics, but did not feel himself to be strong enough to follow their example. In the early 530s John led a quiet life. After the Council of Constantinople in 536, however, Justinian issued sharp legal restrictions against Miaphysites, and the monks of Amida had to go into exile once again. Probably from about 540, John lived and worked in or near Constantinople, also making various journeys as far as Egypt. He seems to have become the abbot of a monastery in Sycai, on the northern bank of the Golden Horn, and may be regarded as the most conspicuous representative of the Miaphysites at this time, even managing to stay in contact with the imperial court and other members of the elite. Presumably in 558, Jacob Baradaeus ordained him bishop of Ephesus. Jacob was the main organiser of the Syriac Miaphysite church, which came to be known as the Jacobite Church. As bishop of Ephesus, John was also called bishop of Asia in Syriac sources. Although Justinian did not defect from the Chalcedonian creed and defended it aggressively at times, he did reach out to other groups, and the emperor and the Miaphysite bishop seem to have found a *modus vivendi*, even though the occasional conflict was unavoidable.

According to Miaphysite sources, Justinian's nephew Justin II (565–578) favoured a unification of the Christian confessions, winning John's support for this endeavour at least for a time. However, the situation of the Miaphysites soon deteriorated, in particular as of 571. The short-lived unity of the churches collapsed. Conflicts flared among the anti-Chalcedonians, possibly more strongly than before, because some agents had compromised themselves during the negotiations on church unity.[16] John, who had probably overestimated his influence among Christians and at court, suffered persecution from the emperors, including imprisonment and once again exile. The latest date in his works refers to the age of Maurice, or more precisely to the year 588.[17] He died shortly afterwards. We should bear in mind that he was not living in Syria at the time he wrote his *Church History*, but in Constantinople, the centre of power that was also a centre of Miaphysitism at this time.

---

[16] Shahîd 1995: 2, 793–6, 860–2; Cameron 1976: 51–67 = Cameron 2001, X; Rosen 2001: 778–801; Whitby 2000: 86–94, 90 rightly warns against taking John's description of the persecutions at face value.
[17] Allen 1979.

Political and Ecclesiastical Space inside the Roman Empire

John wrote his *Church History* while under the impression that the end of the world was near.[18] The history he recounts is one of a church being persecuted by Roman emperors and others on account of the sins of mankind. I cannot discuss his views on the individual Roman emperors of his time.[19] But it is clear that there was no perfect emperor and each of them had his flaws. The praise heaped on Tiberius in the third book is belied by the preceding chapters, which show him vacillating and initiating persecutions of Christian minorities that are open to misuse by the Chalcedonians.[20] However, even an emperor such as Justin II, who is mostly depicted in negative terms by John, shows signs of goodwill towards him.[21] Moreover, there were perfect constellations, such as in the 540s for example, when John was able to convert thousands of pagans to Christianity thanks to Justinian's generous support (an event that is highly stylised by John).[22] Although events of this kind were rare, they were possible.[23] The empire could still function. Once more, we can see that John is convinced that there is a chance to assign the Miaphysites an important role within the political order of the Roman Empire.[24] Thus he might be termed a loyalist historian in regard to politics.[25]

John had grown up in the empire and lived there for most of his life, if not continuously. His mother tongue, Syriac, was not one of the languages of power, but had adapted to the circumstances. The Syriacs used technical terms such as names of provinces and magistratures in their language as loan words, and so did John. When John sets out to describe the whole Roman world he uses three geographical terms in a kind of climax in three steps: *aṭrā,*

---

[18] Esp. John of Ephesus, *Ecclesiastical History* 3.1.3 (p. 5–6 Brooks), 3.2.25, 3.6.1.

[19] See Van Ginkel 1994: 327–9 on Justin. John of Ephesus, *Ecclesiastical History* 3.3.1 for Justin's change for the worse.

[20] John of Ephesus, *Ecclesiastical History* 3.47; on his generally positive view of this emperor, see Van Ginkel 1994, 328–30.

[21] See, e.g., John of Ephesus, *Ecclesiastical History* 3.1.19 (p. 25 Brooks), 3.1.26–8.

[22] See Flusin 2010; Mellon Saint-Laurent 2015: 77–9; Leppin 2017.

[23] It is significant that Justin even tries to console the Miaphysite bishops (John of Ephesus, *Ecclesiastical History* 3.1.26). At first glance, Theodoret employs a similar concept when he deals with Jovian's short but perfect reign (Leppin 1996: 89–90). But he says that God wanted to show that he was able to produce such emperors, and does not claim that human agents can bring about an ideal situation while cooperating.

[24] One should, however, bear in mind that good Persian rulers were conceivable, too: see John of Ephesus, *Ecclesiastical History* 3.6.20 on Khusrau I with Walker 2006: 178–9, 184–6.

[25] Greatrex 2009: 51, underlines the distance John feels to the empire, see also Andrade 2009: 217, but in regard to a *Vita*. For other positions among Miaphysites of the sixth c. see Taylor 2009.

pniṭā and *hūparkia* (Greek: *hyparchia* or *eparchia*), saying that all of them were affected by a schism. These might correspond to the steps of province, diocese and prefecture, which were still relevant at this time although provinces and dioceses often coincided.[26] Normally, John simply transliterates the names of provinces and other geographical units. In the case of the diocese of *Oriens* he is sensitive enough to use the traditional Syriac word for east (*maḏnḥā*), which mirrors the Latin parlance.[27] He seems to be familiar with the structures of the Roman Empire and the relevant *termini technici*.

Military history does not seem to appeal to John (and in any case is not an important feature of church historiography). In the last book, however, John provides long passages about military history, describing Maurice's war against the Persians at length, while also giving details about the conflict between the Jafnids and Nasrids and about barbarian invasions of the Balkans. These passages are unusual in most regards. In the first chapter, John mentions that the subject matter is alien to church historiography. Many chapters look as if they were taken from profane historiography. John touches on numerous very concrete geographical facts that are only of strategic importance for the conflicting armies.[28] As part three of the *Church History* is incomplete, we may perhaps assume that he planned to rework this book.[29] The first chapter, however, gives an idea of what John might have planned because there he delves into an apocalyptic dimension of history. But this does not explain the circumstantiality of his account.

Otherwise, John's description of the Roman Empire is essentially a description of a Christian space that is influenced by politics to a greater or lesser extent.[30] The author does not show any more interest

[26] John of Ephesus, *Ecclesiastical History* 3.4.39 (p. 219 Brooks); Brooks translates *hūparkiya* as *provincia*, which is possible; but see for the meaning of *praefectura* (which is implied in Payne-Smith 1903, 103) Brockelmann 1895, 24a with references from John of Ephesus. The climax (the next step is East and West) supports the interpretation given here (also given by Schönfelder 1862 in his translation). For *atrā* as province cf. John of Ephesus, *Ecclesiastical History* 3.2.17 (p. 57 Brooks), 3.2.44 (p. 80 Brooks); but the word can also have a more general meaning. The hierarchy of provinces, dioceses and prefectures might have become a literary convention by John's time: on the suppression of the dioceses under Justinian, who turned the *comes orientis* into a de facto provincial governor, see Stein 1949: 465–6; however, Justinian rescinded some of his measures, see Leppin 2011: 177–81. On the methodological problems of the development of the administrative structure after Justinian, see Brandes 2002: 123–5.

[27] John of Ephesus, *Ecclesiastical History* 3.1.32. For other meanings of this word see following text.

[28] John of Ephesus, *Ecclesiastical History* 3.6.5–21.

[29] Another argument might be the use of the Greek loan word Constantinople for the capital, cf. John of Ephesus, *Ecclesiastical History* 3.6.10 (p. 302 Brooks), 3.6.11 (p. 305 Brooks); normally he says, 'royal city', see following text.

[30] Interestingly, besides *malkuṭā* (kingdom/empire) he nevertheless also uses the Grecism *puliṭiya*, e.g., John of Ephesus, *Ecclesiastical History* 3.2.11 (p. 73 Brooks), 3.3.5 (p. 126 Brooks), 3.3.26 (p. 153 Brooks); on the meaning see Andrade 2009: 204–12, 207 for the routine use in that sense.

in dogmatic questions than other church historians. Even Theodoret, who knew his theology, did not discuss it extensively in his *Church History*. John's empire as a whole is a Christian empire, whatever the confessional position of the ruling emperor is, but Christianity is fractured into multifarious different groups. John takes the contrast between his co-religionists with the Chalcedonians for granted, without, however, challenging the legitimacy of Chalcedonian bishops.[31] Moreover, he does not exclude common action. The idea of unifying Chalcedonian and non-Chalcedonian Christians persists. Both groups welcome Eutychius on his return as patriarch of Constantinople in 577, so John says, because of his ability to perform miracles.[32] This is an important point for my argument: the short passage shows that the amalgamation of various Christian groups is possible where holiness is concerned. The interest in the veneration of sanctified persons beyond confessional borders is, by the way, a motif that John shares with Socrates. [33]

Then again, it seems to be particularly important for John to define and justify his position among the anti-Chalcedonians because he had reached out to Chalcedonians under Justin II only to be disappointed afterwards. He explains his behaviour in a special chapter and dwells at length on the sufferings he had to endure afterwards.[34] This shows how deep the rifts were even among the Miaphysites.

Readers of the *Church History* are not offered an even picture of the empire. Rather, the church historian gives a nuanced picture of certain parts of the empire that are important for his group. Egypt is frequently mentioned.[35] A passing reference reveals that John is fully aware of its strategic importance for Constantinople's corn supply.[36] But another issue was obviously much more important to him. Alongside Syria, Egypt was a principal centre of Miaphysitism, and the regions often competed for hegemony in their confession – although John consciously conveys the

---

[31] Van Ginkel 1995: 113–14.

[32] John of Ephesus, *Ecclesiastical History* 3.2.31 (*bis*). A similar phrase occurs in 3.2.29 (p. 70 Brooks) and 3.6.49 (p. 261 Brooks), the last sentence of the work; its ascription to John is, however, doubtful; see the footnote by Brooks. This passage implies that the Miaphysites even joined services in the Hagia Sophia. In 3.2.35 the phrase refers only to the Miaphysites. 3.3.31 (p. 119 Brooks): all the Christians stream into the episcopal church. A bishop John, a firm Miaphysite, who possessed the gift of seeing the future, was buried in the presence of Chalcedonians and Miaphysites according to Michael the Syrian, *Chronicle* 10.15 (364) in a passage that is probably derived from the fourth book of John of Ephesus; on the identity of the bishop Van Ginkel 1995: 37 n. 89.

[33] Leppin 1996: 229.   [34] John of Ephesus, *Ecclesiastical History* 3.1.30, 3.2.5.

[35] E.g., John of Ephesus, *Ecclesiastical History* 3.1.33, 35; 40. See Ashbrook Harvey 1990: 76–80 for John on Egypt, especially in the *Lives*.

[36] John of Ephesus, *Ecclesiastical History* 3.1.33, 3.3.45.

impression that there was one orthodox, strong, Miaphysite, Severan-Jacobite church and some deviations.[37] Nevertheless, the schism among the Miaphysites of 575, which was intertwined with the rivalry between Syria and Alexandria, dominates the fourth book.[38] In general, John has a tendency to depict Egypt as a region with problematic, somehow exotic peculiarities. It appears as dangerous and ridden with conflicts. John has to admit that the region is teeming with hermits, holy men who have the reputation of being able to foresee the future. However, when Justin invites them to Constantinople, most of them affirm (perhaps as a pretence) that they do not know anything and give some general advice on God's justice. Others comply with the emperor's request to renounce their asceticism.[39] The region is treated with respect, but the reader gains the impression that John would not see the monks as consistent in their behaviour. Famous heroes of the resistance are much less prominent than in Syria.

John repeatedly refers to incidents in Antioch, the Syrian metropolis, especially in the context of schisms and of the Roman-Persian wars. But unlike the grecophone Chalcedonian church historians from Syria, Theodoret and Evagrius, John does not put Antioch centre stage.[40] In John, the metropolis even plays a negative part at one point, regarded as an enduring centre of paganism supported by the Chalcedonian bishop Gregory (who, by the way, is a pillar of Christian belief in Evagrius's *Church History*).[41] Moreover, Antioch is one of the centres of the tritheist schism, which hit Miaphysitism hard during the second half of the sixth century. The tritheists' opponents insinuated that the tritheists introduced a division of the substances and perhaps even the natures of the Trinity.[42]

The imperial capital, Constantinople, is by far the most important setting in John's account; many influential Miaphysites lived in the capital for some time. Events in the capital are the main focus of the first three

[37] However, Hermann 1928: 263–304, esp. 300, rightly underlines that John's description of the tritheist schism gives the impression that there were closed parties, whereas in fact there were several individual (and wavering) positions. See Wood 2010: 167–75 on the fracturing of the Miaphysite community; Millar 2013: 43–92, esp. 53–6 gives an overview of various expressions used for Christian groups by John.
[38] On the background, see Hermann 1928; Brooks 1929: 468–75; Grillmeier and Hainthaler 1986–2002, 3: 279–91; Allen 2011: 23–38, esp. 32 f.
[39] John of Ephesus, *Ecclesiastical History* 3.1.35.   [40] Leppin 2009.
[41] John of Ephesus, *Ecclesiastical History* 3.1.41, 3.2.8, 3.3.19, 3.3.27–31 (paganism), 3.3.40, 3.4.5, 3.4.31, 3.5.17 (paganism), 3.6.4 (p. 216 Brooks). On the contested Antiochene bishop Gregory, see Lee 2007: 99–106; Leppin 2012: 249–54. The description of the Miaphysite schism in the fourth book includes many allusions to the history of Antioch and Syria; the narration of the Roman-Persian wars also includes references to Antioch, but primarily for strategic reasons.
[42] Allen 1994: 230; on the position of John Philoponus, see Verrycken 1998: 550–1.

books and remain essential for the narrative of the remaining three. The persecution started there.[43] John normally calls Constantinople the 'royal town' (*mdinaṯ malkūṯā*)[44] or simply 'the town', as was usual, and only rarely uses the name Constantinople. As far as I can see, there are only two passages in which he does this, both within his unusually lengthy description of military exploits in the sixth book. This uncommon usage in an uncommon passage may point to a source not previously exploited.[45]

John knows the capital intimately. He alludes to many buildings, not only churches and monasteries but palaces, too, and he expects his readers to be familiar with these edifices likewise.[46] Constantinople was the 'place to be' because it was the city where the court resided and where decisions between differing Christian groups were negotiated. It was all the more so for a man such as John, who did not want to retreat into isolation, but instead struggled to get along with the Roman government although his influence remained limited. In addition, Constantinople is described as a meeting point for various Christian groups. It is, for example, the place where the Armenian *katholikos* informs John about the sufferings of his church.[47] Moreover, Constantinople is a centre of Miaphysitism, with numerous monasteries where monks and nuns from distant regions live.[48] John's co-religionists boasted two infirmaries, which were, as he said, the most important in town until they were taken away during the persecution.[49] This certainly represents the religious importance of this place, which many Miaphysites flocked to even in times when their belief was suppressed by law.

Although religious conflicts in Constantinople are a recurring theme, the Miaphysites can be described as part of the whole town (*kollāh mdyttā*), even during certain occurrences of religious importance, such as when Eutychius returns as a patriarch in 577.[50] John shares his high regard for Constantinople with Socrates as well as with Sozomen, who were based in the capital for a long time. However, in this John differs from both the

---

[43] John of Ephesus, *Ecclesiastical History* 3.1.5. See Ashbrook Harvey 1990: 80–91 on the roles of Miaphysites in Constantinople.

[44] The term might also be translated as 'imperial town' because the Syriac word *malkuṯā* can mean both.

[45] John of Ephesus, *Ecclesiastical History* 3.6.10.

[46] E.g., ibid., 3.2.9 (Hormisdas and monastery), 3.3.7 (Hormisdas outside the palace), 3.3.16–17 (palace of Marina, which serves as a church; other churches), 3.3.23 (Great Palace), 3.3.24 (other buildings in Constantinople), 3.3.30 (palace of Placidia), 3.3.31 (several buildings in Constantinople), 3.3.34 (Hormisdas and Hebdomon), 3.5.13 (Hebdomon), 3.5.18 (various buildings).

[47] Ibid., 3.2.18–24.

[48] Ibid., 3.1.10, 3.1.36 and 3.1.38 (return after persecution); cf. on the presence of Miaphysites also 3.1.5.

[49] Ibid., 3.2.15 f.   [50] Ibid., 3.2.31; see preceding text.

other Syrian historians, Theodoret and Evagrius. They cannot help mentioning the capital repeatedly, but it is much reduced in importance compared to their own regions.

Other towns seem to be considerably less significant to John. He pays only scant attention to Jerusalem – its religious status, which was well-respected among most Miaphysites, is not emphasised in the *Church History*.[51] Perhaps the patriarchs of his time were too closely involved with the Chalcedonian cause. A special case is Arabissus in Cappadocia, where Emperor Maurice (582–602) came from. His building program here is described extensively.[52] The island of Cyprus turns up occasionally as a place that is difficult to control and where Christians who had been Persian subjects are allowed to settle.[53] But these are only scattered notes.

Political and Ecclesiastical Space outside the Roman Empire

John refers to Persia frequently, as it was an important player in the East. The Euphrates is mentioned as the border between the two empires.[54] I already mentioned the long account on the Roman-Persian war under Maurice. Generally speaking, however, Persia does not seem to be paid more attention than is usual for church histories. There is no hint of a concept comparable to that of the 'two eyes of the world' as expressed by Khusrau in a letter to Maurice. [55] John observes that there were a few Miaphysite bishops in Persia, whereas most Persian Christians were Nestorians. But he speaks about their fate only in one instance, when they had a disputation at the court of the Persian king that proved successful.[56] Eventually, the Miaphysites even obtained the right to install their own *katholikos*, but this does not infringe John's loyalty towards the Roman Empire,[57] nor do his sympathies with Khusrau.[58]

---

[51] Ibid., 3.1.32, 3.1.39, 3.2.3, 3.3.35. On the importance of Jerusalem, e.g., Ashbrook Harvey 1990: 74, 77, 122, indirectly 141. Even some of the *Beati orientales* go on pilgrimage to Jerusalem, see John of Ephesus, *Lives of the Eastern Saints* 12 (Mary and Euphemia), PO 17, 167–70, 26 (Susan), PO 18, 543–6.

[52] John of Ephesus, *Ecclesiastical History* 3.5.22.

[53] Ibid., 3.6.15, 3.6.27, 3.6.34 (settling of Christians); for other references 3.1.16, 3.2.3 (cf. 4), 3.4.55 f. (retreat of Paulites).

[54] Ibid., 3.6.9, see also 3.4.35.   [55] Theophylact Simocatta 4.11.2–3 with Canepa 2009: 1, 122–5.

[56] Walker 2006 highlights that in his *Vitae* John depicts Persia as a country teeming with well-trained heretics where many debates took place (176). It is thus no coincidence that Persia appears under this aspect in the *Church History*.

[57] John of Ephesus, *Ecclesiastical History* 3.6.20f. with Van Ginkel 1995: 79.

[58] Ibid., 3.6.20 (p. 316 Brooks).

A key issue is the conflict between Rome and Persia fought out in Armenia under Justin, recommencing in 572. John describes the history of this conflict, which included the persecution of Christians, in a kind of excursus, distinguishing carefully between the two parts of Armenia, although his focus is on the war's religious aspects.[59] The Armenian conflict also serves as a comment on Roman church politics. The Persian representatives explain that the Magi observed the persecution of Christians in the Roman Empire and felt encouraged to do the same in their realm. John does not hesitate to inform his readers about the consequences: the revolt of the Christians of Armenia and the vicissitudes of the war between Rome and Persia.

This sounds like *Schadenfreude*. However, John remains a firm supporter of the Roman cause even though the emperor does not support the right belief in his eyes. Consequently, hostility to single emperors does not result in the condemnation of the political system or of the Roman Empire in general. It is still the empire to which John feels attached. Despite experiencing oppression so often himself, John repeatedly calls the Roman Empire a Christian empire, in contrast to Persia.[60] In addition, he underlines that the Armenians claim loyalty to the Roman emperor, even though they are Persian subjects, because they are Christians like him.[61]

He distances himself from the Roman government in a different way, however. When he underlines, as mentioned previously, that the Persians were motivated to persecute people of a different faith by the Roman Empire's example, he insinuates that Justin's church policy had destructive consequences for Christianity, and not only from a Miaphysite point of view.[62] Sins committed in the Roman Empire have a deep impact on the whole world.

Foreign tribes are a recurrent subject in church historiography. In the second part of John's *Church History* the spread of Christianity is an important issue. The author praises the Christian faith's successes.[63] His interest continues in the third part and there are still some conversions to

---

[59] Ibid., 3.2.18–24. Armenia is also an important theatre of war during the Roman-Persian conflict narrated in the sixth book.
[60] Ibid., 3.2.18 (p. 79 Brooks), 3.2.21 (p. 84 Brooks), 3.2.23, 3.6.2. In contrast to the impious (*raššī*) empire of the Persians (3.2.21).
[61] Ibid., 3.6.12 (p. 233 Brooks; Armenians), 3.6.15 (Persian subjects from the province of Arzon = Arzanene that was inhabited by Armenians).
[62] Ibid., 3.2.18.
[63] See, e.g., *Chronicle of Zuqnin* p. 54–6, 111 Chabot (tr. 50–2, 100 Witakowski = 75–86, 114 Harrak); cf. Chronicle of Zuqnin p. 68 Chabot (tr. 63 Witakowski = 85 Harrak). Cf. Wood 2010: 226–30; Leppin 2017. For the *Lives*, Ashbrook Harvey 1990: 94–100.

speak of, but another aspect of foreign tribes comes to the fore: now, groups endangering the Roman Empire are more prominent, such as the Avars, who arrive from the far end of the world, and Slavonic groups. Often they are called barbarians, using the Greek loan word (*barbarāiā*).[64] Typically, John does not dwell on ethnographic details. He speaks somewhat more extensively about the history of the Avars and their neighbours, especially the Gepids and also the Longobards, but he does not even allude to their conquest of Italy. [65] Another chapter dedicated to the Slavonic groups likewise includes only a few ethnographic details.[66] The Turks who live beyond the Sasanian Empire appear on the horizon, but details remain obscure.[67] John reports that Roman envoys who visited the Turks give accounts of fascinating things, but he does not offer any particulars.[68] He also briefly comments on the Nubian Nobadaeans and Alodaeans, going back to the time of Theodora. [69] But once again, foreign customs do not hold his attention. His work betrays no deeper concern with ethnographic or geographical details.[70]

His interest in the intruders lies elsewhere. They contribute to the fulfilment of God's plans. When the Chalcedonians destroy the churches of the Miaphysites, their own churches suffer the same fate at the hands of the Avars in Thrace. [71] Barbarians can even shame Christians when they feed the hungry, as the Avars do in Sirmium. [72]

Arabs figure more prominently in John's narrative than in the works of earlier authors – for the obvious reason that they had gained importance during the sixth century.[73] John perceives them as an ethnic community, but describes them as politically connected with one of the big empires respectively: Arabs of the Romans (*ṭaiāiē d-rhūmāiē*) and Arabs of the Persians (*ṭaiāiē d-pārsāiē*).[74] This corresponds to the confederations that are usually called the Ghassanids and Lakhmids. More recent research has

---

[64] On those nations John of Ephesus, *Ecclesiastical History* 3.2.30, 3.3.25, 3.5.19, cf. 3.5.21.

[65] Ibid. 3.6.14 (Longobards as Roman troops), 3.6.24, 3.6.30–3. The chapters 3.6.44–9 that mention Avars as well as Slavs are supplemented from Michael the Syrian; Van Ginkel 1998: 351–8 rightly underlines that Michael has reworked John's text and should not be taken as an undistorted source.

[66] Ibid., 3.6.25.   [67] Ibid., 3.6.7, 3.6.12, 3.6.23.   [68] Ibid., 3.6.23 (246 Brooks).

[69] Ibid., 3.4.6–8, 3.4.48–53; see Richter 2002: 42–98.

[70] Witakowski 2007: 219–46 on the limited interest in geography in early Syriac authors in general.

[71] John of Ephesus, *Ecclesiastical History* 3.2.30. There is no confessional bias in 3.6.45–9, where John also deals with invasions by the Avars.

[72] Ibid., 3.6.32.

[73] Ibid., 3.6.3 f. See Fisher 2011: 18–20, 174 and *passim* on John as a source on the Arabs; cf. Fowden 2014: 112 on the question of exaggerations in John's account, distancing himself from Shahid 1995.

[74] Most significantly in John of Ephesus, *Ecclesiastical History* 3.6.3 (p. 212 Brooks).

underlined that political leaders are more important in the sources than ethnic identities, preferring to call them Jafnids and Naṣrids.[75]

The crucial figure is the Arab king al-Mundhir (568/9–581/2).[76] Sporting the title of *patricius*, he was influential at court, albeit only to a certain degree. On the one hand, the Roman Empire was dependent on him. On the other hand, this dependence stirred up mutual distrust. The political dimension shines through John's narration. He underlines that in 580 al-Mundhir received a crown never given to an Arab king before,[77] but this does not attract his main interest, which is again in religion.

Most importantly for John, al-Mundhir is the only powerful political figure at this time to genuinely sympathise with the Miaphysites.[78] He tries to reconcile Jacob Baradaeus with Paul the Black, the contested bishop of Antioch, but to no avail.[79] In 580, he even endeavours to bring various anti-Chalcedonian groups together, as John describes approvingly. They reach an agreement, which is fragile from the beginning, however, and is further undermined by unreliable bishops – something that John notes with disgust.[80] Things become even worse. John maintains that al-Mundhir's followers defect from the true belief because of the Romans' deceitful politics.[81] Al-Mundhir is betrayed by the Romans twice[82] and ends up as an exile in Sicily. After describing the machinations against al-Mundhir under Tiberius, John inserts a long passage that recounts horrifying disasters in Constantinople, culminating in the death of the emperor.[83] According to the conventions of church historiography, the catastrophes attest to God's wrath, which fits with John's ideas about history.

---

[75] Fisher 2011 is the fundamental source on this matter. Millar 2010: 200 highlights that both terms, Ghassanids and Jafnids, are (almost) not attested in contemporary sources. John does not use them either. See, however, Liebeschuetz 2015, who underlines that Jafnid phylarchs claimed Ghassanid identity, but has to rely on late sources.

[76] For the basic dates PLRE III A 34–7, s.v. Alamandurus.

[77] According to John of Ephesus, *Ecclesiastical History* 3.4.39 (p. 164 Brooks), 3.4.42 (p. 168 Brooks) Tiberius bestowed a royal diadem (*tāg̱ā d-malkuṯā*) on him; on this elevation, see Chrysos 1978: 50; Shahîd 1995 i.1, 398–406.

[78] He is often mentioned: John of Ephesus, *Ecclesiastical History* 3.2.8, 3.3.40–3, 3.4.21, 3.4.40 and 42, 3.6.4, 3.6.16–18; see Van Ginkel 1995: 120; Wood 2010: 252–5. On al-Mundhir's political role see Edwell et al. 2015, esp. 254–61 and 263–6 on John's standpoint.

[79] John of Ephesus, *Ecclesiastical History* 3.4.36 with Fisher and Wood et al. 2015: 276–372, esp. 325.

[80] John of Ephesus, *Ecclesiastical History* 3.4.39; on the final breakdown of negotiations, see 43 and Wood 2010: 251; Fisher and Wood 2015: 326–8.

[81] John of Ephesus, *Ecclesiastical History* 3.3.56; with Shahîd 1995: 542; Van Ginkel 1995: 82 is doubtful whether this chapter goes back to John; on the difficulties in using Michael as a witness for John's text, see Van Ginkel 1998.

[82] John of Ephesus, *Ecclesiastical History* 3.6.3 (a kind of flashback), 3.3.40–4; on the historical context cf. Edwell 2015: 254–68 with translations of these passages.

[83] John of Ephesus, *Ecclesiastical History* 3.45–7.

Whereas Roman sources traditionally depict barbarians and Arabs as unfaithful, in John's description of the division between al-Mundhir's Arabs and the empire, the Romans – or more accurately the Roman emperor and his confidantes – prove to be unreliable. The protector of the Miaphysites is the embodiment of a courageous and honest ruler, who builds churches and is generous to the poor,[84] succumbing only to religious and political traitors. In this case it becomes obvious that religious identities override ethnic stereotypes. The best ruler sits not at the centre of the political space, but belongs to a kingdom on the periphery of the Roman Empire.

As in the case of Armenia, the politics of the Roman emperors mean a reversal of Christianisation outside the empire – the opposite of what should have happened under proper Christian rule. Most previous church histories had described the Christianisation of nations outside of the Roman Empire, and John had given some glorious examples in part two. Yet this part already mentions the failures of Christianisation, which are highlighted even more strongly in part three.

Gothic troops appear as a part of the Roman army. When Emperor Tiberius enters the war with Persia, he is forced to fetch troops from the western part of the empire. Being Goths, the soldiers, who are accompanied by their families, still cling to Arianism, which had otherwise been eliminated from the eastern part of the empire. They cause trouble when they demand a church for their wives and children who are to stay in Constantinople. Tiberius, who is still the regent for Justin II, reacts evasively at first and is suspected to have Arian inclinations. In the end, he feels obliged to persecute them along with other heretics. These persecutions are executed unfairly.[85] John certainly was no friend of Arian doctrines, but he seems to have understood how difficult it was for the emperor to steer a clear course between the various factions. John seems even to have sympathised with the Arians when they fell victim to Chalcedonian outrage and their church was looted.[86]

What about the West? As I said, John's Greek predecessors already did not pay much attention to this part of the empire. The disappearance of the West from the intellectual sphere, which is palpable in Theodoret, is quite blatant in John's work. The West is virtually absent from his historiography; there is almost no reflection of what has been called the post-imperial

---

[84] See his praise in ibid., 3.6.4 (p. 217 Brooks).
[85] Ibid., 3.3.13 and 3.3.26 seem to refer to the same incidents, albeit with minor differences.
[86] Ibid., 3.5.16.

world.[87] There is no mention of Gaul or the Iberian Peninsula, Greece is referred to only in passing and Thrace, so close to Constantinople, is primarily featured as a dangerous region where exiles are forced to carve out a miserable existence.[88]

The West in general is a region where dangers loom. The foundation of conventicles in Rome, Corinth, Athens and Africa attests to the menacing spread of the tritheists, but only the city of Rome is more visible. John's main concern, however, is that tritheists will go as far as to attempt to convert the praetorian prefect Narses, whom John regards as a friend to his cause and who is extremely influential in the East.[89] For obvious reasons, the see of Rome appears as a source of erroneous belief, whereas the Chalcedonians highlight the importance of the communication with this see as a matter of course.[90] Worst of all is Pope Leo the Great (440–461), with his notorious *tomus Leonis*. From a Miaphysite point of view, it was impossible not to repudiate him.[91] When John of Ephesus deals with the Council of Constantinople (553), he mentions Vigilius's ambivalent attitude and his change(s) of mind in regard to the *Three Chapters*, obviously to denigrate the synod; he is also aware of the disruptive consequences of the synod's decision in the West.[92] Although John knows about the apostolic, Petrine claims of the bishop of Rome, they do not seem to impress him.[93]

Such a perspective certainly deepened the divide between the eastern and western parts of the Mediterranean world. However, there is no need to connect this attitude with John's Syriac identity. His attitude is first and foremost a result of his being a Miaphysite. The lack of interest in the West is common to the eastern sources at this time, be they Greek or Syriac.

---

[87] Ibid., 3.5.22 (p. 274 Brooks) might be a hint, but the passage puts East and West on the same level in regard to destructions.

[88] Ibid., 3.6.25 on destructions in this region; ibid., 3.4.19, a chapter that describes the divisive effects of the Miaphysite schism, seems only interested in the eastern regions and Constantinople. When he narrates how far the ravages of the plague spread in the 540s he also mentions Ravenna and Carthage: Part 2, ch. 89 (82 Witakowski = p. 101 Harrak). This is a strange exception.

[89] Ibid., 3.5.2; for his sympathies 3.1.39.   [90] Ibid., 3.1.24 (p. 23 Brooks).

[91] See, e.g., ibid., 3.1.18 (p. 14 Brooks), 3.1.24 (p. 22 Brooks), 3.1.42, 3.2.35, 3.5.19. In 3.2.32 the authorities' suppression of the Roman *archidiaconus* of Rome who dares to criticise the reinstallation of Eutychius as uncanonical is used to demonstrate the Chalcedonians' hypocrisy. Cf. for the second part Chronicle of Zuqnin p. 12 Chabot (tr. p. 14 Witakowski = 47 Harrak), 27 Chabot (tr. p. 27 Witakowski = 57 Harrak), 29 Chabot (tr. p. 29 Witakowski = 57 Harrak).

[92] Ibid., 138 f. ch. (p. 123 f. Witakowski = p. 132 Harrak).

[93] Ibid., 3.2.43. Cf. Ps.-Zachariah, whose work even contained a description of remarkable buildings in Rome (10.16).

The Lives of the Eastern Saints

What I have discussed so far about John's concept of Christian space refers to his *Church History*. But this is not the only perspective that John takes. When we look at the *Lives of the Eastern Saints*, it is clear that he is consciously dealing only with a circumscribed area of the late antique world, whereas his *Church History* in principle deals with the empire as a whole as well as its neighbours. In his *Vitae*, John emphasises the importance of his home region,[94] which is only of marginal importance in the *Church History*. The world of the *Vitae* is predominantly rural. Nevertheless, the royal town remains the all-important place of decision-making in regard to persecutions. Thus the desire to convince the emperor residing there of the Miaphysites' cause pervades all the works of this Syriac author, including the *Lives*.[95]

How are we to explain the differences between the two works?[96] We certainly cannot assume that John's attitude changed between them because the texts were written at more or less the same time. It is rather a question of outlook, audience and literary intentions. The *Vitae* describe exemplary lives, true Christians, among them heroes of resistance in the time of persecution. The intended readership consists of John's fellow believers. The *Church History*, by contrast, speaks of many failed attempts to achieve reconciliation not only between the emperor and the Miaphysites but also among the Miaphysites. With its apologetic elements, the *Church History* seems to appeal to a broader readership within the anti-Chalcedonian world. John takes on different literary roles in these texts, corresponding to his different political roles within his community and outside. Thus there is a tension between these works, but not a contradiction because *Kaiserkritik* that is directed towards individual emperors does not disprove a fundamental loyalty to the Roman Empire.

---

[94] Well brought out by Wood 2010: 178–98.

[95] Some remarks on the perception of geography in this world are found in Ashbrook Harvey 1990, esp. chs. 3 and 4.

[96] It is interesting to see that Wood 2010, who pays more attention to the *Vitae* than to the *Church History*, is inclined to stress the distance John feels, especially 229 and 262. ('The experience of the Miaphysites in the sixth century, which led them to displace the authority of the Roman emperors.') But he also emphasises the basic loyalty to the Roman Empire (e.g., 174, 252, 256), a fact that I would highlight even more; on the critical position apparent in some of the *Vitae*, see Taylor 2009, 82f.

A Romano-Syriac Historian

Hitherto, I have made a great deal of detailed observations. I will now try to paint a broader picture. What we have seen so far seems to confirm that John's *Church History* is much less unusual than we might expect. In fact, his work is a variant of Greek Christian historiography as it developed in the late antique Roman Empire. Unfortunately, we know Philostorgius – another representative of a marginalised religious group – only from fragments, precluding a systematic comparison.[97] In my opinion, the analysis of Philostorgius's work would result in similar insights to the ones we gain from the work of John of Ephesus.

Philostorgius wrote in Greek, however, whereas John's language was Syriac, which had gained considerable cultural prestige in the sixth century.[98] He appears to be a Roman historian who happened to write in Syriac, so to speak.[99] In that sense, from a linguistic perspective, I call him a Romano-Syriac historian. His view of the Roman Empire and of the world outside the empire is very similar to that of the imperial church historians writing in Greek, although the Roman West is paid even less attention than in other eastern historians. Significantly, ecclesiastical and political languages diverge on one point. While the Syriac word for West (*ma'rbā*) can mean the western part of the Roman Empire, which is also the traditional usage in Greek church historiography, in John's work, it can also denote the western part of the Miaphysite world, including Constantinople. This is naturally also true for the word for east, which can also technically denote the diocese of *Oriens* and the eastern part of John's church.[100]

Although there seem to be some rifts as regards its western part, the Roman Empire does not appear to be a fracturing power system, but rather, along with the Persian Empire, as the dominant, stable power in its world. John may represent a marginal group, but he certainly does not

---

[97] See now the splendid work of Bleckmann and Stein 2015.

[98] See Ashbrook Harvey 1990: 40–3; Millar 2013, *passim*, 81 on John's *Church History*.

[99] On Roman identity among Syriacs cf. Tannous 2018. He argues that Romanness came to be identified with dyothelete Chalcedonian Christianity (457); John would be an exception to this, which may be explained by the fact that he is a relatively early author who wrote before the monothelete controversy began. On John's position cf. Tannous 2018, 467–8.

[100] John of Ephesus, *Ecclesiastical History* 3.3.26 (political; because they are Arians and assemble in Constantinople, they must stem from a region in the west of Constantinople), 3.4.31 (ecclesiastical), 3.4.39 (ecclesiastical and perhaps political). 3.3.45 uses the word *ma'rbā* for the western part of the eastern empire including Constantinople. This shows that the language has adapted to the ecclesiastical usage. But we should bear in mind that his chapter has only been transmitted by Michael the Syrian and the Chronicle of 1234.

take a peripheral viewpoint. This is especially apparent in the fact that the 'royal city', the see of the emperor, is always the focus, though obviously not as a place that is of huge religious importance in itself, but as the political centre that has a strong impact on church policy. It is not only the place where the dangers for the believers are most formidable but also the place where peace can be made. Many members of the imperial elite are connected with John's church. To give an example, he is proud of three consuls who remain true to his church despite persecution.[101]

This allows us to draw some conclusions about the intended audience. In the second part, he once calls his readers his brothers (aḥen),[102] which indicates that monks were addressed. But they must have been urban monks and clerics, familiar with Constantinople. He seems to have a readership in mind that was attached to the Roman Empire and respected its social hierarchy, albeit perhaps distrustful towards the rulers. Significantly, John thought it necessary to defend his behaviour towards Justin II when the emperor tried to bring a unification of the Christians about in 571. At this time, John was willing to compromise, but changed his position later when he felt he had been cheated.[103] However, John uses some examples (notably his missionary work in Asia Minor) to illustrate that an ideal relationship between emperor and true Christians is possible.[104] Despite all the saddening stories and the apocalyptic visions, there is also an optimistic message in his *Church History* encouraging his co-religionists to try to co-operate and to come to terms with the Roman Empire.[105]

The main difference between the Miaphysite John and the Greek church historians lies not in his view of political space of the Roman Empire, but in his description of ecclesiastical space. The continuity of the church is guaranteed not by certain sees, but by true believers. In that sense, John's church was deterritorialised, although a process of territorialisation had set in.[106] Due to its precarious situation, the church was highly personalised; it did not easily lend itself to a language of space.

---

[101] Ibid., 3.2.11, with some flaws in the details: Eudaemon (3, PLRE III 456); Ioannes (19, PLRE III 676); Petrus (17, PLRE III 1003 f.). He seems to allude to important, well-known people of his confession who were not among the bishops, s. 3.1.22 (p. 29 Brooks).
[102] Chronicle of Zuqnin p. 97 Chabot (tr. p. 89 Witakowski = 106 Harrak).
[103] On this botched attempt see Grillmeier and Hainthaler 1986–2002: 2: 502–11.
[104] Leppin 2017.
[105] Ps.-Zachariah, who ends in 569, seems to have been optimistic, see Greatrex 2006: 40, 2009: 34–5; cf., however, for apocalyptic elements Greatrex 2006: 44.
[106] See Chapter 6 by Philip Wood.

More generally speaking, John's Church was still in the process of establishing itself while suffering almost permanent persecution during the time he was writing. A growing number of bishops were ordained, but compared to the Chalcedonian Church, Miaphysite ecclesial structures were solely based in the East and many bishops were in exile. After 536, the monasteries were the real power centres of the Miaphysite cause.[107] Moreover, John's church was always in danger.

Under these circumstances, it was difficult to maintain continuity in all the episcopal sees. This also has consequences for the literary structure of John's work: the evidence of the apostolic succession that was highlighted in Eusebius's *Church History* was unable to shape the framework of his narration. He is not able to provide uninterrupted lists containing the legitimate incumbents of important sees. Instead he names the heroes and the sufferers, which fits well with the much more individualised structure of the Miaphysite Church.[108] When John gives lists of episcopal successions at the end of the first book of part three, they are striking for the number of interruptions.[109] This makes it all the more interesting that John goes to the effort to offer lists of bishops at all. In the *Chronicle of Zuqnin*, which transmits vast passages from the second part of the *Church History*, the author occasionally provides lists of patriarchs, but they are much less impressive than the Eusebian ones, and I am not even sure whether all of them go back to John. The *Chronicle* regularly names the most important Chalcedonian bishops, whose legitimacy is not fundamentally contested, and highlights the persecuted bishops and the sufferers from John's side.[110]

I have mentioned on various occasions that John was a loyal subject of the Roman Empire aiming at the incorporation of the Miaphysites into the empire. He does not adopt an intermediate position between the empires in his *Church History*. This kind of attitude is by no means to be taken for granted. Syriac speakers are famous for having lived on both sides of the Roman-Persian border, engaged in close exchange between the two sides.

---

[107] Key Fowden 1999: 156.   [108] See, e.g., John of Ephesus, *Ecclesiastical History* 3.1.14–18.
[109] Ibid., 3.1.41–2.
[110] Chronicle of Zuqnin p. 2 Chabot (p. 1 Witakowski = 37 Harrak), 5 Chabot (p. 6 Witakowski = 41 Harrak), 13 Chabot (p. 15 Witakowski = 47 Harrak), 15 Chabot (p. 16. Witakowski = 48 Harrak), 17 Chabot (p. 19 Witakowski = 50 Harrak), 47 Chabot (p. 44 Witakowski = 70 Harrak), 110 Chabot (p. 99 Witakowski = 113 Harrak), 127 Chabot (p. 113 Witakowski = 124 Harrak), 143 Chabot (p. 127 Witakowski = 136 Harrak). See Witakowski 1987: 124–36 on the use of sources in the Chronicle of Zuqnin, who used a main source that he supplemented occasionally from a score of others; on lists of bishops see Greatrex et al. 2011, 44–5, arguing that the lists in John and Ps.-Zachariah derive from a common source.

Roman and Persian rulers competed to win over the Syriac speakers. The strong interest that Persian, Roman and Arab monarchs took in the cult of St Sergius in Rusafa has been interpreted as an expression of this endeavour.[111]

In some passages of his *Vitae*, especially in the *Vita of John of Tella*, John of Ephesus comes close to distancing himself from the Roman Empire.[112] But even highlighting the rulership of Christ, he never condemns the Roman Empire. In his *Church History*, John unambiguously sides with it. His perspective is undoubtedly eastern, but it is a decidedly Roman perspective at the same time. He certainly underlines the sufferings of the Miaphysites under Chalcedonian rule and highlights the shortcomings of the Chalcedonian Empire in fulfilling its responsibility towards the true Christian belief. He criticises most of the emperors he mentions, some of them even severely. However, he remains a loyal subject of the Roman Empire in its wars against Persia[113] and he never questions imperial rule as such.[114]

Later Miaphysite or Jacobite historians were to ascribe the Arab victory over Byzantium to God's wrath against the Romans, who persecuted the true believers. John is sometimes seen as their predecessor,[115] but this is a much too linear concept of Miaphysite historical thinking and Syriac identity.[116] There is no doubt that God sometimes punishes the Roman emperor for his sins against the Miaphysites and that consequently the empire must suffer backlashes. However, the idea of a sweeping defeat of the Romans is certainly against John's wishes and quite unthinkable to him. It seems eminently possible that eventually the Roman Empire will be converted to the true belief. Miaphysitism is the empire's orthodoxy in waiting.[117]

---

[111] Key Fowden 1999: 130–73; Canepa 2009: 26; Fisher and Wood 2015: 329–31. John of Ephesus, *Ecclesiastical History* 3.6.4 (p. 285 Brooks) on Rusafa as a somehow neutral meeting place; see Key Fowden 1999: 172. On contacts across the borders from an east Syriac perspective, see Walker 2006: 174–6.

[112] Esp. *Lives of the Eastern Saints* 24 (John of Tella), PO 18: 318; Andrade 2009: 217; Wood 2010: 163–208.

[113] See Van Ginkel 1995: 207–11. In *Ecclesiastical History* 3.6.11 (p. 305 Brooks) John calls the Roman emperor our king of the Romans (*malkā dilan d-rhūmāiē*); referring to Constantinople John of Ephesus, *Ecclesiastical History* 3.2.18 (p. 79 Brooks) says in our royal city of the Romans (*b-mdinaṭ malkūṭā dilan d-rhūmāiē*).

[114] Van Ginkel 1995: 109.

[115] See the critical remarks by Palmer 2009: 57–87, esp. 75–7. Harrak 2009: 95 shows that the chronicler of Zuqnin is still loyal to Byzantium in military matters.

[116] Van Ginkel 2006a: 171–84 brings out the gradual development of a specifically Syriac Christian identity under the influence of the Arab conquests.

[117] Wood 2010: 252, 256.

Conclusion

John of Ephesus is a Roman imperial historian just like Theodoret (who, by the way, was also persecuted when he wrote his *Church History*, but unlike John did not write about his experiences) or Eusebius. Political space is not identical with religious space: Christianity goes beyond the borders of the empire, but it does not supersede the political order. For John, the political order he identifies with is the order of the Roman Empire. He criticises various imperial acts heavily and even describes them as the reversal of what a Christian emperor should do. Nevertheless, he places his trust in the monarchical order of Rome and has not given up hope that Roman emperors might ally themselves with the true belief. But the best ruler comes from the periphery: al-Mundhir, who committed himself to the unification of the anti-Chalcedonians. He is, however, a figure of honest failure: the agreement he seemed to have reached was subverted and he fell into a trap set by the Roman emperor Tiberius.

John was a Roman imperial church historian who happened to write in an unusual language that he adapted to his needs by using the relevant technical vocabulary.[118] Therefore, I would even go as far as calling his historiography Syro-Roman, in analogy to the expression Greco-Roman.[119] Had political history developed otherwise, had the western Syriac community remained under Roman rule and pursued the tradition of imperial historiography in Syriac, we could perhaps interpret John's *Church History* as an important step in the establishment of Syriac as a language enjoying a similar role within the Eastern Roman Empire as the Greek language during the principate. But these ruminations will remain nothing more than counterfactual history.

---

[118] In *Ecclesiastical History* 3.1.10 (p. 10 Brooks) he explicitly calls soldiers who abuse and imprison Miaphysite nuns (who come from the east) Romans (*rhūmāyē*). Here a negative tone might be heard in the sense that Romans were the persecuting power.

[119] The phrase 'Syro-Roman' is already well established in regard to the Syro-Roman law code, see Selb and Kaufhold 2002 for the Syriac text, which was originally written in Greek, but has been transmitted in Syriac.

CHAPTER 6

Changing Geographies
West Syrian Ecclesiastical Historiography, AD 700–850

Philip Wood

Dorothea Weltecke has remarked that we should not think of ecclesiastical history as a tree that grows from a single root in the Acts of the Apostles and Eusebius. As she argues, we may be better off thinking of churches as networks of individuals or as a bamboo forest, of distinct institutions planted in the same soil.[1] However, as a historiography, ecclesiastical history *does* present itself as a single tree, to follow Weltecke's analogy, some of whose branches withered away as they abandoned 'orthodoxy'. Our challenge, therefore, is to write a history of the historians as image makers, emphasising their continuity with the past, while acknowledging that the raw material from which they constructed this image, often the events of their own times, forced innovation, some of it conscious and some of it unconscious. Here I explore the way that historians structured their work around a specific geography and how changing events gave a regional focus to a genre that, in theory, described a universal church.

My focus is on the twelfth-century Chronicle of Michael the Syrian as a testimony for earlier histories composed between circa 750 and 830. The most significant of these is Dionysius of Tel-Mahre, the Edessene aristocrat, monk of Qenneshre and patriarch of Antioch, writing in the middle of the ninth century.[2] I am particularly interested in how Dionysius and the other Jacobite[3] historians continued the themes of ecclesiastical

---

[1] Weltecke 2017.

[2] There is a substantial gap in complex Jacobite history after the death of Dionysius. Therefore, I would argue that the history of Ignatius of Melitene, which was used by Michael, was not very substantive for the late ninth century (though he may have been a vehicle for earlier unnamed histories who were not available to Michael as extant sources). With this in mind, I read the rich history of c. 740–830 as the product of historians writing before c. 830, though they are likely to have been abbreviated by Michael. On Michael's coverage of his own period see Weltecke 2003 and for discussion of his sources, Chabot 1899 and Debié 2015. For Ignatius of Melitene, see Van Ginkel 2010 and Hilkens 2018: 293–304, and for Michael's role as an editor see Van Ginkel 2006b.

[3] In this essay I use 'West Syrian' to refer to the Christian communities west of the old Roman-Persian frontier who employed Syriac (i.e., including both Miaphysites and Chalcedonians). We may further

historiography of the fourth and fifth centuries, that is of how they understood the genre(s) in which they wrote. I argue that they preserved a long-standing interest in councils and synods as an organising schema for ecclesiastical history, but that their disinterest in doctrine might suggest that they wrote for a much less speculative audience than their predecessors, and that the theological basis for group membership was no longer a controversial problem. I then turn to the geographical focus of the Jacobite histories onto the two patriarchates of Antioch and Alexandria. This, I argue, harks back to an ideal of the older histories, in which the patriarchs act as guarantors of one another's orthodoxy. But this focus is rather different in the Melkite and Maronite histories of the early Islamic period, which still depict a world of five patriarchs, reaching towards Rome, and the expectation that doctrine will be determined in ecumenical councils gathered by an emperor, even for the Christians of the Islamic world. Finally, I examine the significance of the Jacobites' focus on a small number of monasteries in Syria and Mesopotamia, to stress the interesting blind spots of this school of history writing and of the rulers of the church. I argue that Central Asia and Arabia were 'Jacobite places' whose stories were not told, or not continued, and that this reflects the negative aspect of the church's emphasis on its 'Suryaya' identity.

A History of Bishops and Councils

Eusebius and his successors offered a model of history focused on the Roman Empire, where the chief protagonists were the emperor and the patriarchs. The historians gave a prominent role to orthodox emperors as the conveners of councils such as Nicaea and Constantinople, where doctrine was determined by bishops who represented the empire's provinces.[4] Throughout the narratives of Eusebius's successors, synods and councils are key organising features, where the confrontations of different bishops are recorded with documents.[5] In this schema, the beliefs of a universal religion were determined through the administration of a universal empire, in which bishops acted as servants of the orthodox

---

differentiate West Syrian Chalcedonians into the (Dyothelete) Melkites and the (Monothelete) Maronites and West Syrian Miaphysites into Jacobites and Julianists.

[4] On bishops in council see Rapp 2005; Chadwick 1980. Bobertz 1992 sees episcopal succession as the key to the entire narrative of Eusebius's Ecclesiastical history.

[5] Momigliano 2012: 115; Van Ginkel 1995: 65; Van Nuffelen 2004: 207–9; Whitby 2011: 352; Gardiner 2012: 51.

emperor.[6] By time of the narratives set in the fourth century, the key protagonists of this history were the emperor and the incumbents of the patriarchal sees of Constantinople, Alexandria, Antioch and Rome. These interests and expectations are still seen in John of Ephesus, a late-sixth-century historian who wrote in the Eusebian tradition in Syriac instead of Greek and who was a seen as a major predecessor by both Dionysius and Michael. John expected orthodoxy to be maintained by the emperor and a gathering of the patriarchs.[7]

However, there was a significant break with earlier tradition in the West Syrian historians of the early Islamic period who, in various ways, abandoned the model of a history constructed around councils convened by an orthodox emperor. The West Syrian historians of the late Umayyad period, on whom compilers such as Michael drew, wrote on the far side of a gulf of amnesia, rather than as part of a continuous tradition of ecclesiastical history. The texture of the Jacobite material preserved in Michael or in the ecclesiastical History of Bar Hebraeus, is very sparse indeed for the period circa 616–740. I think it likely that, when it came to ecclesiastical material, Dionysius was able to access detailed written histories for the late sixth century but not for the period 616–740.[8]

It is hard to determine exactly which parts of Michael's *Chronicle* stem from Dionysius, though Michael certainly recognises him as a major source. Dionysius deliberately stressed his inheritance of the Eusebian tradition, through John of Ephesus and the little-known sixth-century historian Cyrus of Batna. But Dionysius also employed other writers who wrote material that he found useful but who did not qualify as 'ecclesiastical historians' according to his definition, men such as 'those who have charted the succession of years' and 'those who have written materials resembling ecclesiastical history' (including Daniel of Tur Abdin, John son of Samuel and Theophilus of Edessa).[9]

---

[6] Justin II, novella 6 and 42, order bishops to disseminate imperial law. For bishops as judges and the escalation of the status of canon law see Humfress 2007 and Rapp 2005: ch. 9, with CJ 1.4.29.

[7] Good examples are John's positive treatments of the councils of Sidon (in 508) and Constantinople (in 553): *Chronicle of Zuqnin* 11–13/46–7 and 138–9/132. John continued to expect emperors to intervene to preserve Miaphysite orthodoxy, even when the emperor was not in communion with the Miaphysites.

[8] There are apparent exceptions, such as the account Michael gives of the conflict between Severus bar Mashqa and his bishops (11.13). But this account consists almost entirely of quoted documents, and I suggest that it has been generated through research by a later historian such as Dionysius who had access to an archive, rather than being the record of contemporary analysis of events. The lacuna in historical memory in Jacobite circles is especially clear in the *Chronicle of Zuqnin*, which has little to report between the death of Justinian and the last of the Umayyads.

[9] Michael the Syrian, *Chronicle* 10.21 (IV, 378/ II, 358). Translated with comments in Palmer, Brock and Hoyland 1993: 91–2.

Needless to say, Dionysius (and Michael) were only able to write history on the basis of the sources available to them. In what follows, I also offer some comparative comments on two West Syrian chronicles, the *Chronicle of Zuqnin* and the *Chronicle to 819*, which, in different ways, developed the structure of Eusebius's *Chronicle* and represent other paths which Roman Christian ways of representing church and society were adapted to eighth and ninth century conditions.[10]

For Jacobite historians of the Abbasid period, the history of church councils, such as those reported in Eusebius or Socrates, was a distant history that formed 'orthodox' identity, but it was not a living history, and, unsurprisingly, there was little interest in the 'ecumenical' councils held by Roman emperors in the eighth and ninth centuries.[11] But we should note a marked change in the texture of the material preserved in Michael from the 740s. After a lull of almost two centuries, Jacobite ecclesiastical history becomes a conciliar history like its fifth-century predecessors. Indeed, the church's capacity to organise councils coincided with its ability to sponsor history writing, and both should be seen as the products of its increasing wealth and improved ties with government. The election of new patriarchs, their fraught relations with their bishops, efforts at the union of separated churches, the issuing of canons and, in a few cases, debates over doctrine are all seen through the lens of councils, which are concentrated in Michael's account of the period 743–835.[12]

The frequent councils that are recorded in the West Syrian histories differ in several important ways from those recorded by the fifth-century historians. There are not normally doctrinal issues at stake in these synods. One historian comments that the strife of the period of Athanasius Sandalaya was not due to theological differences, but due to mere ambition.[13] Accounts of the union between the Jacobites and the Armenians and the Jacobites and the Julianists likewise give little account of doctrinal difference.[14] In the union with the Armenians, there is (rather

---

[10] Witakowski 1987: 72, 77 sets out the origins of the Syriac chronicle tradition in Eusebius's *Chronicle* (and the Hellenistic chronographies that underlie it) and in the archival practices of the city of Edessa. In chapter 5, he surveys the many different technical terms used for history writing in Syriac. However, as he notes at 61, all Syriac historical writing shows a mixture of genres: Dionysius employs the chronicles of Jacob of Edessa and John of Litarba and the *Chronicle of Zuqnin* includes large amounts of material from Eusebius, Socrates and John of Ephesus.

[11] The council of Constantinople III in 680 remained a major point of controversy for Chalcedonians because it was the dividing point for Maronites (Monotheletes) and Melkites (Dyotheletes). Michael has received sources composed in a Maronite milieu. I discuss this further in the following text.

[12] The Jacobite councils of this period are usefully summarised in Mounayer 1963.

[13] Michael the Syrian, *Chronicle* 11. 22 (IV, 467/II, 510).

[14] For the realities of doctrinal differences between Severans and Julianists see Draguet 1924 and Moss 2016.

incredibly) no mention of any doctrinal difference. The documents quoted give the impression that the Jacobites and Armenians had simply been unaware of their shared faith because of the slanders of Julianist monks. The Armenians, it is alleged, do not have any recourse to patristics, and their concerns can be dealt with simply by quoting a passage from the Acts of the apostles.[15] And in the case of the Julianists, Gabriel the Julianist patriarch admits that Julian of Halicarnassus had been in the wrong. The only sticking point is that he wants to avoid stripping him out of the diptychs and that this would cause consternation among the Julianists. Our source finds this policy eminently reasonable, but Gabriel's caution means that his overtures are rejected by Jacobite hardliners.[16] We might not expect fifth-century ecclesiastical historians to give balanced accounts of the theological positions of every side in their report of synods, but they still give the impression that the issues at stake are doctrinal and sophisticated. But the record of these attempts at union in the eighth and ninth centuries is that disunity is simply an issue of miscommunication, ignorance or personal ambition: the historians do not present doctrine as controversial.[17]

The second major difference between the Jacobite synods reported in Michael for the eighth and ninth centuries and the pre-Islamic era is the absence of secular authority. This is obviously true in the case of the emperor: this is a world without ecumenical councils, but only with local synods. But neither are there any only forms of lay authority that earlier Jacobites had praised as guarantors of good order, such as the phylarch Mundhir in 570s,[18] Heraclius's cousin Nicetas, who helped to broker the 616 Alexandria agreement[19] or the caliph, who had orchestrated meetings between the Jacobites and Maronites in Aleppo.[20] The absence of lay orchestration for councils can be seen as the consequence of the

---

[15] Michael the Syrian, *Chronicle* 11. 20 (IV, 458–9/II, 494–5). Cf. Abramowski 1940: 92, who sees the background to this union as the changing fortunes for the Byzantines and the disappearance of hopes for a Byzantine reconquest. There would be a second agreement of union with the Armenians in the council of Shirakawan in 862, which suggests that the agreement reported here did not hold very well, perhaps because of the persistence of Julianism and Chalcedonianism in Armenia that is not mentioned in this extract: Nabe-von Schonberg 1977: 137–8. Cf. Griffith 1991 for Nonnus of Nisibis's debates with Theodore Abu Qurrah in Armenia.

[16] Michael the Syrian, *Chronicle* 12.4 (IV, 485/III, 13–15). I read the document discussed by Simonsohn 2013 as a reaction by Cyriacus to the problem of the Julianists, in which he advocates the inclusion of schismatics to further church unity.

[17] Abramowski 1940: 121 comments on the dogmatic certainty that pervades Dionysius's writing.

[18] John of Ephesus, *Ecclesiastical History* 3.4.39–42.

[19] Michael the Syrian, *Chronicle* 10.26 (IV, 394/II, 385). Further on this event see Frend 1972: 340–2.

[20] The Jacobites had come off the worse in this meeting, reported in the *Maronite Chronicle*, and this event seems to have been suppressed in the Jacobite historical record. Recent analyses in Marsham

Islamicate environment and the new expectations of the Abbasid caliphs. The caliph approved patriarchal elections and backed up the patriarch with force against bishops who defied him. One aspect of this state backing was that it gave the patriarch the resources and the legitimacy to raise synods in a way that had eluded his predecessors but did not require the involvement of any Christian lay elites.[21]

The World of the Patriarchs

One feature of the geography of the fifth-century ecclesiastical historians that is closely tied to their interest in the councils is their focus on the patriarchates, on the cities of Constantinople, Alexandria, Rome and Antioch.[22] Their focus is given in this order and the lion's share of the narrative is devoted to affairs in Constantinople, especially in the emperors' relationship with the patriarchs, and in Alexandria.[23]

John of Ephesus offers a vision that is even more eastern and even more focused on Constantinople, a city he lived in and knew well.[24] The deeds of emperors and patriarchs of Constantinople form the spine of his narrative: even where events are set in rural Mesopotamia, they are the outcome of decisions taken in Constantinople to persecute or to negotiate with the Miaphysites. Though he does make the Chalcedonian patriarchs of Antioch or the bishops of Edessa major protagonists in his history, they are often ultimately implementing a policy decided in the capital. Likewise, in his famous account of the plague, which he may have understood as a divine judgement on imperial policy, his description is focused on Constantinople and Alexandria: it is here that God's displeasure is felt most keenly.[25] A similar focus is maintained in the third part of John's history, much of his narrative is really confined to the court, to the circle of bishops and laymen that had clustered around Justinian's wife Theodora

---

2013 and Papaconstantinou 2010. As Tannous argues (2014: 52), Maronites were probably the most significant Christian confession in seventh-century Damascus.

[21] Wood forthcoming.

[22] The patriarchates were at this time aligned to the importance of the cities in the imperial administration and in public prestige. These four are given pride of place in the Peutinger map, for instance, Salway 2005. For the emergence of patriarchal status see Panagiotopoulos 2003.

[23] Blaudeau 2006: 509 stresses that Sozomen and Socrates inserted Constantinople into Eusebius's geo-ecclesiology to reflect changing political circumstances and to emphasise the role of the emperor. Though Theodoret gives considerable space to Antioch, Socrates barely gives it greater attention than metropolitan sees such as Jerusalem (511).

[24] Cf. Leppin (Chapter 5, this volume).

[25] Meier 2003: 321–9 and 373–86. For the role of natural disasters in John more generally, Van Ginkel 1995: 187–90.

and their fate under the rule of Justin II. And when the unity of the Miaphysite movement begins to unravel, a significant part of John's explanation is the inability of the Alexandrians to maintain a single Miaphysite patriarch and the ordination of clergy without appropriate qualifications.[26]

The imagination of the Christian world as divided between the patriarchal sees is also a feature of the episcopal lists given for the sixth century in later West Syrian sources. Part III of the *Chronicle of Zuqnin* mainly consists of part II of John of Ephesus's history, but it also carries brief chronological notes that divide up the narrative according to episcopal reign. As Leppin notes, these probably do not go back to John, but are additions by a later hand.[27] Constantinople, Rome and Alexandria take pride of place in these lists, but they are normally joined by Jerusalem and Antioch, and occasionally by Ephesus and Edessa and by lists of famous theologians (such as Philoxenus of Mabbug) and lists of the monarchs of the time.

The *Chronicle of Zuqnin* is unable to sustain these lists of different patriarchs beyond the reign of Justinian: for the period 600–730 he is reduced to one-line notes on the Jacobite patriarchs of Antioch. But very similar lists are preserved in Michael the Syrian. These begin with the reign of Heraclius at the start of Book 11. Because they are scattered throughout this long work, I gather them here for easy comparison:

11.1 **(IV, 403/ II, 401):** 'The same year that Heraclius began his reign, the Chalcedonian patriarch of Antioch, named Anastasius, was killed and his see remained vacant for 38 years.

For us, the orthodox, we had as a patriarch for the see of Antioch Athanasius [Gamala] who made the union in that era with the Egyptians, with Anastasius, Pope of Alexandria (as we have shown in detail at the end of Book 10).

At Alexandria, the Chalcedonians had as their head Cyrus and at Constantinople, Sergius

He sent Isaiah, a bishop from Persia, to Edessa'.

11.3 **(IV, 408/ II, 411):** 'In this era Anastasius Pope of Alexandria died, and we ordained in his place for the orthodox, Anastasius. It was he who sent anew a letter to Athanasius, patriarch of Antioch, and confirmed the union.

The Chalcedonians had a patriarch named Cyrus at Antioch ... who persecuted the faithful there'.

---

[26] John of Ephesus, *Ecclesiastical History* 3.4.12.   [27] Leppin, Chapter 5, this volume.

11.5 (IV, 414/ II, 419): 'In 942 AG the patriarch Athanasius died and was buried in the convent of the Garumaye. In his place was ordained John Sedra, of the monastery of Eusebona.

At Alexandria after Athanasius came Andronicus and then Benjamin. Both of them sent synodal letters to Athanasius before his death'.

11.7 (IV, 417/ II, 427): 'In this era, the Chalcedonians had Pyrrhus as patriarch of Constantinople. They rejected him and Paul became patriarch.

At Rome, the fourth bishop after the destruction of the city was Martin. All the world testifies to his piety and good conduct.

The patriarch of the orthodox, John Sedra ordained Constantine bishop for the faithful of Edessa and after his death they had Simeon'.

11.10 (IV, 428/ II, 443): 'In AG 960 John Sedra died. His death was on the 14th or 1st Kanun. He was buried in Amda in the monastery of Ze'ora.

In the same month Simeon metropolitan of Edessa died.

In the same year Mar Theodore of the monastery of Qenneshre was ordained for the orthodox of the see of Antioch.

At Alexandria, the orthodox patriarch was Benjamin.

At Rome and Constantinople the bishops had been Chalcedonian for a long time'.

11.16 (IV, 447/ II, 474): 'In AG 995 Athanasius of Balad was ordained and occupied the see for three years and died in AG 998 on the 11th of Elul. It was he who ordained Jacob bishop of Edessa . . .

The same month Julian was ordained patriarch of Antioch'.

11.17 (IV, 450/ II, 480):
'In AG 1020, Elias of the monastery of Gubba Barraya was ordained for the see of Antioch in his own convent . . .

At Alexandria, after Isaac, the patriarch of the orthodox was Alexander'.

11.21 (IV, 462/ II, 503): 'A year after the union between the Armenians and the Suryaye, Iwannis, catholicos of the Armenians, died in AG 1038.

In the same year the patriarch of Alexandria died. Qozma succeeded him, but he lasted only a short time and departed this world.

In AG 1036 Denha, catholicos of Takrit died.

In the same year Athanasius, patriarch of Antioch died.

Then the bishops chose Iwannis, of the monastery of Eusebona, who was bishop of Harran'.

12.11 **(IV, 504/ III, 47)**: 'In the year 1130, in the month of Nisan, Mar Mark, Pope of Alexandria died, ninth months after the election of Mar Dionysius [of Tel-mahre]. Jacob was ordained in his place'.

The first point to note here is that the lists in Michael are not able to sustain a record of the Chalcedonian succession after the Arab conquests. This is the last point that the author is able to describe alternative structures. In a sense, the recording of the patriarchs in the lists of the *Chronicle of Zuqnin* and Michael the Syrian reflect three stages: firstly, a notionally unified church with single incumbents for the patriarchal see, who have a measure of legitimacy whatever their theological views. Secondly, a (brief) period of dual record, where the Chalcedonian patriarch was sufficiently important for Jacobites to record (until c. 640 in these lists). And thirdly, a period of amnesia, where non-Jacobites were simply ignored.

There is an important editorial comment, placed at circa 720 in Michael's *Chronicle* and possibly written by Dionysius, that supports this interpretation, though it implies that the Chalcedonian material was available to him somewhat later than is apparent from the bishop lists that are repeated in Michael's *Chronicle*. Here Michael (or Dionysius) attempts to rationalise his lack of data:

> Up to this point, we find in our books, the names of the archbishops of four sees: Rome, Alexandria, Constantinople and Antioch . . . even those who are Chalcedonian after the synod of Chalcedon. From this point on we do not find the names of the directors of the sees of Rome and Constantinople. But only the two sees of Antioch and Alexandria . . . It is thought that this is the case for two reasons. Firstly because the empire of the Tayyaye occupied Syria and Egypt . . . and [they] did not have need or ability to inform themselves about the Chalcedonians . . . secondly because the Chalcedonians became more and more perverted by the heresies that developed amongst them.[28]

Chalcedonians likely remained much more important in both Egypt and Mesopotamia in the seventh century than our Miaphysite sources let on.[29] But this comment, and the testimony of the bishops' lists, reflects a Jacobite historical tradition in which Chalcedonian patriarchs have been dropped out in the course of the Umayyad period.

---

[28] Michael the Syrian, *Chronicle* 11.18 (IV, 453/II, 486–7). The reference to the deepening of Chalcedonian heresy may be the adoption of Dyotheletism in the seventh century or the ongoing controversies over icons in the eighth and ninth. The tone of the comment, with its animus against differences in confessional theology, suggests that it is made by Michael rather than Dionysius, but it remains an important observation on the state of the sources available to him. Jankowiak 2012: 14 places the breach in contact in the early seventh century.

[29] Booth 2017. Cf. Moorhead 1981.

We should also note the absence of Jerusalem from lists gathered by Michael. Jerusalem was not a patriarchate for the Miaphysites and is absent in all the episcopal lists in Michael for the seventh century and onwards. And Dionysius of Tel-Mahre makes little mention of Jerusalem, as a real place or as a patriarchal see, in his record of his own time in office. Islamic-period Melkite sources, by contrast, place considerable emphasis on Jerusalem and the Sabaite monasteries as the centres of orthodox scholarship and as sites of pilgrimage. [30] And Jerusalem had been major centre of Roman imperial patronage as well as a holy city for Jews and Muslims, believed by many to be the centre of the world. [31] But there is no equivalent in Dionysius: he tells the caliph al-Ma'mun that Christendom has four apostolic patriarchates. [32] Even when he passes from Nisibis to Alexandria he makes no detour to visit Jerusalem but travels by ship from Joppa. [33] We do not need to suppose that there was, in fact, no Jacobite pilgrimage to Jerusalem in this period by laymen or the lower clergy, but it plays no part in Dionysius's imagined geography or in his itinerary as patriarch. [34]

Alexandria and Antioch

A second point that emerges from the patriarchal lists is the strong relationship between the sees of Antioch and Alexandria, which is the central point of their 'geo-ecclesiology'. [35] They are constant features of the lists, and provide a link to the world of four 'orthodox' patriarchs imagined by the fifth-century historians. The stress they place on the mutual confirmation of the patriarchs in synodal letters functions as an assurance of a Severan Miaphysite orthodoxy that is internationally recognised. [36]

This link between Alexandria and Antioch is a key concern of Dionysius's history. The account of the 616 agreement asserts that the sees are like Israel and Judah, and that in their union, the union of God's chosen people is restored. [37] The 'evangelical see of Alexandria and the

---

[30] Griffith 2001: esp. 161; Griffith 2008.   [31] Silverstein 2009; Elad 1995.
[32] Michael the Syrian, *Chronicle* 12.14 (IV, 519/III, 68).   [33] Ibid., 12.13 (IV, 514/II, 62).
[34] See Johnson, Chapter 7, this volume.
[35] Blaudeau 2017 defines 'geo-ecclesiology' as the use of the vocabulary of international relations to describe competition between different parts of the church. He stresses that this does not deny the significance of doctrine. That said, the relative insignificance of doctrinal debate in the Jacobite histories of this period makes Blaudeau's methods particularly attractive here.
[36] Innemée notes that both the patriarchs of 'Syria and Egypt', Dionysius and Jacob, were mentioned in frescos and manuscript colophons at the monastery of Deir es-Surian in the Wadi Natrun, which was heavily patronised by monks from Takrit. Innemée and Van Rompay 1998: 182.
[37] Michael the Syrian, *Chronicle* 10. 26 (IV, 392/II, 382).

apostolic see of Antioch' acknowledge a shared faith, rooted in the councils of Nicaea and Constantinople and in shared veneration of the saints Severus, Anthimus, Theodosius and Peter, patriarchs of Alexandria, Paul and Julian, patriarchs of Antioch and Jacob (Baradeus). [38] These figures included all of the notable Miaphysite patriarchs of Antioch, Constantinople and Alexandria. The effect of the document is to present the two sees as heirs to an orthodoxy that had once been shared with Constantinople. As Athanasius Gamala says in his encyclical letter, in an allusion to their shared Miaphysite creed, 'God should not be separated or divided, just like his united people'.[39]

Later in Dionysius's history, when he relates his own visit to Egypt, he alludes back to this union. During his visit to Egypt to ask for help from his patron Abdallah ibn Tahir, Dionysius reports on his official visit to the Alexandrian patriarch Jacob. Jacob says that the Egyptians had not received a Syrian since Severus, but Dionysius reminds him of the visit of Athanasius Gamala and his union with Andronicus.[40] Shortly afterwards, Dionysius makes a second trip to Egypt during a failed attempt to negotiate peace with the Bashmuraic rebels in the Delta. Here he meets again with his Alexandrian counterpart and stresses that he was treated as a patriarch and that he acknowledged the holy customs of Cyril and Dioscurus, patriarchs of Alexandria during the formative councils of the fifth century at Ephesus and Chalcedon.[41] But he also makes a number of critical comments at how the church has been forced to practice simony thanks to high levels of taxation and how poor the levels of scriptural knowledge are in Egypt.[42]

Dionysius's autobiographical narrative shows him keen to show that Alexandria's recognition of Antioch is a living sentiment, rather than merely a theoretical statement. The fact that Dionysius opens and closes his history with affairs in Egypt shows how important he thought the relationship between Antioch and Alexandria was. This focus for his history could even be read as Dionysius's response to John of Ephesus's account of the schisms between and within Antioch and Alexandria of the time of Damian and Jacob Baradeus. [43] Where John had reported

[38] Ibid., 10. 26 (IV, 399/II, 392). The exception here is Damian, who is retrospectively condemned for his role in promoting schism (e.g., Athanasius's encyclical letter at MS (IV, 398, II, 392). This version of history would not have been one that was endorsed in Alexandrian circles: Booth 2017.

[39] Michael the Syrian, *Chronicle* 10.27 (IV, 400/II, 395).   [40] Ibid., 12.13 (IV, 516/III, 63).

[41] Ibid., 12.17 (IV, 525/III, 80)   [42] Ibid., 12.17 (IV, 525–6/III, 80).

[43] John of Ephesus, Part III, Book IV.

a movement in crisis, Dionysius is able to write of two unified patriarchs whose mutual recognition is a guarantee against both heretical ideas and schismatic internal opponents. Indeed, in visiting Alexandria himself and being recognised as patriarch, he places himself in the company of only two other patriarchs, Severus and Athanasius Gamala. [44] This is a clear statement of his legitimacy vis-à-vis his rivals in Mesopotamia, such as the anti-patriarch Abraham of Gubba Barraya, who had attempted to secure Alexandrian condemnation of Dionysius's predecessor Cyriacus. [45]

However, Dionysius's account is not simply a familiar reaffirmation of a long-standing relationship between the patriarchates. As Dionysius indicates in his statement to Jacob, the history of the relationship between Antioch and Alexandria was not necessarily widely known (at least in Egypt). And while there is a complete record of Alexandrian patriarchs in the lists preserved in Michael, it is hard to know from when these date. In other words, it is possible that a historian writing in a Jacobite context in the seventh or eighth centuries would *not* have had access to such information, and that it has been filled in later when contact was resumed in the ninth century. The absence of material on Egypt in Michael the Syrian until Dionysius's own lifetime suggests that it had not been possible to maintain a practical connection between Antioch and Alexandria. Dionysius's history certainly includes earlier Syriac texts that described Egyptian affairs in some detail for the late sixth and early seventh century. But it seems likely that Dionysius deliberately sought out such material, partly in response to his own visits to Egypt and the opportunities afforded by the union of Syria and Egypt under the government of Abdallah. [46]

Mission and Its Absence in the Jacobite Ecclesiastical Histories

Another important feature of the geographical imagination of the Theodosian historians had been the expansion of Christianity beyond

---

[44] Michael the Syrian, *Chronicle* 12.13 (IV, 515/III, 63).   [45] Ibid., 12.7 (IV, 492/III, 25).

[46] Ibid., 12.13 (IV, 513/III, 61) for Dionysius's visit to Egypt to seek out Abdallah to prevent his brother Muhammad from destroying churches in Mesopotamia. Abdallah was the son of the Khurasani *mawla* Tahir, to whom al-Ma'mun owed his victory in the fourth fitna. Abdallah was in Egypt to quell revolts in the Delta, after already holding the governorship of Mesopotamia, where he had defeated the revolt of Nasr b. Shabath and defended Dionysius from the claims of the anti-patriarch Abraham of Cyrrhus. His career is described in some detail in Michael the Syrian, *Chronicle* 12.12, which suggests his importance to Dionysius.

the borders of the empire. They recount Frumentius's fourth-century mission to Axum, the miraculous conversions of the kings of Iberia and Armenia and the conversions of the Burgundians, which was followed by victory in battle.[47] These conversions fit a broader model of Rome's civilising mission: though great emperors like Augustus and Trajan had failed to subdue these distant territories, now they were civilised through true religion.[48] A Christian Roman Empire could exceed the limits of pagan Rome and surpass it by the criteria it had set for itself: 'God's light shone for the first time on India (Axum). The courage and piety of the emperor became celebrated throughout the whole world and the barbarians, having learnt by experience to prefer peace over war, were able to enjoy social intercourse and many people embarked on long journeys.'[49]

This interest in mission is developed in John of Ephesus. John had been a missionary in Anatolia, where Justinian had commissioned him to convert pagans and Montanists.[50] He devotes significant scenes to conversion of King Andug of Ethiopia, where he describes the king's victory as a repetition of Constantine's success at the Milvian bridge,[51] and tells of the baptism of barbarian kings at Constantinople.[52] Several chapters describe the activities of Longinus in Nubia and Simeon beth Arsham in the Arabian peninsula.[53] And the missionary travels of John of Tella, Jacob Baradeus and Ahudemmeh are significant pieces of sixth-century hagiography, which draw on earlier tropes of missionary travel in Syriac literature.[54]

Yet the Jacobite historians of the early Abbasid period are curiously silent on the subject. The expansion of Jacobitism to Central Asia is passed over: we only hear of the presence of Jacobites there because of the longstanding difficulty in recruiting bishops for places like Segestan.[55] There is nothing here that continues John of Ephesus's interest in mission. In part this reflects an altered political situation. There were fewer polytheist populations, who had been the main targets of sixth-century missions, in

---

[47] Socrates, *Ecclesiastical History* 1.19 (on Axum), 1.20 (on Iberia), 7. 30 (Burgundians). Cf. Fowden 1993: 110–11.
[48] Wood 2010: 33–7; Merrills 2000: 28.   [49] Theodoret, *Ecclesiastical History* 1.23.
[50] *Chronicle of Zuqnin* 125/123.
[51] Ibid., 55–6/77. John has probably translated an extended version of the scene extant in John Malalas 18.15 (433–4/251).
[52] *Chronicle of Zuqnin* 53–4/75 Cf. Engelhardt 1974.
[53] *Chronicle of Zuqnin* 10/45; John of Ephesus, *Ecclesiastical History* 3.4.8. Cf. Fowden 1993: 117–18.
[54] Menze 2008: 153; Wood 2010: 167–72; 212; Saint-Laurent 2015: 72–128.
[55] Michael the Syrian, *Chronicle* 11.22 (IV, 465/II, 507).

the Middle East by the ninth century and there seems to have been little wish to target other monotheists.

But the centrality of missions in John's history had also been a response to the disintegration of political patronage in Constantinople after the death of Theodora. Missionaries like Longinus and travelling bishops like John of Tella were important because they harkened back to an earlier era of pre-Constantinian Christianity, who suffered publicly for the faith and provided sources of legitimacy in a world where the regular structures of church authority had been disrupted and clergy and monks expelled from their sees.[56] We know from the legislation of George of Beltan and Cyriacus that they were rather more wary about travelling ascetics than their sixth-century predecessors had been: whatever the earlier history of the Miaphysite movement, they were keen to regulate the obedience of the lower clergy.[57]

Here there is an interesting contrast with the contemporary situation in the Church of the East. Thomas of Marga, writing in the 860s, describes missions to Daylam and Gilan that are launched from the monasteries of northern Iraq.[58] In part, this reflects different political realities: the proximity of unconverted polytheist populations made such missions a possibility for these monasteries. But the fact that we are told about such missions is also an issue of genre. Missionary endeavour and the risk of martyrdom did not have to be mediated through the concerns of the higher clergy about potential threats to authority.

Instead of offering a continuation of John's missionary interest, some Jacobite historians present a version of the Miaphysite commonwealth present in some parts of the sixth-century hagiography, which had celebrated the Christianisation of polities on the edge of the Roman world where orthodoxy was preserved in an era of Roman imperial heresy. John's work had celebrated a circle of new Christian rulers. We can see the impact of this message in the episcopal lists present in *Chronicle of Zuqnin* part

---

[56] Wood 2012.

[57] Note especially bans on peripatetic monks travelling with relics (George, canon 15; Cyriacus, canon 20; Dionysius II, canons 17 and 18); the ban of monks living among laymen (John, canon 3) and on monks leading churches and running the business of the church (Ignatius canon 6 and Dionysius II canon 5). These are published in Vööbus 1975–6.

[58] Thomas of Marga, *Book of Governors*, 5.4 (259–61/478–82). Thomas describes how Shubhalisho was consecrated bishop before his mission, and how lay notables paid to equip him so that that the Daylamites would be suitably impressed. In Gilan and Daylam, Shubalisho converts the people through miracles and establishes churches and ordains priests and deacons. His rivals include Marcionites and Manichees as well as local pagans. Also note the accounts of seventh-century missions in the *Chronicle of Seert*, PO 13: 45, 50, 54, 76.

three (themselves a gloss on part 2 of John of Ephesus), where the list of patriarchs is supplemented by a list of kings (the Persians, the Romans, the Jafnid Arabs, the Axumites and the Himyarites) and a list of Miaphysite bishops, headed by the Catholicoi of Persia and Armenia, Ahudemmeh and John.[59]

Echoes of this vision of a Miaphysite commonwealth and of a greater patriarchate of Antioch are not common in the later histories, but we may find one in the episcopal list for AG 1083 in Michael the Syrian, which mentions the Catholicoi of Armenia and Takrit alongside the patriarchs of Antioch and Alexandria.[60] Another, more substantial, echo may be found in Dionysius's extensive account of the mission of George, king of Nubia, to visit the caliph al-Mu'tasim. Dionysius stresses the Christian character of George's entourage, with its priests and crosses, and his rich presents for the caliph.[61] One reason for this scene is to celebrate Dionysius's own proximity to the centre of universal power at Baghdad. But a second reason to include the scene may be that Dionysius wrote as a continuator of John of Ephesus, and it may be that his representation of Nubia's peace and prosperity under a Christian king harked back to John's descriptions of the Nubian mission of Longinus.

The Chalcedonian Imagination of the Patriarchates

We have seen thus far how, in Dionysius's history, the Antioch-Alexandria axis was the only survival from an idealised world of four orthodox patriarchs. But it is worth reflecting that this does not represent all forms of geo-ecclesiological imagination in the West Syrian world. West Syrian Chalcedonian geo-ecclesiology remained tied to the Mediterranean world, and to the emperor and the pentarchy for longer than their Jacobite counterparts and provide an important contrast to what we have seen this far.[62]

From the perspective of the Chalcedonians, the seventh century was significant not only for the Arab conquests but also for the attempt of Heraclius and his patriarch Sergius to forge a compromise formula, Monotheletism, that could reconcile neo-Chalcedonians and Miaphysites. One aspect of this was the use of a version of the Trisagion prayer that had

---

[59] *Chronicle of Zuqnin* 110/114.   [60] Michael the Syrian, *Chronicle* 11.21 (IV, 462/II, 503).
[61] Ibid., 12.19 (IV, 531–3/III, 90–4).
[62] The Chalcedonians recognised Jerusalem as a patriarchate, unlike the Miaphysites. For the pentarchy see Herrin 2013: 240–2, building on Peri 1988 and Blaudeau 1996.

become widespread in Syrian Miaphysite circles.[63] This policy was pursued by his son Constans as part of a wider attempt to repeat Heraclian policies and bring together Christian allies to overthrow the Arabs, as Heraclius had done before with the Persians. Constans's failure led to the reversal of his policies by his successor Constantine IV at the council of Constantinople III in 680.[64] Under Constans, Monotheletism was opposed by the Palestinian monk Maximus the Confessor, who gathered allies in North Africa and Italy, and later generations would celebrate him as a martyr of imperial tyranny.

However, we should remember that Monotheletism did enjoy considerable success in the Levant, where Miaphysites and Chalcedonians lived in close proximity, and had encouraged many Christians in Syria to adhere to what was then the imperial orthodoxy.[65] Bar Hebraeus reports adhesion of many Jacobites to Monothelete Chalcedonianism in the era of Heraclius.[66] Though he ascribes this to the use of force, it also seems likely that many found the formula convincing. Here, in the Levant, the shift towards Dyotheletism took a generation longer than in the Byzantine empire. The sources ascribe this to the influence of Byzantine prisoners of war and the proselytising efforts of a Christian elite in Damascus that looked towards Byzantium in the early eighth century.[67]

Michael the Syrian includes a history written from a Monothelete ('Maronite') perspective that runs from circa 600 to 750, roughly from Heraclius[68] and the establishment of Monotheletism as an imperial orthodoxy to the persecutions of Monotheletes in Damascus by the Chalcedonian patriarch Theophylact bar Qanbara in the 740s.[69] This

[63] Horn 2006: 393–5. The patriarch of Antioch, Peter the Fuller, had introduced the words 'who was crucified for us' into the prayer as a test against Nestorianism, but the pro-Miaphysite emperor Anastasius had triggered great controversy when he tried to introduce this into Constantinople. This past history made its use in Chalcedonian circles potentially controversial.
[64] See the narratives of Booth 2013; Tannous 2014; Haldon 2016.
[65] Later sources present the origin of Monotheletism in an act of compromise between Chalcedonians and Miaphysites. Note the accusations of Dyotheletes that it was practically Miaphysite (e.g., Theodore abu Qurra, quoted in Griffith 1993: 292), and in the editorial statement in Michael the Syrian that it was less heretical than Dyotheletism (Michael the Syrian, *Chronicle* 11.12 [IV, 434–5/ III, 453]). Jankowiak 2013 suggests that this was false, emphasising the chronology of Heraclius's attempts to achieve union with Athanasius Gamala and the articulation of doctrines on Monenergism and Monotheletism. Tannous 2014, by contrast, situates the development of Monotheletism within the context of Levantine neo-Chalcedonianism.
[66] Bar 'Ebroyo, Ecclesiastical Chronicle II, 269–74.
[67] Gribomont 1974: esp. 107–9 collects the evidence.
[68] For the Dyothelete Chalcedonian historian Eutychius, Heraclius could simply be termed a Maronite: a good indication of how the term was synonymous with Monothelete. Griffith 2004.
[69] Gribomont 1974.

records a series of flashpoints in northern Syrian cities where Monotheletes and Dyotheletes refused to worship together, resulting in the division of churches and sometimes the seizure of the church by the Dyotheletes, with the agreement of the Muslim governors. This, together with the imposition of fines and the attempts of Bar Qanbara to stop the use of the Trisagion prayer, prompted the consecration of a rival Monothelete patriarch of Antioch. The use of the term 'Maronite' to describe the Monotheletes dates from this period,[70] and probably refers to the dominance of the monastery of Beth Maron in Syria II.[71]

Though there is little extant Maronite history from before the period of the Crusades, it seems likely that this was an independent composition in Syriac that has been included in Michael and glossed for a Jacobite audience.[72] To its later Jacobite editor, it illustrated the descent of the Chalcedonians into further heresy through the adoption of Dyotheletism (called Maximism by the author of this text, referring to the theologian Maximus the Confessor).[73] In the first section of this history preserved in Michael it describes how Origenism and crypto-paganism flourished among the Sabaite monks near Jerusalem, and how this lay the background of the Dyothelete theology of the Palestinian theologian Maximus the confessor. The whole history can be read as a polemical description of the spread of this Maximite doctrine. The historian speaks approvingly of how the patriarch Menas gathered the fifth synod (i.e., the ecumenical council of Constantinople II in 553) to anathematise any who confessed two wills in Christ (Dyotheletes) and to condemn both Origen and Theodore of Mopsuestia, the Dyophysite theologian who was seen as a 'Nestorian' heretic by Miaphysites.[74] Next it relates how the emperors Heraclius and Constans II opposed Dyotheletism, while Maximus persuaded Pope Martin in Rome and the monks of Africa to join his heresy

---

[70] The term is first used by John of Damascus in a polemical treatise in c. 726. Gribomont 1974: 109.

[71] These monks are accorded a central role in bringing Jacobites to Chalcedonianism in the time of Heraclius and are the key targets of Bar Qanbara's attempts to ban the Trisagion.

[72] This absence may be the result of deliberate destruction after the Maronites converted to Roman Catholicism in the period of the Crusades: Salibi 1962: 213.

[73] Note the editorial statement at Michael the Syrian, *Chronicle* 11.12 (IV, 434–5/II, 453).

[74] Ibid., 11.9 (IV, 424–6/ II, 434–5). The approval of the Three Chapters by a Maronite historian, and its inclusion by Jacobite historian, is a good indication of how Justinian's policy was capable of building bridges between Chalcedonians and Miaphysites in the sixth century. Menas's phrase 'only one will and operation' was later quoted by Sergius in the era of Heraclius to support the Monothelete position (Tannous 2014: 37). Menas's letters in 553 were rejected as forgeries at Constantinople III (Davis 1988: 280–1), so Menas may be mentioned here as a *cause célèbre* of the Maronites.

and borrowed the ideas of Nestorians he met in the West.[75] Constans
gathers a synod where bishop Constantine of Perge tries and fails to win
over Maximus and the emperor is eventually forced to have Maximus
mutilated. The historian seems to approve: the final sentence of the
section observes that Maximus 'never achieved any rank within the
church'.[76] A later section of the same history is equally unsympathetic
to Martin, who is imprisoned by the emperor Constans after anathema-
tising the emperor Heraclius and the patriarch of Constantinople.[77]

Here the author approves of the actions of the emperors, even when they
act with violence, and follows earlier ecclesiastical historians in centring his
narrative around councils and synods.[78] But this situation is inverted under
Constantine IV when 'Maximism' is confirmed 'at a council called the
sixth in Constantinople'. He describes how Theodore, the papal legate,
wins over the emperor with gold and leads him to accept the definition,
though neither the patriarchs of Antioch nor Constantinople accept it and
are deposed. Though there are 250 bishops in attendance, he notes that
there none from 'Egypt, Syria, Palestine or Armenia' and that 'they took
a man called Peter and established him in the place of Peter of Alexandria
and another in the place of the bishop of Jerusalem'.[79] There follows
a series of bitter arguments in which Macarius of Antioch uses Cyril of
Alexandria to show the heresy of declaring two wills in Christ, for which he
is labelled a Severan by his opponents and imprisoned in Rome.[80]

Taken as a whole, this narrative offers a much more traditional,
Mediterranean geography than the Jacobite histories of the Islamic period.
Authority is ideally vested in the emperor, together with the patriarchs
acting in concert, who should determine doctrine through ecumenical
councils.[81] In this sense it preserves a Justinianic model of the pentarchy.
We see this ideal most clearly in its comments on Constantinople III, when

---

[75] For the relationship between Maximus and Rome see Booth 2013: 269–328. McCormick 1998 traces
the extensive links between the Levant and Italy in the seventh and eighth centuries, especially the
foundation of Greek-speaking monasteries in Rome and the south of Italy and the Roman Popes
who came from Syrian backgrounds.

[76] Michael the Syrian, *Chronicle* 11.9 (IV, 427/II, 436).

[77] Ibid., 11.10 (IV, 429/II, 444). For the imprisonment of Martin see Booth 2013: 301–3.

[78] Compare John of Ephesus, embedded in *Chronicle of Zuqnin* 138–9/132, which is enthusiastic about
the condemnation of the Three Chapters and the presence of representatives of the five patriarchs.
John does not mention the role of Menas in this council.

[79] The presence of the pentarchy of patriarchs, through their representatives, was also an important
part of the self-fashioning of Justinian II at the Quinisext council in 692: Herrin 2013: 242;
Humphreys 2014: 74.

[80] Michael the Syrian, *Chronicle* 11.12 (IV, 434–5/II, 452–3).

[81] Booth 2013: 332 notes that, at the time, a major embarrassment for Maximus's supporters was his
rejection by a consensus of the patriarchs, which forced them to assert the existence of an

the author expresses shock at the removal or replacement of the eastern patriarchs to accord with the policy of Rome. A key element of the critique of Maximus is that he has no priestly rank: implicitly, it is proper for the higher clergy to determine doctrine, but not an unordained monk.[82] Unlike the Jacobite material we have examined so far, there is an expectation that all five patriarchs will determine doctrine together. Furthermore, this source gives an authority to the emperors Heraclius and Constans that has no parallel in the Jacobite sources: they are seen acting legitimately against heretics like Maximus and Martin in their efforts to stop Dyotheletism spreading.

This view of the sources of authority is linked, of course, to the author's own Christology. Though he approves of Constans punishing a recalcitrant Pope of Rome, he is horrified at Constantine IV's behaviour to the eastern patriarchs. But this divergent analysis is also framed against an eastern focus to his history: the sense of shock at Constantine is about his abandonment of the normal episcopate of Egypt, Palestine, Syria and Armenia. On the one hand, we can read this as a statement of resentment of the abandonment of parts of the Roman world that had fallen to the Arabs some forty years before and the use of imperial appointees to speak for its bishops. On the other, it suggests that this author thought of Egypt, Palestine, Syria and Armenia as a single unit, which had a shared experience in following the doctrine set out by Heraclius and Constans and was now forsaken by Constantine IV in his search for a rapprochement with Rome. There is a sense then of the emperor reorienting himself towards the 'Maximism' and 'Nestorianism' of the West and leaving the post-Roman East behind. It is a breach of trust and of expectations in the imperial office and the structures of the pentarchy that is much more visible for the Maronites than for Jacobites, perhaps because it was so sudden. Certainly, the later parts of Michael's *Chronicle* that seem to derive from the same source are much more restricted in focus to Syria, and seem to reflect the rapid loss of power of Maronites in the face of Umayyad support for the Maximites.[83]

---

unchanging orthodoxy that was not subject to the vagaries of episcopal politics or the will of the emperor. Winterhager 2016: 197–8 stresses that Maximus was not a supporter of Roman primacy per se, but simply sought out Roman support because of the pope's opposition to Monotheletism. The apostles, the patristics and the councils collectively constitute true belief for Maximus, 'but there is no certainty that it is at any certain place in every historical situation'.

[82] Though Maronite condemnation of Maximus could be much more violent than this: the Syriac *Life of Maximus* condemns him as the son of Samaritan.

[83] Michael the Syrian, *Chronicle* 11.20 (IV, 458–61/II, 492–6) for conflicts in Aleppo; ibid., 11.22 (IV, 467/II, 511) for persecution of Maronites in Mabbug.

The Melkites (i.e., Dyothelete Chalcedonians in the Levant) had a very different experience of the loss of links to Constantinople and the lands still ruled by Christian kings. Agapius of Mabbug, writing in the tenth century, clearly intended to follow the Eusebian canons and give the succession of the different patriarchates. He gives these until the mid-sixth century[84] alongside the reign lengths of Roman emperors, supplementing them with the Arab kings after the coming of Muhammad and abandoning them entirely after the death of Constans.

Agapius's interest in church affairs is minimal from the late sixth century: his overwhelming interest is in military conflict between Rome and the Persians and then the Arabs. He abandons his record of episcopal succession after the reign of Justinian and gives a cursory note on the council of Constantinople III (680): 'only the Melkites accept its canons, to the exclusion of all other Christian communities'.[85] And though he states the council's importance, he does not know the name of the patriarch of Constantinople who convened it.[86]

Eutychius of Alexandria's chronicle, also composed in the tenth century, is ignorant of the patriarchs of Constantinople in the eighth and ninth centuries (even the famous polymath Photius), and of the ecumenical councils of Hieria (753) and Nicaea II (787) that first established and then overturned Iconoclasm.[87] But unlike Agapius he seems conscious of this absence, and he has invented additional patriarchs and emperors to fill the gaps in his lists. Both men inherited historical traditions that imagined a world based on Constantinople, but they found it hard to sustain that geography when they wrote of history after the seventh century. There is the feeling that imperial decisions had produced the confessional divisions of the present day, but little sense that the imperial office continued to matter in this way and little interest in the oscillating imperial policies on icons.[88]

---

[84] Agapius PO 8: 428.

[85] Ibid., 493–4. Though he does note that Pope Agathon gave his consent.

[86] Griffith 1982: 173. Griffith also notes Agapius's ignorance of matters to do with iconoclasm, even to his ignorance of the role of John of Damascus in these controversies, who was a major Melkite iconodule.

[87] Ibid., 174.

[88] Theodore abu Qurrah offers a more sophisticated defence of the basis of Christianity in the decisions of church councils, partly in reaction to Muslim criticism of councils as state-sponsored innovation: Griffith 1993. Signes-Codoñer 2014 suggests that modern historians have ignored the extent to which iconoclasm had appeal among Levantine Chalcedonians during the eighth century.

Monasteries in the Jacobite Histories

One novel feature that emerges in the patriarchal lists preserved in Michael is that new patriarchs are described by their monastery as well as their episcopal see.[89] Indeed, in the sparse coverage of the late-seventh- and early-eighth-century Jacobite patriarchs in Bar Hebraeus, one of the few details given are the monasteries in which patriarchs were ordained and buried.[90] This interest in monasteries has no precedent in the Eusebian episcopal lists and deserves some emphasis, given that this was a terse and conservative genre.

We should also note that, unlike the synods described in fifth-century ecclesiastical history, the many synods recorded for the period 740–830 mostly take place in (rural) monasteries or villages and primarily in the Tur Abdin. [91] Though the Jacobite patriarch ruled the see of Antioch, we hear very little of the city. When the patriarch Elias was able to consecrate a church in Antioch during the reign of al-Walid I, it appears as a major coup, made in the teeth of Melkite opposition.[92] But its significance seems to have been symbolic, and Antioch never became a Jacobite centre or a place of interest for Jacobite historians.[93]

One of the best examples of the monastic domination of ecclesiastical life in this period is the Syriac *Chronicle to 819*. This history begins with Jesus and relates the history of the church in the first six centuries. From the sixth century onwards, it gives increasing space to political narratives, to the wars between the Romans and Persians and then the internal affairs of the caliphate. From this point too, ecclesiastical history is increasingly seen through the lens of the monastery of Qartmin. Thus the struggles of the followers of Severus in the sixth century emphasise the role of John of Qartmin, [94] and the Persian invasions devastate 'the monastery of Qartmin, as well as Callinicum, Tella, Harran and Edessa'.[95] The *Chronicle* has used a number of earlier Edessene sources and relates a number of fourth-century Edessene bishops (many of them famous from the works of Ephrem). But by the sixth century, its episcopal lists are almost exclusively monks of Qartmin. It traces their monopoly over the

---

[89] The lists of ordinations given for the ninth-century patriarchs show that most bishops were ordained in a small number of Mesopotamian monasteries, rather than in their own sees.

[90] Bar 'Ebroyo, *Ecclesiastical Chronicle* II.   [91] Mounayer 1963.

[92] Michael the Syrian, *Chronicle* II.19 (IV, 456/II, 490). Cf. Hage 1964: 11.

[93] Note in particular the strong association between Severus and the city of Antioch that Severus made in his own sermons (Alpi 2009: 168) and that is still made in his seventh-century biography by George of the Arabs: *Memra on Severus*, 19–20.

[94] *Chronicle to 819*, AG 795.   [95] Ibid., AG 891.

sees of Harran and the Tur Abdin (the latter often based in the monastery) and occasional incumbents of the patriarchate (Isaac, Athanasius Sandalaya and David of Dara, though it is silent about the controversial rule of all three of these men).

The *Chronicle of 819* is dominated by a single monastery (we might equally call it the chronicle of Qartmin). But it is interesting that even the more expansive Jacobite history found in Michael the Syrian, much of which comes from Dionysius of Tel-Mahre, is heavily rooted in four or five monasteries: Qenneshre, Qartmin in the Tur Abdin, Gubba Barraya (near Cyrrhus), Mar Mattai (near Mosul) and the monastery of the pillars (in Raqqa). The events of 740–80 can be understood as the transition of power from patriarchs controlled by or trained in Qartmin to those trained in Qenneshre or the monastery of the pillars. Thus when David of Dara and George of Beltan feuded over the patriarchate, Mesopotamia followed David while 'the west' (the lands west of the Euphrates) went to George.[96] Similarly, the major strife of Dionysius's days was against the anti-patriarch Abraham, supported by Gubba Barraya, and the over-mighty Catholicos of Takrit, Basil of Mar Mattai.[97]

The integration of these monasteries into Jacobite ecclesiastical history writing offers an interesting contrast to the situation in the Church of the East. Here we certainly see monks from the great monasteries of northern Iraq proceed to the office of patriarch. But we also see countervailing trends in the writing of history that stressed the differentiation of history writing based on the patriarchate (in the tradition of Mari ibn Sulayman or Amr ibn Matta) and that based on the monasteries (such as the *Book of Chastity* or Thomas of Marga's *Book of Governors*). This differentiation is not absolute, and both Thomas and Mari emphasise the monastic backgrounds of patriarchs. But Thomas does incorporate and acknowledge monastic historians with a much more antagonistic attitude. For instance, Thomas writes of one of his own predecessors, Sergius of Beth Rasthaq, whose hagiographic collection of the monks of Beth Garmai, composed in 640s. Thomas notes that Sergius called his work 'Destroyer of the Mighty' because he did not write about the great men of the church but those who were victorious in the houses of their fathers or the churches of their own villages, who were men of simple spirit.[98]

One reason for this difference between Jacobite and Church of the East narratives may be that the Church of the East had a much more attenuated

---

[96] Michael the Syrian, *Chronicle* 11.25 (IV, 476/II, 525).   [97] Ibid., 12.11–12 and 18–19.

[98] *Book of Governors*, I, 33 (61/109–10).

relationship to the Eusebian tradition of history writing.[99] One feature of the Eusebian tradition was that it had the capacity to incorporate local historical traditions (of ascetic or philosophical movements in Eusebius's case) and subordinate these to a broader structure centred on the succession of bishops and emperors.[100] This model of a universal history that subordinated the histories of specific institutions (such as monasticism) may have encouraged the conception of monastic history as part of ecclesiastical history in general, rather than something to be separated from the history of the great men of the church.

Places Unmentioned

An unstated, but nonetheless striking feature of the Jacobite narratives, is the monopoly over the patriarchate held by a small number of monasteries concentrated in Mesopotamia and northern Syria. There must have been a large number of settlements with Jacobite populations who could only have provided a patriarch by sending a monk to the great monasteries (as in the case of George of Beltan, a native of Emesa)[101] or were simply excluded from the higher circles of power. Thus the Jacobite episcopal lists record bishops in Palestine, southern Syria and Cilicia and for the Jacobite colonies in the east in Khurasan, Segestan, Zaranj and Herat.[102] But these men are absent from the narratives of the chronicles. The only exception, where an eastern bishop appears in the 'centre', is when Cyriacus of Segestan tries to arrange his transfer to the Tur Abdin with the help of Athanasius Sandalaya.[103] The disjuncture between the episcopal lists and the historical narrative gives the impression that various parts of the Jacobite communion were disenfranchised, in the sense that these territories were not places where the events that mattered occurred, they were simply places that required administration and provided tithes.[104] In

---

[99] For the proximity between hagiography and historiography in the Church of the East see Debié 2010.

[100] Van Nuffelen 2004: 194–204.   [101] Michael the Syrian, *Chronicle* 11.25 (IV, 475/II, 525).

[102] Ibid., Appendix III, with commentary in Honigmann 1954. For the distribution of Jacobite sees in Central Asia, as well as those of the other confessions, see Fiey 1973 and Fiey 1993.

[103] Michael the Syrian, *Chronicle* 11.22 (IV, 465/II, 507). Also note the difficulty in obtaining a bishop for Aphrah in Khurasan (ibid., 12.17 (IV, 525/III, 79)).

[104] We can note something similar in the Melkite tradition, which seems unaware of the presence of Melkites in Central Asia. Yet these Melkites were clearly important informants for al-Biruni and had their own distinctive hagiographic tradition that celebrated the evangelists, martyrs and Catholicoi in Merv and Nishapur: al-Biruni, *Chronology of the Ancient Nations*, 286–98. For the Melkite Catholicoi in Khurasan see the useful summary of older references in Parry 2017: 97. Historians of the Church of the East based in Ctesiphon are rather more conscious of the world east

part, this amnesia over Central Asia may reflect the Mediterranean bias of the Eusebius, which encouraged his continuators to focus their commentary towards the west.[105]

A particularly interesting example where a population is attested in episcopal lists but unmentioned in contemporary chronicles are the Tayyaye (Saracen/Arab). Some of the first footholds of the Severans in Sasanian world were allegedly established through the missions of Simeon beth Arsham and Ahudemmeh to 'Saracen' populations living on the borders of Rome and Persia (to the regions of Hira and Beth Arabaye respectively).[106] His hagiographer makes Ahudemmeh responsible for a major shrine at Qasr Serj, intended to draw pilgrims away from the famous shrine to St Sergius at Rusafa.[107] According to his *Life*, his exorcisms among the tribes eventually prompts the Saracen leaders to convert and to fund churches and monasteries, as well as the ordination of Saracen priests and deacons.[108] His *Life* celebrates the charity and asceticism of the Arabs, as well as their fortitude in the face of martyrdom: 'each time the orthodox church was persecuted they gave their heads for the church of Christ, above all the numerous chosen people of the Aqulaye, the Tanukh and Tu'aye'.[109]

Though our histories for the seventh and early eighth centuries are not detailed, the historians mention two famous intellectuals, George (d. 724) and Trokos, who were bishops of the Arabs, which George enumerates in his own writings as the Aqulaye, Tanukh and Tu'aye.[110] One Joseph, bishop of the Taghlib, causes problem for the patriarch Julian by helping the 'Catholicos' of Takrit ordain bishops without patriarchal consent.[111] And the 'Aqulaye, Tanukh and Tu'aye' are involved in the translation of the Bible from Syriac into Arabic so that it can be used to resolve the questions of a Muslim emir to the patriarch John Sedra.[112] Perhaps the best example of the significance of the Tayyaye for the self-representation of the

---

of Fars: the *Chronicle of Seert* gives a full section to the evangelisation of Merv and Merv features as a part of monastic networks (if a very distant one): Wood 2013: 152.

[105] Johnson 2016a: 131. Cf. Brock 1992.

[106] For Simeon see PO 18 and for Ahudemmeh, PO 3. In general see the comments of Trimingham 1979; Saint-Laurent 2015: ch. 7; Fisher and Wood 2015: 350–7 (with further references); Pierre 2017.

[107] For Qasr Serj see Fiey 1958, and for Rusafa, Fowden 1999.　　[108] PO 3: 26–7.　　[109] Ibid., 28.

[110] Michael the Syrian, *Chronicle* 11.12 (IV, 435/II, 453).　　[111] Ibid., 11.16 (IV, 448/II, 475).

[112] Ibid., 11.9 (IV, 422/II, 432). This colloquium is also attested independently in Syriac. Griffith 1985 initially saw this as a genuine seventh-century account of a recent debate, but Reinink 1993 persuasively dates it to the Marwanid period. Nevertheless, as Tannous 2009 argues, we should still emphasise the fact that an eighth-century author sought to stress the role of these three groups as occupying a key position between Muslim Arabs ('Tayyaye' in the language of the text) and Christian Syriac speakers.

Jacobite patriarchate is the statement of unity given by the bishops in their letter to the patriarch Severus bar Mashqa on his deathbed: 'God has made peace in all the lands of the West, among the Tanukh, the Tu'aye and the Aqulaye, [and] in Mesopotamia, in Edessa'.[113] The sentence could be read in various ways depending on which nouns are taken in apposition to one another, but I interpret this list as identifying three equal units: the West (i.e., the urban sees of Syria and Palestine), the three Arab groups and Mesopotamia, with its capital in Edessa (which had traditionally held the metropolitanate).[114]

It is hard to specify who these Arab groups were and whether and when the list of three groups (Aqulaye, Tanukh and Tu'aye) reflect actual Christian populations or are archaising claims to authority. Chase Robinson notes that Tu'aye is a term that is not used in Arabic and was used for Sasanian clients in the Jazira.[115] He suggests that it is a collective term that includes tribal groups such as the Banu 'Ijl, the Bakr bin Wa'il and the Taghlib.[116] The Aqulaye and Tanukh are generally located farther to the south, in the vicinity of Kufa and Hira, and it may be that their inclusion in the lists of Ahudemmeh's converts is an exaggeration.[117] Simon Pierre makes the suggestion that the *Life of Ahudemmeh*, with its stress on the ability of the new converts to resist conversion, is a Marwanid-era composition and relates that the Christian 'Arab' groups it describes were recent migrants from the south.[118]

Whatever the precise distribution of these groups, we should stress their importance in these early sources. Ahudemmeh was revered in the medieval sources as the founder of Miaphysitism in the east, whose successors would hold bishoprics in Ctesiphon and then in Takrit, where a major church held his relics.[119] But his *Life* associates him more with the mission to the nomads of the Jazira than his activities in Ctesiphon (or his links to

---

[113] Michael the Syrian, *Chronicle* 11.14 (IV, 441/II, 463).

[114] The 'East' is probably unmentioned here because this was a schism that did not affect the lands of the former Sasanian empire, and the Catholicos; John of 'Beth Parsaye' functions as an intermediary between the different parties.

[115] They are described raiding the region near Nisibis during a drought in the 480s. Trimingham 1979: 151; Edwell and Fisher 2015: 217–18.

[116] Robinson 1996: 433–4; Morony 1984: 374.

[117] Robinson 1996: 434 n. 40. The Tanukh are normally identified as clients of the kings of Hira (Toral-Niehoff 2014) and 'Aqulaye' is an ethnonym derived from Aqula (Kufa), the Islamic-era miṣr built next to Hira in the *sawad*. Shahid 1984 had placed the Tanukh in Syria on the basis of al-Mas'udi, but note the criticisms of Pierre 2017: 167–9.

[118] Pierre 2017. For instance, he stresses the report in Al-Tabari, *Ta'rīkh al-rusul wa-al-mulūk*, Vol. 1: 2673–4 of Kufans moving to the Jazira in the seventh century.

[119] Bar 'Ebroyo, *Ecclesiastical Chronicle* 99 represents Ahudemmeh as a monk of the monastery of Mar Mattai. This text also places him in the lineage of the Catholicoi of the east: the first 'orthodox'

the Miaphysites of Mar Mattai). And the letter of union between Bar Mashqa and the bishops, which may preserve an older document, takes the significance of these Arab groups for granted. But this relatively prominent position for the Christian 'Arabs'[120] is not maintained in the later, more extensive Jacobite histories that are extant for the period after 740. One reason for this could be that many Christian Arabs converted to Islam soon after the conquests or were targeted by early efforts at forced conversion.[121] The caliph Walid I was said to have eaten the flesh of one Taghlibi martyr, Sham'allah, who refused to convert to Islam. And another, Muadh, chief of the Taghlib, died in prison and his relics were preserved in a purpose-built monastery by one Eustathius of Dara.[122] But there were still Christian Tanukh living a semi-nomadic life in the environs of Aleppo in the 780s, who were targeted by al-Mahdi in forced conversion.[123] And bishops are mentioned in the ordination lists of the ninth-century patriarchs as bishops of 'the tribes' or 'Arabia and the Taghlib'[124] (with a see in the village of Daqla), as well as a bishop of Palmyra, who may have ministered to semi-nomads, and a bishop of 'Najran and the Ma'adaye'.[125]

Thus there seems to have been a significant amnesia concerning the Christian Arabs. Though they had seemed a relatively prominent part of

catholicos after the 'apostasy' of the Church of the East in the fifth century and the predecessor of Samuel and Marutha, Jacobite Catholicoi of Ctesiphon in the reign of Khusrau II. For the installation of his relics at Takrit see Bar 'Ebroyo, *Ecclesiastical Chronicle* III, 148 with Fiey 1963: 313. The end of the *Life of Ahudemmeh* refers to the transfer of Ahudemmeh's body, but this is an afterthought to the main action of the text.

[120] Pierre 2017 notes that sources like the *Life of Ahudemmeh* seem to deliberately avoid the term 'Tayyaye', long used in Syriac to describe the Jafnid and Nasrid allies of the Romans and Persians (many of whom were Christian). He suggests that this because of the increased association of this term with Arab *Muslims*.

[121] Sources are surveyed in Caetani 1926: IV, 58–9 and 226–32.

[122] Michael the Syrian, *Chronicle* 11.17 (IV, 451–2/II, 481). Monasteries associated with the Taghlib were still widespread in the region between Circesium, Mosul and Takrit when Yaqut wrote in the twelfth century: *Mu'jam al-Buldan*, II, 640–709.

[123] Michael the Syrian, *Chronicle* 12.1 (IV, 479/III, 1). Al-Mahdi was said to have been motivated by their ostentatious wealth. The conversion only applied to the men, and the women were allowed to remain Christian 'until this day' (which is likely to be the middle of the ninth century). This population was later forced to flee to Qinnasrin: ibid., 12.8 (IV, 497/III, 31). An earlier forced conversion of the Tanukh is recorded in the seventh-century Ehnesh inscription: Palmer, Brock and Hoyland 1993: 71.

[124] Sometimes the see is specified as 'the Taghlib of the Jazira of Mosul' (e.g., III, p. 457, no. 78). Honigmann 1954: 148 suggests that they may have had two different sees at some points, at the fortified village of Daqla on the Tigris and at Jazirat Umar.

[125] The Ma'ad probably refers to the Arabs of the interior of the Arabian peninsula. Sometimes the term can be pejorative, but it does not seem to be here. Both Jacobite and 'Nestorian' bishops operated here at various points in the ninth and tenth centuries: Fiey 1968: 148–9. It is unclear whether 'Najran' here refers to the ancient city on the border of modern Saudi Arabia and Yemen or the new Najran founded near Kufa in the Islamic period: Tardy 1999: 84–108.

the Jacobite confession in the Marwanid period, their importance had not persisted in the accounts of later periods. One indication of this may be the shift in language employed in Michael the Syrian: where the seventh-century passages speak of Aqulaye, Tanukh and Tu'aye, later parts of the narrative just describe the Tanukh and the Taghlib, which might suggest that parts of the Christian Arabs had become Muslim. Thus we may simply be witnessing the demographic erosion of the Christian Arabs, who were targeted for conversion by al-Walid, Umar II and al-Mahdi and who were not always accorded the same protections as other Christians in law.[126] But there were still bishops dedicated to Arab groups, and there were still Christian Arab populations even after al-Mahdi's persecution, such as the Tanukh of Bostra who joined the anti-patriarch 'Abraham'.[127] I suggest, therefore, that the disappearance of the 'Christian Arabs' could be a reflection of the blindness of our sources in addition to conversion to Islam. As with the omission of Palestine or Central Asia, this blindness may be linked to the restriction of avenues of promotion to a small number of key monasteries or to a new emphasis on the role of the Syriac language and Suryaya ethnicity, which left less and less room for non-Suryaye in the Jacobite imagination.

Conclusion

The Jacobite material preserved in Michael witnesses a marked contraction of 'the world that mattered' from an ecclesiastical perspective. The wish and capacity to record the affairs of the church and continue earlier ecclesiastical history was restored in the works of Daniel of Tur Abdin, the Zuqnin chronicler and Dionysius of Tel-Mahre. But there was little interest in the world of the surviving Roman Empire from an ecclesiastical perspective.[128] Indeed, the overwhelming focus is on the small group of monasteries that produced the church's bishops and patriarchs, to the exclusion of many territories where Jacobites lived. Dionysius appears as a well-connected patriarch, who used his close proximity to high-ranking Muslims like Abdallah ibn Tahir to re-establish a link to Alexandria. In his time, the Jacobite patriarch of Antioch was affirmed through the recognition of one of his peers. And in his record of the visitation of George of

---

[126] Friedmann 2004: 62–8.   [127] Michael the Syrian, *Chronicle* 12.8 (IV, 495/III, 32).

[128] The *Zuqnin Chronicle* does continue to show an interest in (and appreciation for) the military victories of Leo III and Constantine V, but it is ignorant of (or disinterested in) the affairs of the Byzantine church. The absence of Byzantine ecclesiastical material in Michael should be contrasted to the numerous (albeit brief) references to Byzantine military and political affairs.

Nubia it is possible to catch a glimpse of Dionysius's awareness of earlier Miaphysite missionary activity that established Miaphysite populations even further afield. Nevertheless, I think that our assessment of the geographical imagination of the Jacobite world in the first Abbasid century should stress the fact that it was so short-lived. For all Dionysius's ambition in looking back to earlier history for models or his importance for later writers like Michael and Bar Hebraeus, he had no immediate successors. It was not until Ignatius of Melitene wrote his history in the eleventh century that Dionysius found anything like a continuator, and by then the Jacobite world, and the political circles of its chroniclers, had been altered radically by migration towards the west and the establishment of new links with Byzantium.

CHAPTER 7

Where Is Syriac Pilgrimage Literature in Late Antiquity?

Exploring the Absence of a Genre

Scott Johnson

The title of my chapter asks a seemingly innocuous question. Why do no examples of a formal written genre of Syriac pilgrimage from late antiquity survive to today? Various answers could be offered to quickly dismiss the question: Syriac authors simply chose not to write about pilgrimage; or, they did write about it but their texts have not survived; or further, they did write about it, but chose to do so only within the context of other literary arenas, such as hagiography or historiography. These responses, as we shall see, all have some descriptive truth to them, but they do not offer a completely satisfactory answer. The genre of pilgrimage literature was vibrant in late antiquity in neighboring languages and cultures. The option of developing a genre of pilgrimage literature was certainly available to Syriac authors, but they appear not to have capitalized on that availability for their own tongue. Further, it seems from the surviving evidence that no Latin or Greek pilgrimage narratives were translated into Syriac.

The larger context of the absence of Syriac pilgrimage literature in late antiquity is the development of indigenous concepts of Christian space, particularly with regard to the Holy Land.[1] No complete study has been made to date of Syriac perceptions of physical and/or holy space. This is

---

[1] I have discussed several of the relevant issues in Johnson 2016a. The subject is vibrant, and many scholars have approached the topic of Christian views of physical space from different viewpoints (movement, trade, colonialism, cartography, geographical science, etc.). See, for instance, Leyerle 1996; Constable 2003; A. Jacobs 2004; Talbert and Unger 2008; Merrills 2005. Pilgrimage nevertheless remains a primary mode of investigation. A valuable collection of essays on pilgrimage — examining the practice, literature, and nomenclature, and covering both antiquity and late antiquity — is Elsner and Rutherford 2005. See also Hunt 1982; Frankfurter 1998; Elsner 2000; Frank 2000; Maraval 2002a; Dietz 2005; Bitton-Ashkelony 2005; Limor 2006 and Caseau et al. 2006. Maraval 1985 is still fundamental. Religious travel among Jews and Muslims has also been studied, though comparative scholarship across religions is notably lacking: see Hezser 2011; Martin Jacobs 2014 and Zadeh 2011. See, however, the big-picture cultural history of pilgrimage in Coleman and Elsner 1995, which interacts with anthropological frameworks developed by Turner and Turner 1978 and Eade

partly due (I would suggest) to the fact that no pilgrimage literature exists as such. However, as will be shown, ample material evidence exists that Syriac Christians did go on pilgrimage to the Holy Land, even though these real-world pilgrimages seem not to have been connected to a ritualized way of writing about such journeys. By contrast, the study of pilgrimage in the late antique and medieval West often *begins* by asserting a relationship between modes of writing and the movement of pilgrims on the ground. The texts, some of which circulated widely, served to 'script' the experiences of western pilgrims, especially in the medieval period. Without the 'script', the methodology for investigating Syriac perceptions of space, at least as far as pilgrimage goes, is made more complicated.

I would like to emphasize, however, that the word 'script' to describe pilgrimage literature is somewhat misleading. The relationship between pilgrimage text and religious activity was not (and is not today) stable or predictable, and examples exist of pilgrimages in late antiquity that appear to challenge reigning norms of Christian pilgrimage.[2] Perhaps it is better to say that while one can delineate certain emergent norms – specifically, which sites were visited and in what order – these norms were unstable. It is therefore worth asking whether Syriac pilgrimage – especially the absence of formalized pilgrimage literature – is part of a larger instability with regard to Christian views of holy sites. In other words, it is possible to approach the absence of Syriac pilgrimage texts from a broader cultural-historical viewpoint, which accords with a reading of the texts that is less genre-based and more concerned with the anthropology of early Christian pilgrimage. In what follows, I attempt to explore the absence of the genre of pilgrimage in Syriac from both literary- and cultural-historical points of view. Suffice it to say that the two cannot be easily separated. Pilgrimage literature was both a product of and a stimulus to the real-world movement of Christians in late antiquity. Pilgrimage literature was thus both descriptive and prescriptive.[3] While exploring its absence in Syriac is necessarily an argument about silence, the investigation of the silence is not a fool's errand because the issues raised are fundamental to Christian views of the physical world, of movement and travel, and ultimately of literature and creative endeavor.

and Sallnow 1991, among others. For an updated and reframed anthropological discussion, see Coleman and Eade 2004.

[2] One example, I have argued, is the Piacenza Pilgrim from c. 570: Johnson 2016b.

[3] A description which might be posited of much literature from late antiquity. This formulation, with varying emphases (didacticism, antiquarianism, experimentation, etc.), has been applied by several scholars: for example, Cameron 1992; Formisano 2007. See also the papers in Johnson 2006.

Christian pilgrimage texts show up in a variety of languages in late antiquity, though the most numerous and familiar are in Latin. Written from the fourth to ninth centuries, eight independent Holy Land pilgrimage narratives survive in Latin. These texts are the Bordeaux Pilgrim (333), Egeria (381–4), the anonymous Breviary of Jerusalem (c. 400), Ps.-Eucherius (c. 440), Theodosius (c. 518), the Piacenza Pilgrim (c. 570), Adomnán (before 683), and Willibald of Eichstätt (c. 787).[4] Only one related Greek text survives from the period: Epiphanius Hagiopolites from around 800, to which I will return in my conclusion.[5] In Armenian, we have at least two independent pilgrimage accounts: that of the Joseph the Hermit from around 660 preserved in the tenth-century history of Moses Kalankatuac'i and an anonymous description of Mt. Tabor, surviving as part of a treatise on the Transfiguration attributed to Eliše Vardapet, though probably dating to around 630.[6] Similarly, Georgian pilgrimage accounts, such as that of David Garedjeli (sixth-century founder of the famous Garedji Lavra in eastern Georgia), seem to have circulated independently in late antiquity, even though we know them through later hagiographical compilations (in David's case, the tenth-century cycle known as the *Lives of the Syrian Fathers*). The independent pilgrimage account of Saint Hilarion the Iberian from the tenth century shows a very mature form of pilgrimage narrative, encased within his *Life*, which was composed on Mount Athos in the circle of St. Euthymius the Hagiorite.[7] The sites Hilarion visited are described in considerable detail showing the well-developed Georgian pilgrimage networks of the time, complementary to the clearly established genre in which it is written, and comparable to the established form in Latin.[8]

Despite all these important comparanda, there is no evidence of Syriac pilgrimage literature in late antiquity.[9] Why is this? To explore the question further, let us begin with what does exist. Numerous short, integrated accounts of late antique pilgrimage survive in Syriac saints' lives and collected hagiography. In the East Syriac tradition these include accounts related to Abraham of Kashkar and numerous East Syrian saints collected

---

[4] All of these except Willibald appear in Geyer et al. 1965. For the standard critical editions of these texts, see the following appendix.

[5] Ed. and trans. Donner 1971. See Külzer 1994: 14–17.

[6] Joseph the Hermit: trans. Brooks 1896. Treatise on the Transfiguration: trans. Thomson 1967. This is by no means an exhaustive list of Armenian accounts of pilgrimage incorporated into other texts.

[7] Ed. and trans. Peeters 1913.   [8] On all the Georgian texts, see Tchekhanovets 2011.

[9] Perhaps as a consequence of this absence, no modern history of Syriac literature includes pilgrimage as a genre or category of Syriac writing. The standard encyclopedia of Syriac Studies – the *Gorgias Encyclopedic Dictionary of the Syriac Heritage* – likewise does not include an entry on pilgrimage.

by Isho'dnah of Basra and Thomas of Marga in the ninth century. In the West Syrian tradition, examples include the *Lives* of Peter the Iberian and Barsauma of Samosata and the *Life of Theodota of Amid* (early eighth century), all of which contain episodes of pilgrimage. One might also add the wide range of travels in John of Ephesus's *Lives of the Eastern Saints*, both by the subjects of his biographies and also by the author. A handful of these journeys are specifically described as pilgrimages: one example is his notice about the annual pilgrimage from Amid to Jerusalem made by a Mary, one of two sisters John calls the 'Daughters of the Gazelle'.[10]

The earliest and most well studied of the integrated pilgrimage accounts is the narrative of Peter the Iberian's tour of the Holy Land. His *Life* was written around 500 by Peter's disciple John Rufus, and the 'pilgrimage' section has been discussed several times in recent scholarship.[11] Peter, son of an Iberian king but held hostage in Constantinople, decided to escape the capital and go to the Holy Land. In Jerusalem he met Melania the Younger and became a monk in the monastery of Gerontius on the Mount of Olives. He subsequently established his own monastery on Christian Mt. Zion, for the specific benefit of poor pilgrims. He left Jerusalem around 444 and moved to Gaza, where he was ordained a priest and seven years later became bishop of Maiuma. After an active career of ecclesiastical involvement and many journeys around the eastern Mediterranean, he died there in 491. After leaving Constantinople for the Holy Land, Peter's journey becomes more pilgrimage-like and he treats holy sites with reverence – the language used to describe his actions and attitude is reminiscent of the language in Latin pilgrimage accounts, though told in the third person and incorporated into the longer narrative.

> When they were in the neighborhood of Jerusalem, the holy city beloved to them, they saw from atop a hill about five stadia away, like the flashing of the sunrise, the high roof of the holy and worshipful churches, that of the saving and worshipful Cross, of the holy Anastasis, and again of the worshipful Ascension, which is the mountain opposite it. They cried out aloud fulfilling the prophetic word, 'Behold Zion, the city of our salvation. Your eyes shall see Jerusalem' (Isaiah 33:20). They sent up praise and thanksgiving as their strength allowed to Christ whom they loved, to him who called them,

---

[10] Ed. and trans. Brooks 1923–5: 1.166–86. In his manner of compiling short biographical entries John differs little from the later East Syriac collective hagiography, but pilgrimage does not play the same structural role in John that it does in Isho'dnah and Thomas.

[11] See Horn 2004; Perrone 2009; Kofsky 1997; Bitton-Ashkelony 2004. More generally on Peter the Iberian, see Horn 2006.

brought them out, guided them, and preserved them. They cast themselves upon their faces and did not cease worshipping from on that height. Crawling on their knees, they greeted continuously with their lips and with their eyes this holy land full of assurance of the love that was kindled in them until they were inside the holy walls and embraced the foot of the venerable cross.[12]

The prostrations, kissing, and sense of worship upon arriving at the holy city are very reminiscent of independent pilgrimage accounts from the period, such as the Piacenza Pilgrim. It might also be noted that one of Peter's benefactors, Melania the Younger, is described with similar language in her *Life* by Gerontius.[13] Jerome's *Epitaphium Paulae*, a hagiographical letter describing her arrival into and tour of the Holy Land, uses similar descriptions.[14] While the language and interpretation of Peter's early movements in the Holy Land are shared with a wide range of texts from the period, both hagiographical texts and pilgrimage accounts, neither the Syriac nor the later Georgian versions of the *Life of Peter the Iberian* are pilgrimage accounts in narrative form.[15] The *Life* betrays knowledge of the practice and value of pilgrimage for late antique Christians, but in terms of overall form Peter's pilgrimage is very different from the familiar Latin narratives of the period. The pilgrimage episodes are, like the rest of the life, told in the third person and do not offer Peter's own viewpoint on what he was seeing Jerusalem and what he was doing in response.

Abraham of Kashkar, the sixth-century founder of the Great Monastery on Mount Izla near Nisibis, was celebrated as the renovator of East Syrian Monasticism.[16] He became such an important figure in later generations that the biography of the legendary Mar Awgen, supposed founder of all Syrian monasticism, subsequently became confused with his: Florence Jullien has discussed this aspect of Abraham in two recent articles.[17] Although it is mentioned very briefly, Abraham's pilgrimage is a fundamental part of his biography in the ninth-century *Liber Castitatis* of Isho'dnah of Basra.[18] '[Abraham the Great] journeyed all the

---

[12] Trans. Horn and Phenix 2008: 50–3.
[13] Greek version: ed. and trans. Gorce 1962. Latin version: ed. and trans. Laurence 2002; Clark 1984. On Melania's travels and relationship to the space of the Holy Land, see Andrew Jacobs 2017 and Shoemaker 2017.
[14] Ed. and trans. Cain 2013. See also Cain 2010 and Johnson 2016a: 37–8.
[15] Interestingly, the Georgian translation of Peter's *Life*, which is somewhat later than the Syriac translation of the original Greek, seems to have been a model for some Georgian pilgrimage accounts: see Tchekhanovets 2011.
[16] Jullien 2008b.   [17] Jullien 2006, 2008a.   [18] Ed. and trans. Chabot 1896: §14.

way to Egypt, to Scetis, and to Mount Sinai, then he returned to the schools of Nisibis'. Abraham is one of ten East Syrian saints in Isho'dnah, out of 140 mini-biographies in the work, who go to the West on pilgrimage. Martin Tamcke has argued against the older interpretation by Theodor Hermann that Abraham's pilgrimage to Scetis was used to legitimate changes to the monastic rule at Mt. Izla.[19] Whatever the rationale, Abraham's pilgrimage to Scetis and Sinai sets a pattern in Isho'dnah whereby several subsequent founders of monasteries in Iraq, from the seventh to ninth centuries, make pilgrimages to the West (not just to Egypt but also to Jerusalem and other holy places). These pilgrimages are not described in great detail, but their formulaic nature suggests that the pilgrimage was a constituent part, at least in Isho'dnah's conception, of a monastic founder's spiritual formation. I have analyzed these pilgrimages collectively elsewhere – comparing Isho'dnah to his older contemporary Thomas of Marga – so I will not go into further detail here.[20] The salient point is that the pattern of Abraham's pilgrimage is, on the one hand, less detailed and emotive than the *Life of Peter the Iberian*, and, on the other hand, also distinct from the Latin model. It does not stand on its own but serves the collective biographical pattern used by Isho'dnah throughout his work.

Barsauma of Samosata, an archimandrite and energetic supporter of the Miaphysite/anti-Chalcedonian cause, is said to have visited Jerusalem four times during the fifth century.[21] These pilgrimages are embedded in the sixth-century Syriac *Life of Barsauma* (*Vita Barsumae*).[22] Hagith Sivan has recently argued that these were politically motivated, determined in part by Jewish-Christian polemics and the presence of the Empress Eudocia in Jerusalem in the mid-fifth century.[23] Barsauma's pilgrimages collectively represent 'the metamorphosis of pilgrimage from a personal experience, basically a meditative prayer on the sacred, into a subversive model of interaction with peoples and places'.[24] Barsauma was very active in the Christological controversies surrounding the Council of Chalcedon in 451 and even offered an address in Syriac on the floor of the council.[25] According to Sivan, these pilgrimages are narrative devices that lend support to his aggressiveness towards Jews, Samaritans, pagans, and Chalcedonians in and around the

---

[19] Tamcke 2007; Hermann 1923.   [20] Johnson 2016a: 115–32.
[21] On Barsauma, see Brock et al. 2011: 59 (s.v. 'Barṣawmo' by Luk van Rompay).
[22] The date and authorship are contested: see the references at Sivan 2018b, 53 n. 1.
[23] Sivan 2018b.   [24] Ibid., 54.
[25] For the context of Barsauma speaking in Syriac at Chalcedon – the only example of this in the Acta – see Millar 2006: 113–15.

Holy Land. [26] As with other Syriac hagiographical texts, Barsauma's *Life* is not written as a pilgrimage narrative, but the pilgrimages play a structural role in the exaltation of this violent and revered Miaphysite monk.

As a final example, *The Life of Theodota of Amid* was written in the early eighth century and describes Theodota's monastic career, which spanned several monasteries. He began at Zuqnin, moved to Qenneshre, was consecrated bishop of Amid, and finally founded his own monastery of Mar Abay at Qeleth. [27] During his time at Qenneshre he conceived a desire to go on pilgrimage to Sinai and Jerusalem. As with the east Syrian biographies collected by Isho'dnah, his visit to the Holy Land seems more about the legitimization of his own authority as a holy man (namely, as a healer) than it is about the sites. Consider the following example:

> From there, [Theodota] went to Jerusalem. He entered in and was blessed by the Holy Places. But as for God, for Whom all things are easy and Whose wonders are not hidden, He wanted to make clear to the inhabitants of Jerusalem some of the righteousness of the Blessed Theodota and the wonders which God had worked through him. When Theodota was walking and visiting the Holy Places in which Our Lord had walked, he saw a paralytic. He placed his hand upon him and he was restored.... Word of him went out into all the city and in all its frontiers and the sick and the paralytic began coming to him ... the Blessed One would take some dirt in the name of Our Lord and sprinkle it over them and they would be healed. [28]

Whatever Theodota's own motivation was for going to the Holy Land, the narrative goal of his *Life* is to show his authority as a healer and to allow him to work miracles in the very place and manner that Jesus did. In this pilgrimage the dirt is not holy because of the *loca sancta*, but because Theodota is the one sprinkling it over the suppliants. After this he travels to Egypt and spends five years there: his presence is so valuable that the Egyptian bishops try to make him a bishop. Instead, guided by a vision, he returns to his homeland and becomes bishop of Amid. In this way the pilgrimage from Theodota's *Life* resembles both that of Peter the Iberian and Abraham of Kashkar. The pilgrimage is told in the third person and is functional for the overall argument of the *Life*.

These varied episodes of pilgrimage embedded in Syriac hagiography from late antiquity, while important for understanding the way the texts

---

[26] Sivan 2018b: 60: 'By linking demolition with pilgrimage, the biographer lends a canonical expression to lawless actions. He inscribes ruin in the idealization that exalts pilgrimage. The so-called second pilgrimage elevates violence as an extension of piety and "orthodoxy".'

[27] Brock et al. 2011: 408–9 (s.v. 'Theodotos of Amid' by Jack Tannous).

[28] §§ 42–3, trans. Jack Tannous forthcoming.

operate, do not constitute independent narratives and seem not to have circulated on their own. Nevertheless, they show an awareness of the cultural importance of pilgrimage to Syriac Christians and they also signal that certain patterns of movement and ritualized travel were known in various Syriac communities throughout the Middle East.

Indeed, ample material attests to pilgrimage among Syriac Christians. The famous inscriptions/graffiti on the columns at the western entrance to the Church of the Holy Sepulchre, published by Sebastian Brock and others, make it clear that Syriac Christians were visiting the Holy Sepulchre complex in the early Ottoman period.[29] This is later evidence of habits we know were in place much earlier. Syriac pilgrim inscriptions have turned up alongside Armenian and Georgian inscriptions in Nazareth from the fifth century, and from Sinai a century later.[30]

Anecdotal confirmation of this material evidence can be found in Syriac letters wherein mention is made of pilgrims to the Holy Land. Andrew Palmer notes a letter by Philoxenos of Mabbug (d. 523) wherein he states that seven visits to the monastery of Qartmin were equal in spiritual value to one visit to Jerusalem.[31] Brock has drawn attention to evidence of pilgrimage in the letters of Timothy 1 (d. 823).[32]

Many other examples could be added to this list of evidence for the practice of pilgrimage in Syriac circles – I would point the reader to seminal articles by Jean-Maurice Fiey, Herman Teule, and Andrew Palmer on pilgrimage to Jerusalem that survey the surviving testimonies to the practice.[33] Even during periods in which the practice of pilgrimage was criticized, it seems there was a steady stream of Syriac Christians visiting the Holy Land from outside Palestine.[34]

It is worth noting that Syriac travel narratives from the high medieval period appear more developed than those from late antiquity. Around 1275 Rabban Sauma embarked on a pilgrimage to Jerusalem with his disciple, Rabban Markos (later patriarch Mar Yahbalaha III).[35] The pilgrimage account and Sauma's later travels are framed as a dual biography of the two.[36]

---

[29] Brock 2001, 2006; Brock, Haim and Kofsky 2006–7.   [30] Tchekhanovets 2011: 457–65.
[31] Palmer 1991: 18, with bibliography in n. 6.   [32] Brock 2001: 202.
[33] Fiey 1969; Teule 1994, 2005; Palmer 1991.
[34] On attempts to limit the practice of pilgrimage in late antiquity, see Bitton-Ashkelony 2005.
[35] Brock et al. 2011: 360–1 (s.v. 'Ṣawma, Rabban' by Joseph Amar); and 429 (s.v. 'Yahbalaha III' by Joseph Amar).
[36] First edited and translated into French by Bedjan 1893, translated into English by Montgomery 1927 and Budge 1928, re-edited and translated into Italian by Borbone 2000 (subsequently translated into French: Borbone and Alexandre 2008), and translated into German by Toepel 2008.

Residents of Yuan Beijing, the pair left Mongol-controlled China and traveled across the Mongol Empire to Ilkhanate Persia. [37] They never reached the Holy Land due to regional conflicts with the Mamluks but instead visited numerous monasteries in Mesopotamia and Armenia, and they even tried to reach Georgia. When they reached Baghdad the patriarch (katholikos) of the Church of the East died and Markos was appointed as his successor because he knew the language of the ruling Mongols (even though he knew no Syriac). [38] After his installation, and at the urging of Arghun Khan, Mar Yahbalaha sent Rabban Sauma as ambassador to Europe (because 'he was acquainted with the languages'). [39] He toured the whole continent, including state visits to Constantinople (Andronikos II Palaiologos), Rome (twice, in 1287 and 1288; Pope Nicholas IV), Paris (Philip IV), and Gascony (King Edward I), before returning to Baghdad. [40] While this text is biographical in nature and not an exemplar of a strict pilgrimage genre, it is couched as a pilgrimage to Jerusalem from the beginning, and Sauma seeks out churches and relics while in the West.

Remarkably, this work corresponds closely to familiar medieval narratives of travel in the West, not least Marco Polo's reverse journey (in precisely the same years). There are also substantial Jewish travel narratives from the Middle Ages that resemble it and that circulated in similar milieux. [41] I am not postulating knowledge of contemporary Latin, Greek, or Jewish pilgrimage accounts among medieval Syriac authors, but comparatively speaking, both Western and Far Eastern traditions are evidenced by exempla of a mature type. [42] This literary maturation takes time to develop. So, if there is truly no native genre of pilgrimage in Syriac, where does such a narrative come from? Should we assume a native Mongolian or Chinese tradition behind this text? Perhaps its proper setting is amidst broader Asian literary trends, such as the substantial Buddhist pilgrimages, or the travel narratives, some overtly religious, from Japan and Korea surviving from medieval Asia? [43] These include, for example, a tenth-century Buddhist pilgrimage account surviving among the Sino-Tibetan manuscripts discovered at Dunhuang and a diplomatic mission from Japan to Silla (Korean peninsula) in 736/7, described in 145 early Japanese

---

[37] On Christianity under the Mongols, see Baumer 2016: 195–233 and Tang 2014.

[38] Montgomery 1927: 44.

[39] Montgomery 1927: 51. Argun Khan, who was very friendly to the Christians, sent four embassies to the West, of which this was the second, to secure support for capturing Jerusalem.

[40] Ibid., 52–72.   [41] Adler 1987.

[42] On the emergence of formulaic modes of travel writing in the high medieval and early modern periods, both East and West, see Brummett 2009.

[43] On Buddhist pilgrimage from a comparative perspective, see Coleman and Elsner 1995: 170–95.

poems.[44] The pilgrimage of Sauma and Markos purports to be a redaction and translation from a Persian original into Syriac, so perhaps Middle Persian is the proper literary world, or even Uighur/Turkic, which was Sauma and Markos's ethnic background.[45] Regardless of the specific context, influence from outside Syriac seems likely in this case. Nevertheless, the text has been preserved only in Syriac, so the search for comparanda within the Syriac tradition remains tempting.

Along these same lines, the text known as *Kalila and Dimna* – in the main a collection of animal and other stories – originated in Sanskrit but found its way into Middle Persian in the sixth century, translated by a Burzoy (Barzaway).[46] The first Syriac translation seems to have been made soon thereafter from the Middle Persian.[47] The second Syriac translation was made from a ninth-century Arabic translation by Ibn al-Muqaffaʿ. The original Sanskrit, the Middle Persian, and the ninth-century Arabic are lost. But the two Syriac versions (among later Arabic, Turkish, Hebrew, and other translations) survive, and the later Syriac one includes an autobiography of Burzoy, which recounts his travels to India.[48] In the narrative, Burzoy is commissioned by the king of the Persians, Khusroy Anoshagruwan (Khosrow I, 501–79), to go to India in search of plants and herbs that can produce a medicine to bring the dead back to life, a medicine that his books have told him exists. He finds no such medicine in the end, but during his sojourn the Indian sages reveal a metaphorical interpretation that leads him to seek out their knowledge and translate their books of wisdom (from Sanskrit to Persian). One of these books of wisdom ends up being the book *Kalila and Dimna*, in which this narrative of Burzoy's travels is embedded. The journey thus becomes an etiology of the book. The multitude of translations of *Kalila and Dimna* into medieval languages attests to the popularity of the book: in Syriac, as mentioned, there are no fewer than two surviving versions, and it seems to have had wide appeal. As with the narrative of Rabban Sauma, *Kalila and Dimna* demonstrates that stories of journeys were available in Syriac through the medieval period. In neither case, however, can we definitively say these are pilgrimage narratives in a formal sense. As with hagiographical texts, the accounts of movement/pilgrimage are embedded in a larger narrative

---

[44] See Van Schaik and Galambros 2012 and Horton 2012, respectively.

[45] Originally written in Persian: Montgomery 1927: 73.

[46] Brock et al. 2011: 241–2 (s.v. 'Kalila and Dimna' by Sebastian Brock).

[47] Ed. and trans. Schulthess 1911. See also Rundgren 1996.

[48] See de Blois 1990: esp. 81–95 (edition and translation of Burzoy's journey). Later Arabic version: ed. and trans. Wright 1884.

framework. The journeys of Rabban Sauma and Burzoy are written in the third person, reinforcing the distinction between them and, in particular, the Latin accounts from the late antique and medieval periods.

No distinct genre of pilgrimage literature has survived in Syriac, despite the fact that the literary and religious cultures Syriac interacted with in late antiquity apparently recognized such a genre. Nevertheless, pilgrimage narratives are embedded in a range of Syriac literature. In most cases, they seem to be used as a legitimization of the subjects of biography, especially for monastic founders and prominent saints. Moreover, Syriac Christians regularly visited the Holy Land and other locales, visits for which we have a variety of literary and epigraphical testimonia, up through the Ottoman period. This much is relatively well known and has been studied from various points of view. How then do we explain the absence of a genre of Syriac pilgrimage literature where we would be completely justified in expecting it?

I will confess that I see no easy answer to the question – barring new discoveries or texts I am unaware of – but I would like to pose some further questions to try to triangulate an answer. First, despite the shared patterns of narration across languages, direct cross-linguistic influence (through translation or multilingualism) seems to have occurred less in this literary arena. In contrast, one could point to the cross-pollination of liturgy in Palestinian monasteries, evidenced early on by the casual observations of pilgrim Egeria in 381–4, but which has been explored at a detailed level by scholars studying the manuscript history of the Jerusalem liturgy as it survives in multiple eastern Christian languages.[49] One could also mention here the easy fluidity of hagiography and theological treatises between Greek, Syriac, Armenian, Georgian, Arabic, and other languages throughout the period.[50] So, why not cross-linguistic influence in the realm of pilgrimage literature? Is this because Syriac-speaking and Latin- or Greek-speaking pilgrims did not mix in the way that monks resident in the multilingual monasteries did? Within the sociology of religion, pilgrimage is often seen as a community-defining event and studies of modern pilgrimage confirm that visitors to holy sites tend to stay in their ethnic or linguistic groups and do not mix in the way that local residents around the site do. I would point to Candace Slater's excellent study of Brazilian pilgrimage, *Trail of Miracles*, for a modern anthropologist's close reading of this phenomenon.[51]

[49] Galadza 2018. [50] Johnson 2015.
[51] Slater 1986. I have attempted to apply some of the themes of the anthropological study of pilgrimage to the Piacenza Pilgrim: Johnson 2016b.

Second, it is worth noting that many of the later stories of pilgrimage in Syriac come from East-Syrian monastic hagiographers from the ninth century, namely Isho'dnah of Basra and Thomas of Marga. As noted, they use visits to the West as a common motif, especially for famous monks prior to donning the habit.[52] Likewise, the letters of Timothy I seem to regard pilgrimage as a normal part of Church of the East relations with the West.[53] With this in mind, could we say that there was less impetus to write about pilgrimage among Christian groups originating closer to the Holy Land? Clearly, Syrian Orthodox pilgrims were frequent visitors to (and inhabitants of) Jerusalem, to a degree not definitive of the Church of the East.[54] However, the Syrian Orthodox do not write about pilgrimage with the frequency that East Syrian writers do.[55] Does relative proximity to the Holy Land have something to do with this? One answer has been proposed by Teule, who notes the restrictions on pilgrimage in monastic rules among West Syrians.[56] In the East, such proscriptions (if they were ever adopted) seem to have been less ideologically potent than they were in the West. In other words, perhaps there are fewer surviving notices of Syrian Orthodox pilgrimage because it was explicitly forbidden in their monastic culture.

This line of argument brings to the fore one major distinctive of the Latin tradition: the majority of the early pilgrimage texts appear to have been written by laypeople. By contrast, the Syriac literature that survives – especially from the fifth century on – was written by monks and clerics. Is pilgrimage literature in the Latin world therefore a phenomenon attributable to a literate lay class of Christians who had the means and ability to take such journeys and record them (and, by extension, a readership intent on preserving them)? The best known of these pilgrims, Egeria, seems to have been a wealthy laywoman and one, moreover, who possessed a library of texts related to early Christianity back home in the west.[57] One reason we might not find pilgrimage literature in Syriac is because it was not a common monastic form of writing.

This thought, however, is complicated by the fact that, across the large corpora of late antique Latin, Greek, Syriac, Coptic, Armenian, and Georgian, episodes of pilgrimage are incorporated into hagiographical

---

[52] Fiey 1969; Teule 1994; Tamcke 2007; Johnson 2016a: 115–32. [53] Brock 2001: 202.
[54] Palmer 1991.
[55] I quote above from the early-eighth-century *Life of Theodota of Amid*, but the handful of examples given by Palmer 1991 are sixth century and earlier. This does not seem to have been a major theme in Syrian Orthodox writing after the sixth century.
[56] Teule 1994, 2005. [57] Sivan 1988a, 1988c.

texts. As noted previously, the embedded pilgrimage accounts in such texts are usually told in the third person, in contrast to the first-person narratives of, for instance, Egeria and the Piacenza Pilgrim. A more complete picture, therefore, of pilgrimage as a Christian literary activity might show that, while real-world, on-the-ground pilgrimage was happening among many different communities of late antique Christians, monastic writers learned how to blend or mediate those experiences into more familiar hagiographical genres, such as saints' lives or miracle collections. This phenomenon is, of course, evident in both western and eastern monastic literatures. Independent pilgrimage texts in Latin become, on this view, a more surprising form of writing and less connected to shared developments in Christian literature through the period.

Nevertheless, it is important to emphasize that western modes of writing about territory and space were not the only modes that could be employed, and indigenous ways of investigating space developed among various groups. Other genres in Syriac take up some of the work of describing holy sites and the individual Christians' views of the physical world around them. Poetry, historiography, and formal liturgical texts in Syriac all incorporate notions of space and location.[58] Poetry is perhaps the most valuable for understanding how late antique conceptions of territory and holiness intersected Syriac literature. Julian Saba (d. 367), an ascetic from Osrhoene, was said to have made a pilgrimage to Sinai circa 362, and became the subject of twenty-four *madrashe* attributed to Ephrem and one *memra* attributed to Jacob of Serugh.[59] The Ephremic poems and the one by Jacob (in addition to the biography by Theodoret of Cyrrhus) all speak of Julian's journey to Sinai and claim he built a church there.[60] From the *memra* attributed to Jacob of Serugh:

> So then,
> look upon Saba
> as upon Moses...
> The humility of the great Moses
> Saba possessed...
> Saba too

---

[58] For Syriac historiography, see now Debié 2015, esp. the chapter on 'Historiographie et Genres Connexes': 403–39. See also Debié 2004 (on views of Antioch in Syriac historiography); and 2006 (on the flood of Nisibis in 350). On technical geographical literature in Syriac, see Defaux 2014.

[59] Griffith 1994. On the authenticity of these poems, see Griffith 1994: 198–203. Most of the Ephremic poems are of later composition and attribution, but the first four in the collection seem to be authentic.

[60] Griffith 1994: 191–2.

                              was raised up
to Mt. Sinai…
He anointed and designed
a holy church
in that splendid place.[61]

After he died in the desert, Julian's body was carried to the city of Edessa, whereupon a cult grew up that was centered around his tomb. One Ephremic *madrasha* memorializes this cult:

Rise up, O country of ours, fulfill your vows on your feasts.
Within you their feasts resound like trumpets,
of Guria, Habib, and Shmona.
And now the fair Saba is added to you,
the voice of whose trumpet a new assembly sings for you.[62]

In the same poem Ephrem claims a superiority of Edessa, even over the Holy Land:

The name of our country is even greater than that of her consort.
For in her was born Levi, the chief of the priests,
and Judah, the chief of royalty,
and Joseph, the child who went forth and became
the lord of Egypt. In the light from her
the world is enlightened.

For the new sun which appeared in creation
was of Judah, who was born in our country.
And within our country,
his light appeared and was brought to shine
from Bethlehem. As from you there sprang the beginning,
so in you he enriches the end.[63]

Thus, the figure of Julian Saba and the cult that was attached to his tomb in Edessa becomes a literary opportunity for Ephrem to tout the significance of Edessa as a holy site over and against the revered holy sites of Jerusalem. He incorporates biblical geography into a metrical celebration of northern Mesopotamia and, especially, his adopted home city of Edessa (after 363).[64] This is just one of many examples of how Syriac views of territory or space

---

[61] Trans. Griffith 1994: 191. See ibid., n. 28 for manuscript information.
[62] Ed. Beck 1972: 1.10 (*madrasha* 4.7); trans. Griffith 1994: 195. This is one of the four poems on Julian Saba that Griffith considers to be genuine.
[63] Ed. Beck 1972: 1.10 (*madrasha* 4.9–10); trans. Griffith 1994: 202.
[64] The *Carmina Nisibena*, mostly written before his exile to Edessa, could also be approached from the point of view of location and space.

were incorporated into various types of literature. In Julian's case the legend that is celebrated in verse includes memory also of his pilgrimage to Sinai, and Ephrem's poem offers an intriguing opportunity to consider the overlap of pilgrimage literature, the celebration of pilgrimage as part of a saint's biography, and a broader view of literary cartography within the Syriac tradition.

As a final way of triangulating the absence of pilgrimage literature in Syriac, let us compare the Greek tradition. Only one meager example of an independent pilgrimage genre survives in Greek from before 1000. This is the account of Epiphanius Hagiopolites from around 800.[65] Labeled by later manuscripts as a *proskunetarion*, the text only distantly resembles those later 'prayer circuits' known in middle- and late-Byzantine literature.[66] Instead, it corresponds very closely with the Latin *itinerarium* genre that was already very well developed by that time. Epiphanius travels from Constantinople to Jerusalem through Cyprus and Tyre, making extended journeys from there to Alexandria, Raithou, and Sinai, in addition to visiting numerous holy sites in and around the Holy Land. When combined with the Syriac tradition surveyed in the preceding text, can we posit that this sole surviving Greek pilgrimage reinforces the view of a generally weak eastern interest in a distinct genre?

Another way of asking the question is, if Epiphanius Hagiopolites were in Syriac, would it significantly alter our perception of Syriac interest in the genre? I think it would, and the survival of at least one example of a formal pilgrimage genre in Greek (with many examples from later centuries) is suggestive of a broader familiarity with pilgrimage literature in Greek than what we see in Syriac.[67] Above all, this one extant text in Greek should recommend caution about presuming the genre of pilgrimage never existed in Syriac. The precariousness of manuscript preservation, even amidst a corpus as large as Syriac, is an important element in any literary history, and no argument from silence can prove that a Syriac pilgrimage account was never written. And, of course, there is still much paleographical and editorial work to be done on Syriac literature. However, on current

---

[65] Ed. and trans. Donner 1971.   [66] See Mullett 2002.

[67] Indeed, we could cite Cosmas Indicopleustes as an exception proving the rule here: while he does not include a pilgrimage narrative in his Greek *Christian Topography* from the sixth century, his chapter on the flora and fauna of the Red Sea coast, signaling what appears to be very close knowledge of the trade routes to India, demonstrates without doubt familiarity with the Greco-Roman genre of the *periplous*, or the ocean-going *itinerarium*, a vibrant ancient genre that extended back to Hanno the Carthaginian in the sixth century BC. See Johnson 2016a: 29–60.

evidence, no such account has survived. This remains something of a surprise given the ample surviving texts in neighboring languages, particularly Latin and Armenian. Why Syriac authors did not develop for themselves a formal genre of pilgrimage literature remains a literary historical problem.

Appendix: Pilgrimage Narratives Discussed

Pilgrims/Religious Travelers in Syriac Texts (examples only, not comprehensive)

Peter the Iberian (c. 417–91), pilgrimage to the Holy Land, as part of the *Life of Peter the Iberian* by John Rufus (c. 500): ed. and trans. Horn and Phenix 2008.

Abraham of Kashkar (c. 500–88), pilgrimage to Scetis, Sinai, and Jerusalem, as part of his biography in the *Liber Castitatis* by Ishoʻdnah of Basra (mid-9th cent.): ed. and trans. Chabot 1896, §14. (One of ten East Syrian pilgrims among 140 mini-biographies in the work.)

Theodota of Amid (d. 698), pilgrimage to Sinai, Jerusalem, and Egypt, as part of the *Life of Theodota of Amid* (early 8th cent.): trans. Tannous forthcoming.

Rabban Sauma and Mar Yahbhallaha (c. 1275), pilgrimage/embassy to the West: ed. and Fr. trans. Bedjan 1893; Eng. trans. Montgomery 1927; Eng. trans. Budge 1928; ed. and It. trans. Borbone 2000; Fr. trans. Borbone and Alexandre 2008; Ger. trans. Toepel 2008.

Kalila and Dimna (6th–7th cent./10th–11th cent.): ed. and Ger. trans. Schulthess 1911 (translation from Middle Persian = earlier Syriac version without travel narrative); ed. and Eng. trans. Wright (translation from Arabic = later Syriac version including Burzoy's travels to India); de Blois 1990: 81–95 (edition and Eng. translation of Burzoy's journey).

Latin Pilgrimage Narratives

Bordeaux Pilgrim (333): eds. Geyer et al. 1965: 1.1–26.

Egeria (381–4): eds. Geyer et al. 1965: 1.29–90; ed. and trans. Maraval 2002b.

Breviary of Jerusalem (c. 400): eds. Geyer et al. 1965: 1.109–112.

Ps.-Eucherius, *De situ Hierusolimae* (c. 440): eds. Geyer et al. 1965: 1.237–43.

Theodosius, *De situ terrae sanctae* (503): eds. Geyer et al. 1965: 1.115–25.

Piacenza Pilgrim (c. 570): eds. Geyer et al. 1965: 1.129–74; ed. Milani 1977.

Adomnán, *De locis sanctis* (before 683): eds. Geyer et al. 1965: 1.183–234.

Willibald of Eichstätt, *Hodoiporicon* (c. 787), preserved as part of Willibald's *Life* (BHL 8931): ed. Holder-Egger 1887.

Greek Narrative

Epiphanius Hagiopolites, *Proskunetarion* (c. 800): ed. and trans. Donner 1971.

Armenian Narratives

Joseph the Hermit (c. 660), pilgrimage to Holy Land, surviving as part of the *History* of Moses Kalankatuac'i (10th cent.): trans. Brooks 1896.

Anonymous description of pilgrimage to Mt. Tabor (c. 630), surviving as part of a treatise on the Transfiguration (late 7th cent.) attributed to Eliše Vardapet (5th cent.): trans. Thomson 1967.

Georgian Narratives

David Garedjeli (6th cent.), preserved in the *Lives of the Syrian Fathers*, composed by the Patriarch of Georgia Arsenius II (c. 955–80): trans. Lang 1976: 81–93.

Saint Hilarion the Iberian (9th cent.), surviving as part of his *Life* composed on Mount Athos in the circle of St. Euthymius the Hagiorite (10th cent.): trans. Peeters 1913.

Bibliography

Abbreviations

ACO: *Acta Conciliorum Oecumenicorum* (1927–), eds. E. Schwartz e.a. Berlin
BNJ: *Brill's New Jacoby*, ed. I. Worthington, http://referenceworks
      .brillonline.com/browse/brill-s-new-jacoby.
PO: *Patrologia orientalis* (1903–), eds. R. Graffin, F. Nau and F. Graffin.
      Paris-Turnhout.

Sources

Agatʻangełos *A*: Tēr-Mkrtčʻean, G. and Kanayeancʻ, S. (eds.) (1914) *Agatʻangełay Patmutʻiwn Hayocʻ*. Tiflis; reprinted (1980) Delmar, NY.

Agatʻangełos *Syriac Vs*: van Esbroeck, M. (ed.) (1977) 'Le résumé syriaque de l'Agathange, *Analecta Bollandiana* 95: 291–358.

Al-Biruni, *Chronology of the Ancient Nations*: Sachau, E. (tr.) (1879) *The Chronology of Ancient Nations: An English Version of the Arabic Text of the Athar-ul-bakiya of Albiruni*. London.

Al-Tabari, *Taʼrīkh al-rusul wa-al-mulūk*: de Goeje, M. J. (ed.) (1879–1901) *Annales quos scripsit Abu Djafar Mohammad ibn Djarir al-Tabari*. 15 vols. Leiden, The Netherlands.

Ašxarhacʻoycʻ (Long Recension): Soukry, A. (ed.) (1881) *Ašxarhacʻoycʻ Movsesi Xorenacʻwoy Yaweluacovkʻ Naxneacʻ*. Venice; reprinted (2003) *Ašxarhacʻoycʻ* (1), in *Matenagirkʻ Hayocʻ 5 dar* vol. 2. Antʻilias: 2137–61.

Ašxarhacʻoycʻ (Short Recension): Abrahamyan, A. G. (ed.) (1944) 'XXIII. Širakacʻu Ašxarhacʻoycʻ-ě', in *Anania Širakacʻu Matenagrutʻyuně*. Erevan: 336–54; reprinted (2003) *Ašxarhacʻoycʻ* (3), in *Matenagirkʻ Hayocʻ 5 dar* vol. 2. Antʻilias: 2176–92.

Bar Hebraeus, *Ecclesiastical History*: Wilmshurst, D. (tr.) (2015) *Barhebraeus: The Ecclesiastical Chronicle: An English Translation*. Piscataway, NJ.

Basil of Caesarea, *Hexaemeron*: Mouradyan, K. (ed.) (1984) *Hexaemeron: Barsēł Kesaracʻi: Yałags vecʻawreayararčʻutʻean*. Erevan.

Chronicle to 819: Chabot, J.-B. (ed. and tr.) (1916) *Anonymi auctoris Chronicon ad annum Christi 1234 pertinens*. Corpus Scriptorum Christianorum Orientalium 81/109, Scriptores Syri 36/56. Louvain.

Chronicle of Seert: Scher, A. (ed.) and Graffin, F. (tr.) (1908–19) *Histoire nestorienne inédite*. Patrologia orientalis 5, 7, 9, 13. Paris.

Chronicle of Zuqnin: Chabot, J.-B. (ed.) (1927–33) *Chronicon anonymum pseudo-Dionysianum vulgo dictum*. Corpus Scriptorum Christianorum Orientalium 91/104, Scriptores Syri 43/53. Paris; Harrak, A. (tr.) (1999) *The Chronicle of Zuqnin, Parts III and IV A.D. 488–775, translated from Syriac with notes and introduction*. Toronto.

Constantine Porphyrogenitus, *De Ceremoniis*: Reiske, J. J. (ed.) (1829–30) *Constantini Porphyrogeniti imperatoris de cerimoniis aulae byzantinae*, 2 vols. Bonn.

Dexippus: Mecella, L. (ed.) (2013) *Dexippo di Atene: testimonianze e frammenti*. I frammenti degli storici greci 6. Tivoli (Roma); Martin, G. (2006) *Dexipp von Athen: Edition, Übersetzung und begleitende* Studien. Classica Monacensia 32. Tübingen.

Egeria: Maraval, P. (ed.) (2002) *Égérie, journal de voyage: Itinéraire*. Sources chrétiennes 296. Paris.

Epic Histories: Patkanean, K. (ed.) (1883) *P'awstosi Buzandac'woy' Patmut'iwn hayoc'*. St Petersburg, reprinted (1912) Tiflis, reprinted (1984). Delmar NY; (1933) *P'awstosi Buzandac'woy Patmut'iwn Hayoc' i č'ors dprut'iwns*. St Petersburg, 4th revised edition, reprinted (2003) in *Matenagirk' Hayoc' 5 dar* vol. 1. Ant'ilias: 273–428.

George, bishop of the Arabs, *Memra on Severus*: McVey, K. (ed. and tr.) (1993) *George, Bishop of the Arabs, a Homily on Blessed Mar Severus, Patriarch of Antioch*. Corpus Scriptorum Christianorum Orientalium 530 Syr. 216. Louvain.

Girk' T'łt'oc' I: Izmireanc', Y. (ed.) (1901) *Girk' T'łt'oc'*. Tiflis.

Girk' T'łt'oc' II. Połarean, N. (ed.) (1994) *Girk' T'łt'oc'*. Jerusalem.

Hesychius, *Patria*: Preger, T. (ed.) (1901) *Scriptores originum Constantinopolitanarum*. Leipzig.

John of Biclaro, *Chronicle*: Campos, J. (ed.) (1960) *Juan de Biclaro, Obispo de Gerona. Su vida y su obra. Introduccion, Texto critico y comentarios*. Madrid; Cardelle de Hartmann, C. (ed.) (2001) *Victoris Tunnunensis Chronicon cum reliquiis ex Consularibus Caesaraugustanis et Iohannis Biclarensis Chronicon*. Corpus Christianorum. Series latina 173A. Turnhout.

John of Ephesus, *Ecclesiastical History*: Brooks, E. W. (ed.) (1935–6) *Iohannis Ephesini historiae ecclesiasticae pars tertia*. Corpus Scriptorum Christianorum Orientalium 105/6, Syr. 54/5. Louvain.

John of Ephesus, *Lives of the Eastern Saints*: Brooks, E. W. (ed.) (1923–5) *John of Ephesus: Lives of the Eastern Saints*. 3 vols. Patrologia Orientalis, 17.1, 18.4, 19.2. Paris.

John Lydus, *On the Magistracies*: Bandy, A. C. (ed.) (1983) *Ioannes Lydus: On Powers*. Philadelphia.

John Lydus, *On the Months*: Wünsch, R. (ed.) (1898) *Ioannis Laurentii Lydi Liber de mensibus*. Leipzig.

John Malalas, *Chronicle*: Thurn, I. (ed.) (2000) *Ioannis Malalae Chronographia*. Berlin and New York.

John Rufus, *Life of Peter the Iberian*: Horn, C. B. and Phenix, R. R. (eds.) (2008) *John Rufus: The Lives of Peter the Iberian, Theodosius of Jerusalem, and the Monk Romanus*. Society of Biblical Literature: Writings from the Greco-Roman World 24. Atlanta.

Łazar, *History of the Armenians*: Tēr-Mrktč'ean, G. and Malxasean, S. (eds.) (1904) *Łazaray P'arpec'woy Patmut'iwn Hayoc'*. Tiflis; reprinted 1986, Delmar, NY; reprinted *Łazar P'arpec'i Patmut'iwn Hayoc'* (2003) in *Matenagirk' Hayoc'* 5 *dar* vol. 2, ed. K. Yuzbašean and P. Mouradean. Ant'ilias. 2197–375.

Life of Ahudemmeh: Nau, F. (ed. and tr.) (1909) *Histoires d'Ahoudemmeh et de Marouta, métropolitains jacobites de Tagrit et de l'Orient (VIe et VIIe siècles)*. Patrologia Orientalis 3. Paris.

Life of Melania: Clark, E. A. (ed.) (1984) *The Life of Melania, the Younger: Introduction, Translation, and Commentary*. Studies in Women and Religion 14. New York.

Life of Willibald: Holder-Egger, O. (ed.) (1887) 'Vitae Willibaldi et Wynnebaldi auctore sanctimoniali Heidenheimensi', *Monumenta Germaniae Historica, Scriptores* 15.1: 80–117. Hanover.

Lives of the Fathers of Emerita: Fear, A. T. (ed.) (1997) *Lives of the Visigothic Fathers*. Translated Texts for Historians 26. Liverpool, UK.

Marcellinus Comes, *Chronicle*: Croke, B. (tr.) (1995) *The Chronicle of Marcellinus*. Sydney.

Michael the Syrian: Chabot, J.-B. (reproduced and tr.) (1899–1910) *Michel le Syrien. Chronique*. Paris.

Nicephorus, *Short History*: Mango, M. (ed. and tr.) (1990) *Nikephoros Patriarch of Constantinople, Short History*. Dumbarton Oaks Texts 10. Washington, DC.

Procopius, *Wars*: Dewing, H. B. (ed. and tr.) (1914) *Procopius of Caesarea, History of the Wars*. Loeb Classical Library. Cambridge, MA, and London.

Pseudo-Zachariah, *Chronicle*: Brooks, E. W. (ed. and tr.) (1919–24) *Pseudo-Zachariah of Mitylene, Historia ecclesiastica Zachariae Rhetori vulgo adscripta*. Corpus Scriptorum Christianorum Orientalium 83–4, 87–8 Syr. 38–9, 41–2. Paris; Greatrex, G., Phenix, R. R. and Brock, S. P. (2011) *The Chronicle of Pseudo-Zachariah Rhetor: Church and War in Late Antiquity*. Translated Texts for Historians 55. Liverpool, UK.

Sebēos, *History*: Abgaryan, G. V. (ed.) (1979) *Patmut'iwn Sebēosi*. Erevan.

Themistius: Downey, G. (ed.) (1965) *Themistii orationes quae supersunt*. Bibliotheca scriptorum graecorum et romanorum teubneriana. 3 vols. Leipzig.

Theophanes, *Chronicle*: de Boor, C. (ed.) (1883–5) *Theophanes, Chronographia*. 2 vols. Leipzig.

Socrates, *Ecclesiastical History*: Hansen, G. C. (ed.) (1995) *Sokrates. Kirchengeschichte*. Griechische christliche Schriftsteller NF 1. Berlin.

Stephanus of Byzantium, *Ethnika*: Billerbeck, M. (ed.) (2006) *Stephani Byzantii Ethnica*. Berlin and New York.

Theodoret, *Ecclesiastical History*: Parmentier, L. and Hansen, G. (eds.) (1998) *Theodoret. Kirchengeschichte*. Griechische christliche Schriftsteller. Berlin.

Thomas of Marga, *Book of Governors*: Wallis Budge, E. (ed. and tr.) (1893) *The Book of Governors: The Historia Monastica of Thomas, Bishop of Marga, A.D. 840*. London.

Victor of Tunnunna, *Chronicle*: Cardelle de Hartmann, C. (ed.) (2001) *Victoris Tunnunensis Chronicon cum reliquiis ex Consularibus Caesaraugustanis et Iohannis Biclarensis Chronicon*. Corpus Christianorum. Series latina 173A. Turnhout.

Literature

Abramowski, R. (1940) *Dionysius von Tellmahre. Jakobitischer Patriarch von 818–845: zur Geschichte der Kirche unter dem Islam*. Nendeln, Liechtenstein.

Abulaże, I., et al. (1963) *Żveli K'art'uli Agiograp'iuli Literaturis Żeglebi [Monuments of Ancient Georgian Hagiographic Literature]*. 6 vols. T'bilisi.

Adams, C. and Laurence, R. (2001) *Travel and Geography in the Roman Empire*. London.

Adler, E. N. (1987) *Jewish Travellers in the Middle Ages: 19 Firsthand Accounts*. New York.

Adontz, N. G. (1970) *Denys de Thrace et les commentateurs arméniens*. Louvain.

Ahl, F. (1984) 'The Art of Safe Criticism in Greece and Rome', *American Journal of Philology* 105: 174–208.

Allen, P. (1979) 'A New Date for the Last Recorded Events in John of Ephesus' Historia Ecclesiastica', *Orientalia Lovaniensia Periodica* 10: 251–4.

(1994) 'Monophysiten', *Theologische Realenzyklopädie* 23: 219–33.

(2011) 'Episcopal Elections in Antioch in the Sixth Century', in *Episcopal Elections in Late Antiquity*, ed. J. Leemans et al. Berlin and New York: 23–38.

Almagor, E. and Skinner, J. (eds.) (2013) *Ancient Ethnography: New Approaches*. New York.

Alpi, F. (2009) *La route royale: Sévère d'Antioche et les églises d'Orient (512–18)*. Beirut.

Álvarez García, F. (1997) 'Tiempo, religión y política en el "Chronicon" de Joannis Biclarensis', *En la España Medieval* 20: 9–30.

Anderson, B. (2011) 'Leo III and the Anemodoulion', *Byzantinische Zeitschrift* 104: 41–54.

(2014) 'Public Clocks in Late Antique and Early Medieval Constantinople', *Jahrbuch der österreichischen Byzantinistik* 64: 23–32.

Anderson, B. R. (2006) *Imagined Communities Reflections on the Origins and Spread of Nationalism*. 2nd ed. London and New York.

Andrade, N. J. (2009) 'The Syriac Life of John of Tella and the Frontier Politeia', *Hugoye: Journal of Syriac Studies* 12: 199–234.

Arnaud, P. (2014) 'Mapping the Edges of the Earth: Approaches and Cartographical Problems', in *The Periphery of the Classical World in Ancient*

Geography and Cartography, ed. A. V. Podossinov. Colloquia Antiqua: Supplements to the Journal Ancient West and East 12. Leuven: 13–30.

Ashbrook Harvey, S. (1990) *Asceticism and Society in Crisis: John of Ephesus and the Lives of the Eastern Saints*. The Transformation of the Classical Heritage 18. Berkeley, CA.

Ashbrook Harvey, S. and Brakmann, H. (1998) 'Johannes von Ephesus', *Reallexikon für Antike und Christentum* 18: 553–64.

Bagnall, R. S., Cameron, Al., Schwartz, S. R. and Worp, K. A. (1987) *The Consuls of the Later Roman Empire*. Atlanta.

Barnes, T. D. (1981) *Constantine and Eusebius*. Cambridge, MA.

(2011) *Constantine: Dynasty, Religion and Power in the Later Roman Empire*. Chichester, UK, and Malden, MA.

Baumer, C. (2016) *The Church of the East: An Illustrated History of Assyrian Christianity*. 2nd ed. London.

Beck, E. (ed.) (1972) *Des Heiligen Ephraem des Syrers Hymnen auf Abraham Kidunaya und Julianos Saba*. 2 vols. Corpus Scriptorum Christianorum Orientalium 322–3, Scriptores Syri, 140–1. Louvain.

Bedjan, P. (ed.) (1893) *Histoire de Mar-Jabalaha: De trois autres patriarches, d'un prêtre et de deux laïques, nestoriens*. Paris.

Bell, P. N. (2009) *Three Political Voices from the Age of Justinian: Agapetus, Advice to the Emperor; Dialogue on Political Science; Paul the Silentiary, Description of Hagia Sophia*. Translated Texts for Historians 52. Liverpool, UK.

Benoist, S. (2016) 'The Emperor beyond the Frontiers: A Double-Mirror as a "Political Discourse"', in *Rome and the Worlds beyond Its Frontiers*, ed. D. Slootjes and M. Peachin. Leiden, The Netherlands: 45–64.

Berzon, T. S. (2016) *Classifying Christians: Ethnography, Heresiology, and the Limits of Knowledge in Late Antiquity*. Berkeley, CA.

Bitton-Ashkelony, B. (2004) '*Imitatio Mosis* and Pilgrimage in the *Life of Peter the Iberian*', in *Christian Gaza in Late Antiquity*, ed. B. Bitton-Ashkelony and A. Kofsky. Jerusalem Studies in Religion and Culture 3. Leiden, The Netherlands: 51–70.

(2005) *Encountering the Sacred: The Debate on Christian Pilgrimage in Late Antiquity*. Transformation of the Classical Heritage 38. Berkeley, CA.

(2010) 'From Sacred Travel to Monastic Career: The Evidence of Late Antique Syriac Hagiography', *Adamantius* 16: 353–70.

Blaudeau, P. (1996) 'Timothée Aelure et la direction ecclésiale de l'Empire post-chalcédonien', *Revue des Etudes byzantines* 54: 107–33.

(2006) *Alexandrie et Constantinople 451–491: de l'histoire à la géo-ecclésiologie*. Bibliothèque des Écoles françaises d'Athènes et de Rome 327. Rome.

(2012) *Le siège de Rome et l'Orient 448–536: étude géo-ecclésiologique*. Rome.

(2017) 'What Is Geo-ecclesiology: Defining Elements Applied to Late Antiquity', in *Late Antiquity in Contemporary Debate*, ed. R. Lizzi Testa. Newcastle: 156–64.

Bleckmann, B. and Stein, M. (2015) *Philostorgios Kirchengeschichte*. Kleine und fragmentarische Historiker der Spätantike E 7. 2 vols. Paderborn.

Blockley, R. C. (1981–2) *The Fragmentary Classicising Historians of the Later Roman Empire: Eunapius, Olympiodorus, Priscus and Malchus.* 2 vols. Liverpool, UK.

Bobertz, C. (1992) 'The Development of Episcopal Order', in *Eusebius, Christianity and Judaism*, ed. H. Attridge and G. Hata. Detroit: 183–211.

Booth, P. (2013) *Crisis of Empire: Doctrine and Dissent at the End of Late Antiquity.* Berkeley, CA.

(2017) 'Towards a Coptic Church: The Making of a Severan Episcopate', Millennium Jahrbuch 14: 151–90.

Borbone, G. (2000) *Storia di Mar Yahballaha e di Rabban Sauma: Un orientale in occidente ai tempi di Marco Polo.* Turin.

Borbone, G. and Alexandre, E. (2008) *Un ambassadeur du Khan Argun en Occident: Histoire de Mar Yahballaha III et de Rabban Sauma (1281–1317).* Peuples et cultures de l'Orient. Paris.

Börm, H. (2007) *Prokop und die Perser. Untersuchungen zu den römisch-sasanidischen Kontakten in der ausgehenden Spätantike.* Oriens et Occidens 16. Stuttgart.

(2014) 'Hydatius von Aquae Flaviae und die Einheit des Römischen Reiches im 5. Jahrhundert', in *Griechische Profanhistoriker des fünften nachchristlichen Jahrhunderts*, ed. B. Bleckmann and T. Stickler. Frankfurt: 195–214.

(2015) 'Procopius, His Predecessors, and the Genesis of the *Anecdota*', in *Antimonarchic Discourse in Antiquity*, ed. H. Börm. Stuttgart: 305–45.

Bosworth, C. E. (1992) 'Abdallah ibn Tahir', *Encyclopedia of Islam*, 2nd ed., http://referenceworks.brillonline.com/browse/encyclopaedia-of-islam-2

Bowersock, G. W. (1996) 'The Vanishing Paradigm of the Fall of Rome', *Bulletin of the American Academy of Arts and Sciences* 49.8: 29–43.

Brandes, W. (2002) *Finanzverwaltung in Krisenzeiten. Untersuchungen zur byzantinischen Administration im 6.–9. Jahrhundert.* Forschungen zur byzantinischen Rechtsgeschichte 25. Frankfurt.

Brandt, H. (2014) 'Zur historiographischen Tradition des Isaurers Candidus', in *Griechische Profanhistoriker des fünften nachchristlichen Jahrhunderts*, ed. B. Bleckmann and T. Stickler. Stuttgart: 163–73.

Brauer, R. W. (1995) *Boundaries and Frontiers in Medieval Muslim Geography.* Philadelphia.

Brock, S. P. (1969) 'Notes on Some Texts in the Mingana Collection', *Journal of Semitic Studies* 14: 205–26.

(1992) 'Eusebius and Syriac Christianity', in *Eusebius, Christianity and Judaism*, ed. H. Attridge and G. Hata. Leiden, The Netherlands: 212–34.

(2001) 'Syriac into Greek at Mar Saba: The Translation of St. Isaac the Syrian', in *The Sabaite Heritage in the Orthodox Church from the Fifth Century to the Present*, ed. J. Patrich. Orientalia Lovaniensia Analecta 98. Leuven: 201–8.

(2006) 'East Syrian Pilgrims to Jerusalem in the Early Ottoman Period', *ARAM* 18–19: 189–201.

Brock, S. P., Haim, G. and Kofsky, A. (2006–7) 'The Syriac Inscriptions at the Entrance to Holy Sepulchre, Jerusalem', *ARAM* 18–19: 415–38.

Brock, S. P., Butts, A. M., Kiraz, G. A. and van Rompay, L. (eds.) (2011) *The Gorgias Encyclopedic Dictionary of the Syriac Heritage*. Piscataway, NJ.

Brockelmann, C. (1895) *Lexicon Syriacum*. Berlin and Edinburgh.

Brodersen, K. (1995) *Terra cognita: Studien zur römischen Raumerfassung*. Spudasmata 59. Hildesheim.

Brodka, D. (2013) 'Die Wanderung der Hunnen, Vandalen, West- und Ostgoten – Prokopios von Kaisareia und seine Quellen', *Millennium* 10: 13–37.

Brooks, E. W. (1896) 'An Armenian Visitor to Jerusalem in the Seventh Century', *The English Historical Review* 11: 93–7.

 (1907) *Chronica minora III*. Corpus scriptorum christianorum Orientalium. Scriptores Syri 5–6. Leuven.

 (1929) 'The Patriarch Paul of Antioche and the Alexandrine Schism of 575', *Byzantinische Zeitschrift* 30: 468–75.

Brown, P. (2002) *Poverty and Leadership in the Later Roman Empire*. London.

Brummett, P. M. (ed.) (2009) *The 'Book' of Travels: Genre, Ethnology, and Pilgrimage, 1250–1700*. Leiden, The Netherlands.

Bruns, P. (2006) 'Kirchengeschichte als Hagiographie? Zur theologischen Konzeption des Johannes von Ephesus', *Studia Patristica* 42: 65–72.

Budge, E. A. W. (1928) *The Monks of Kûblâi Khân, Emperor of China, or, the History of the Life and Travels of Rabban Ṣâwmâ, Envoy and Plenipotentiary of the Mongol Khâns to the Kings of Europe, and Markôs – Who as Mâr Yahbh-Allâhâ III Became Patriarch of the Nestorian Church in Asia*. London.

Burgess, R. W. (1993) *The Chronicle of Hydatius and the Consularia Constantinopolitana*. Oxford Classical Monographs. Oxford.

 (1996) 'Hydatius and the Final Frontier: The Fall of the Roman Empire and the End of the World', in *Shifting Frontiers in Late Antiquity*, ed. R. Mathisen and H. Sivan. Aldershot, UK: 321–32.

Burgess, R. W. and Kulikowski, M. (2013) *Mosaics of Time: The Latin Chronicle Traditions from the First Century BC to the Sixth Century AD. Vol. I: A Historical Introduction to the Chronicle Genre from Its Origins to the High Middle Ages*. Studies in the Early Middle Ages 33. Turnhout.

Burn, A. R. (1955) 'Procopius and the Island of Ghosts', *English Historical Review* 70: 258–61.

Caetani, L. (1926) *Annali dell'Islam*, 10 vols. Milan.

Cain, A. (2010) 'Jerome's Epitaphium Paulae: Hagiography, Pilgrimage, and the Cult of Saint Paula', *Journal of Early Christian Studies* 18: 105–39.

 (2013) *Jerome's Epitaph on Paula: A Commentary on the Epitaphium Sanctae Paulae with an Introduction, Text, and Translation*. Oxford Early Christian Texts. Oxford.

Cameron, A. M. (1976) 'The Early Religious Policies of Justin II', *Studies in Church History* 13: 51–67 = (2001) *Continuity and Change in Sixth-Century Byzantium*. London.

 (1992) 'New Themes and Styles in Greek Literature: Seventh-Eighth Centuries', in *The Byzantine and Early Islamic Near East: Papers of the First Workshop on*

Late Antiquity and Early Islam. Studies in Late Antiquity and Early Islam 1, ed. A. M. Cameron and L. I. Conrad. Princeton, NJ: 81–105.

Cameron, Al. (2011) *The Last Pagans of Rome.* Oxford.

(2015) *Wandering Poets and Other Essays on Late Greek Literature and Philosophy.* Oxford.

Camplani, A. (2015) 'The Religious Identity of Alexandria in Some Ecclesiastical Histories of Late Antique Egypt', in *Historiographie tardo-antique et transmission des savoirs*, ed. P. Van Nuffelen and P. Blaudeau. Berlin: 85–120.

Canepa, M. P. (2009) *The Two Eyes of the Earth: Art and Ritual of Kingship between Rome and Sasanian Iran.* The Transformation of the Classical Heritage 45. Berkeley, CA.

Cardelle de Hartmann, C. (1994) *Philologische Studien zur Chronik des Hydatius von Chaves.* Palingenesia 47. Stuttgart.

(1999) 'The Textual Transmission of the Mozarabic Chronicle of 754', *Early Medieval Europe* 8: 13–29.

Carlson, D. (2017) 'Procopius's Old English'. *Byzantinische Zeitschrift* 110: 1–28.

Carolla, P. (2008) *Priscus Panita: Excerpta et fragmenta.* New York and Berlin.

Caseau, B., Cheynet, J.-C. and Déroche, V. (eds.) (2006) *Pèlerinages et lieux saints dans l'antiquité et le moyen âge: Mélanges offerts à Pierre Maraval.* Monographies 23. Paris.

Cassidy, V. H. de P. (1963) 'The Voyage of an Island', *Speculum* 38: 595–602.

Cassin, M., Debié, M. and Perrin, M.-Y. (2012) 'La question des éditions de l'Histoire ecclésiastique et le livre X', in *Eusèbe de Césarée. Histoire ecclésiastique. Commentaire, tome 1, Etudes d'introduction*, ed. S. Morlet and L. Perrone. Paris: 185–206.

Chabot, J.-B. (1899–1905) *La chronique de Michel le syrien, patriarche jacobite d'Antioche (1166–99).* Paris.

Chabot, J.-B. (ed.) (1896) '*Livre de la Chasteté*, composé par Jesusdenah, Évêque de Basra', *École Française de Rome: Mélanges d'archéologie et d'histoire* 16: 1–79, 225–91.

Chadwick, H. (1980) *The Role of the Christian Bishop in Ancient Society.* Eugene, OR.

Chin, C. M. and Schroeder, C. T. (eds.) (2017) *Melania: Early Christianity through the Life of One Family.* Christianity in Late Antiquity 2. Oakland, CA.

Christensen, A. S. (2002) *Cassiodorus, Jordanes and the History of the Goths: Studies in a Migration Myth.* Copenhagen.

Christophilopoulou, A. (1956) Ἐκλογή, ἀναγόρευσις καὶ στέψις τοῦ βυζαντινοῦ αὐτοκράτορος. Athens.

Chrysos, E. K. (1978) 'The Title Basileus in Early Byzantine International Relations', *Dumbarton Oaks Papers* 32: 29–75.

Clarke, K. (1999) *Between Geography and History: Hellenistic Constructions of the Roman World.* Oxford.

Coleman, S. and Eade, J. (eds.) (2004) *Reframing Pilgrimage: Cultures in Motion.* London.

Coleman, S. and Elsner, J. (1995) *Pilgrimage: Past and Present in the World Religions*. Cambridge, MA.

Collins, R. (2001) 'An Historical Commentary on Iohannis Biclarensis *Chronicon*', in *Victoris Tunnunensis Chronicon cum reliquiis ex Consularibus Caesaraugustanis et Iohannis Biclarensis Chronicon*, ed. C. Cardelle de Hartmann. Corpus Christianorum. Series latina 173A. Turnhout: 110–48.

(2004) *Visigothic Spain 409–711*. Oxford.

Constable, O. R. (2003) *Housing the Stranger in the Mediterranean World: Lodging, Trade, and Travel in Late Antiquity and the Middle Ages*. Cambridge.

Conterno, M. (2014) *La 'descrizione dei tempi' all'alba dell'espansione islamica: Un'indagine sulla storiografia greca, siriaca e araba fra VII e VIII secolo*. Berlin.

Coumert, M. (2007) *Origines des peuples. Les récits du Haut Moyen Age occidental (550–850)*. Collection des Etudes Augustiniennes. Série Moyen Age et Temps Modernes 42. Paris.

Croke, B. (1983) 'A.D. 476: The Manufacture of a Turning Point', *Chiron* 13: 81–119.

(1984) 'Marcellinus on Dara: A Fragment of His Lost "De temporum qualitatibus et positionibus locorum"', *Phoenix* 38: 77–88.

(1990a) 'City Chronicles of Late Antiquity', in *Reading the Past in Late Antiquity*, ed. C. Clarke et al. Sydney: 165–203.

(1990b) 'Malalas, the Man and His Work', in *Studies in John Malalas*, ed. E. Jeffreys. Sydney: 1–26.

(2001) *Count Marcellinus and His Chronicle*. Oxford.

(2005a) 'Dynasty and Ethnicity: Emperor Leo and the Eclipse of Aspar', *Chiron* 35: 147–203.

(2005b) 'Procopius' Secret History: Rethinking the Date', *Greek, Roman and Byzantine Studies* 45: 405–31.

(2010) 'Review of Treadgold, *Early Byzantine Historians*'. *English Historical Review* 125: 133–5.

Cunliffe, B. (2001) *The Extraordinary Voyage of Pytheas the Greek*. London.

Curta, F. (ed.) (2006) *Borders, Barriers, and Ethnogenesis: Frontiers in Late Antiquity and the Middle Ages*. Turnhout.

Dagron, G. (1968) 'L'empire romain d'orient au IVe siècle et les traditions politiques de l'hellénisme', *Travaux et mémoires* 3: 1–242.

(1971) 'Discours utopique et récit des origines. I: Une lecture de Cassiodore-Jordanes: les Goths de Scandza à Ravenne', *Annales: Economies, Sociétés, Civilisations* 26: 290–305.

(1974) *Naissance d'une capitale; Constantinople et ses institutions de 330 à 451*. Paris.

(1984) *Constantinople imaginaire: Études sur le recueil des 'Patria'*. Paris.

(1987) '"Ceux d'en face": Les peuples étrangers dans les traités militaires byzantins', *Travaux et Mémoires* 10: 207–32.

Davis, L. (1988) *The First Seven Oecumenical Councils (325–787): Their History and Theology*. Wilmington, DE.

Debié, M. (2004) 'Place et image d'Antioche chez les historiens syro-occidentaux', in *Antioche de Syrie: Histoire, images et traces de la ville antique*, ed. B. Cabouret, P.-L. Gatier and C. Saliou. Topoi Supplément 5. Lyon and Paris: 155–70.

(2006) 'Nisibe sauvé des eaux: Les sources de Théodoret et la place des versions syriaques', in *Pèlerinages et lieux saints dans l'antiquité et le moyen âge: Mélanges offerts à Pierre Maraval*. Monographies 23, ed. B. Caseau, J.-C. Cheynet and V. Déroche. Paris: 135–51.

(2009) 'L'héritage de l'historiographie grecque', in *L'historiographie syriaque*. ed. M. Debié. Etudes syriaques. Paris: 11–31.

(2010) 'Writing "History" as Histories: The Biographical Dimension of East Syrian Historiography', in *Writing 'True Stories': Historians and Hagiographers in the Late Antique and Medieval Near East*, ed. A. Papaconstantinou, H. Kennedy and M. Debié. Leiden, The Netherlands: 43–75.

(2015) *L'écriture de l'histoire en Syriaque: transmissions interculturelles et constructions identitaires entre hellénisme et islam, avec des répertoires des textes historiographiques en annexe*. Late Antique History and Religion 12. Louvain.

de Blois, F. (1990) *Burzōy's Voyage to India and the Origin of the Book of Kalīlah Wa Dimnah*. London.

Defaux, O. (2014) 'Les textes géographiques en langue syriaque', in *Les sciences syriaques*, ed. É. Villey. Études syriaques 11. Paris: 107–47.

de Jong, I. J. F. (ed.) (2012) *Space in Ancient Greek Literature: Studies in Ancient Greek Narrative*. Mnemosyne Supplements 339. Leiden, The Netherlands.

de Ligt, L. and Tacoma, L. E. (eds.) (2016) *Migration and Mobility in the Early Roman Empire*. Studies in Global Social History 23. Leiden, The Netherlands.

Demacopoulos, G. (2013) *The Invention of Peter: Apostolic Discourse and Papal Authority in Late Antiquity*. Philadelphia.

Destephen, S. (2008) 'Iôannès 43', in *Prosopographie Chrétienne du Bas-Empire 3: Diocèse d'Asie (325–641)*. Paris: 494–519.

DeVore, D. (2013) 'Genre and Eusebius' Ecclesiastical History: Towards a Focused Debate', in *Eusebius of Caesarea: Tradition and Innovation*, ed. S. Johnson and J. Schott. Washington, DC: 19–45.

Dietz, M. (2005) *Wandering Monks, Virgins, and Pilgrims: Ascetic Travel in the Mediterranean World, A.D. 300–800*. University Park, PA.

Dignas, B. and Winter, E. (2007) *Rome and Persia in Late Antiquity: Neighbours and Rivals*. Cambridge.

Dillemann, L. and Janvier, Y. (1997) *La cosmographie du Ravennate*. Collection Latomus 235. Brussels.

Donner, H. (1971) 'Die Palästinabeschreibung des Epiphanius Monachus Hagiopolita', *Zeitschrift des deutschen Palästina-Vereins* 87: 42–91.

Draguet, R. (1924) *Julien d'Halicarnasse et sa controverse avec Sévère d'Antioche sur l'incorruptibilité du corps du Christ: étude d'histoire littéraire et doctrinale suivie des fragments dogmatiques de Julien*. Louvain.

Eade, J. and Sallnow, M. J. (eds.) (1991) *Contesting the Sacred: The Anthropology of Christian Pilgrimage*. London.

Edwell, P. and Fisher, G., et al. (2015) 'Arabs in the Conflict between Rome and Persia, AD 491–630', in *Arabs and Empires before Islam*, ed. G. Fisher. Oxford: 214–75.

Eger, A. A. (2015) *The Islamic-Byzantine Frontier: Interaction and Exchange among Muslim and Christian Communities*. London.

Elad, A. (1995) *Medieval Jerusalem and Islamic Worship: Holy Places, Ceremonies, Pilgrimage*. Leiden, The Netherlands.

Ellis, L. and Kidner, F. (eds.) (2004) *Travel, Communication and Geography in Late Antiquity: Sacred and Profane*. Aldershot, UK.

Elsner, J. (2000) 'The Itinerarium Burdigalense: Politics and Salvation in the Geography of Constantine's Empire', *Journal of Roman Studies* 90: 181–95.

Elsner, J. and Rutherford, I. (eds.) (2005) *Pilgrimage in Graeco-Roman and Early Christian Antiquity: Seeing the Gods*. Oxford.

Engelhardt, I. (1974) *Mission und Politik in Byzanz. Ein Beitrag zur Strukturanalyse byzantinischer Mission zur Zeit Justins und Justinians*. Munich.

Evans, J. A. S. (1996) 'The Dates of Procopius' Works: A Recapitulation of the Evidence', *Greek, Roman and Byzantine Studies* 37: 301–13.

Featherstone, M. (2012) 'Theophanes Continuatus: A History for the Palace', in *La face cachée de la littérature byzantine: Le texte en tant que message immédiat*, ed. P. Odorico. Paris: 123–36.

Feld, K. (2012) *Barbarische Bürger: Die Isaurier und das Römische Reich*. Berlin.

Ferreiro, A. (1986) 'The Omission of St Martin of Braga in John of Biclaro's Chronica and the Third Council of Toledo', in *Los visigodos. Historia y civilización*. Antigüedad y Cristianismo 3. Murcia, Spain: 145–50.

(1987) 'The Sueves in the *Chronica* of John of Biclaro', *Latomus* 46: 201–3.

Fiey, J.-M. (1958) 'Identification of Qasr Serej', *Sumer* 14: 125–7.

(1963) 'Tagrit. Esquisse de l'histoire chrétienne', *L'Orient Syrien* 8: 289–342.

(1968) *Assyrie chrétienne: contribution à l'étude de l'histoire et de la géographie ecclésiastiques et monastiques du nord de l'Iraq*. Beirut.

(1969) 'Le pèlerinage des Nestoriens et Jacobites à Jérusalem', *Cahiers de civilisation médiévale, Xe–XIIe siècles* 12: 113–26.

(1973) 'Chrétientés syriaques du Horasan et du Segestan', *Le Muséon* 86: 75–104.

(1993) *Pour un Oriens Christianus Novus: répertoire des diocèses syriaques orientaux et occidentaux*. Stuttgart.

Fisher, G. (2011) *Between Empire: Arabs, Romans, and Sasanians in Late Antiquity*. Oxford.

(ed.) (2015) *Arabs and Empires before Islam*. Oxford.

Fisher, G. and Wood, P., et al. (2015) 'Arabs and Christianity', in *Arabs and Empires before Islam*, ed. G. Fisher. Oxford: 276–372.

Flusin, B. (2010) 'Christianiser, rechristianiser: Jean d'Éphèse et les missions', in *Le problème de la christianisation du monde antique*, ed. H. Inglebert, S. Destephen and B. Dumézil. Paris: 293–306.

Focanti, L. (2018a) 'Looking for an Identity: The Patria and the Greek Cities in Late Antique Roman Empire', *Revue belge de Philologie et d'Histoire* 96: n.a.

(2018b) 'The Fragments of Late Antique Patria'. PhD Diss. Ghent University and University of Groningen.

Formisano, M. (2007) 'Towards an Aesthetic Paradigm of Late Antiquity', *Antiquité Tardive* 15: 277–84.

Fotheringham, J. K. (1905) *The Bodleian Manuscript of Jerome's Version of the Chronicle of Eusebius*. Oxford.

Fowden, E. K. (1999) *The Barbarian Plain: Saint Sergius between Rome and Iran*. Berkeley, CA.

Fowden, G. (1993) *Empire to Commonwealth: Consequences of Monotheism in Late Antiquity*. Princeton, NJ.

(2014) *Before and after Muḥammad*. Princeton, NJ.

Frank, G. (2000) *The Memory of the Eyes: Pilgrims to Living Saints in Christian Late Antiquity*. Transformation of the Classical Heritage 30. Berkeley, CA.

Frankfurter, D. (1998) *Pilgrimage and Holy Space in Late Antique Egypt*. Religions in the Graeco-Roman World 134. Leiden, The Netherlands.

Frankopan, P. (2015) *The Silk Roads: A New History of the World*. London.

Frend, W. H. C. (1972) *The Rise of the Monophysite Movement: Chapters in the History of the Church in the Fifth and Sixth Centuries*. Cambridge.

Friedmann, Y. (2004) *Tolerance and Coercion: Interfaith Relations in the Muslim Tradition*. Cambridge and New York.

Fuller, A. (2009) 'Rebel with a Cause? From Traitor Prince to Exemplary Martyr: Sor Juana Inés de la Cruz's Representation of San Hermenegildo', *European Review of History – Revue européenne d'histoire* 16: 893–910.

Furlani, G. (1927) 'Andronikos über die Bewohner der Grenzen der Erde in syrischer Sprache', *Zeitschrift für Semitistik und verwandte Gebiete* 5: 238–49.

Fürst, A. (2007) 'Bis ans Ende der Erde. Der geographische Horizont des antiken Christentums', in *Räume und Grenzen: topologische Konzepte in den antiken Kulturen des östlichen Mittelmeerraums*, ed. R. Albertz, A. I. Blöbaum and P. Funke. Munich: 267–91.

Galadza, D. (2018) *Liturgy and Byzantinization in Jerusalem*. Oxford Early Christian Studies. Oxford.

Gardiner, L. (2012) 'The Truth Is Bitter: Socrates Scholasticus and the Writing of the History of the Roman Empire'. PhD Diss. Cambridge University.

Garitte, G. (1952) *La narratio de rebus Armeniae*. Corpus Scriptorum Christianorum Orientaliam 132. Subsidia 4. Louvain.

Garsoïan, N. G. (1981) 'The Locus of the Death of Kings: Iranian Armenia – the Inverted Image', in The Armenian Image in History and Literature, ed. R. G. Hovanissian. Malibu, CA: 27–64; reprinted in Garsoïan 1985, no. XI.

(1983) 'Nersēs le grand, Basile de Césarée et Eustathe de Sébaste', *Revue des études arméniennes* 17: 145–69; reprinted in Garsoïan 1985, no. VII.

(1985) *Armenia between Byzantium and the Sasanians*. London.

(1988) 'Some Preliminary Precisions on the Separation of the Armenian And Imperial Churches: I. The Presence of "Armenian" Bishops at the First Five Œcumenical Councils', in Kathēgētria: Essays presented to Joan Hussey on her Eightieth Birthday. Camberley, UK: 249–85, reprinted in Garsoïan 1999b, no. III.

(1989) *The Epic Histories (Buzandaran Patmutʻiwnkʻ).* Harvard Armenian Texts and Studies 8. Cambridge, MA.

(1999a) *L'Église arménienne et le grand schisme d'Orient.* Corpus Scriptorum Christianorum Orientalium 574. Subsidia 100. Louvain.

(1999b) *Church and Culture in Early Medieval Armenia.* Aldershot, UK.

(2009) 'Armenian Sources on Sasanian Administration', in *Res Orientales XVIII Sources pour l'historie et la géographie du monde iranien (224–710)* ed. R. Gyselen. Paris: 91–114.

Gautier Dalché, P. (2014) 'L'enseignement de la géographie dans l'Antiquité Tardive', *Klio* 96: 144–82.

Gero, S. (1981) *Barṣauma of Nisibis and Persian Christianity in the Fifth Century.* Corpus Scriptorum Christianorum Orientalium 426. Subsidia 63. Louvain.

Geus, K. and Rathmann, M. (eds.) (2013) *Vermessung der Oikumene.* Topoi. Berlin Studies of the Ancient World 14. Berlin.

Geyer, P., et al. (eds.) (1965) *Itineraria et Alia Geographica.* 2 vols. Corpus Christianorum. Series Latina 175–6. Turnhout.

Ghosh, S. (2016) *Writing the Barbarian Past: Studies in Early Medieval Historical Narrative.* Brill's Series on the Early Middle Ages 24. Leiden, The Netherlands.

Gignoux, P. (1991) *Les quatre inscriptions du mage Kirdīr.* Paris.

Gillett, A. (2003) *Envoys and Political Communication in the Late Antique West, 411–533.* Cambridge Studies in Medieval Life and Thought, 4th ser. 55. Cambridge.

Goffart, W. (1971) 'Zosimus, the First Historian of Rome's Fall', *American Historical Review* 76: 412–41.

(1988) *The Narrators of Barbarian History (A.D. 550–800): Jordanes, Gregory of Tours, Bede and Paul the Deacon.* Princeton, NJ.

Gorce, D. (ed.) (1962) *Vie de Sainte Mélanie.* Source chrétiennes 90. Paris.

Greatrex, G. (1994) 'The Dates of Procopius' Works', *Byzantine and Modern Greek Studies* 18: 101–14.

(2000) 'Procopius the Outsider?', in *Strangers to Themselves: The Byzantine Outsider,* ed. D. C. Smythe. Burlington, VT: 15–228.

(2003): 'Recent Work on Procopius and the Composition of Wars VIII', *Byzantine and Modern Greek Studies* 27: 45–67.

(2006) 'Pseudo-Zachariah of Mytilene: The Composition and Nature of His Work', *Journal of the Canadian Society of Syriac Studies* 6: 39–52.

(2009) 'Le Pseudo-Zacharie de Mytilène et l'historiograhie syriaque au sixième siècle', in *L'historiographie syriaque.* ed. M. Debié. Etudes syriaques 6. Paris: 33–55.

(2014) 'Perceptions of Procopius in Recent Scholarship', *Histos* 8: 76–121.

(2016) 'Réflexions sur la date de composition des Guerres perses de Procope', in *Libera curiositas. Mélanges d'histoire romaine et d'Antiquité tardive offerts à*

Jean-Michel Carrié, ed. C. Freu, S. Janniard and A. Ripoll. Bibliothèque de l'antiquité tardive 31. Turnhout: 363–6.

Greatrex, G., et al. (2011) 'Introduction', in *The Chronicle of Pseudo-Zachariah Rhetor: Church and War in Late Antiquity*, ed. G. Greatrex et al. Translated Texts for Historians 55. Liverpool, UK: 1–74.

Greenwood, T. W. (2002) 'Sasanian Echoes and Apocalyptic Expectations: A Re-evaluation of the Armenian History Attributed to Sebeos', *Le Muséon* 115: 323–97.

(2004) 'A Corpus of Early Medieval Armenian Inscriptions', *Dumbarton Oaks Papers* 58: 27–91.

(2008) 'New Light from the East: Chronography and Ecclesiastical History through a Late Seventh-Century Armenian Source', *Journal of Early Christian Studies* 16.2: 197–254.

(2015a) 'Oversight, Influence and Mesopotamian Connections to Armenia across the Sasanian and Early Islamic Periods', in *Mesopotamia in the Ancient World Impact, Continuities, Parallels. Proceedings of the Seventh Symposium of the Melammu Project Held in Obergurgl, Austria, November 4–8, 2013*, ed. R. Rollinger and E. van Dongen. Münster: 509–22.

(2015b) 'A Corpus of Early Medieval Armenian Silver', *Dumbarton Oaks Papers* 69: 115–46.

(2017) 'A Contested Jurisdiction: Armenia in Late Antiquity', in *Sasanian Persia: Between Rome and the Steppes of Eurasia*, ed. E. W. Sauer. Edinburgh: 199–220.

Gribomont, J. (1974) 'Documents sur l'origine de l'église maronite', *Parole de l'Orient* 5: 95–132.

Grig, L. and Kelly, G. (eds.) (2012) *Two Romes: Rome and Constantinople in Late Antiquity*. Oxford.

Griffith, S. (1982) 'Eutychius of Alexandria on the Emperor Theophilus and Iconoclasm in Byzantium: A Tenth Century Moment in Christian Apologetics in Arabic', *Byzantion* 52: 154–90.

(1985) 'The Gospel in Arabic: An Inquiry into Its Appearance in the First Abbasid Century', *Oriens Christianus* 69: 126–67.

(1991) 'The Apologetic Treatise of Nonnus of Nisibis', *ARAM* 3: 115–38.

(1993) 'Muslims and Church Councils: The Apology of Theodore abu Qurrah', *Studia Patristica* 28: 270–99.

(1994) 'Julian Saba, "Father of the Monks" of Syria', *Journal of Early Christian Studies* 2: 185–216.

(2001) 'The Life of Theodore of Edessa: History, Hagiography and Religious Apologetics in Mar Saba Monastery in Early Abbasid Times', in *The Sabaite Heritage in the Orthodox Church from the Fifth Century to the Present*, ed. J. Patrich. Leuven: 147–70.

(2004) 'Apologetics and Historiography in the Annals of Eutychius of Alexandria: Christian Self-Definition in the World of Islam', in *Studies on the Christian Arabic Heritage*, ed. R. Ebied and H. Teule. Leiden, The Netherlands: 65–90.

(2008) 'John of Damascus and the Church in Syria in the Umayyad Era: The Intellectual and Cultural Milieu of Orthodox Christians in the World of Islam', *Hugoye* 11: 207–37.

Grillmeier, A. and Hainthaler, T. (1986–2002) *Christus im Glauben der Kirche* II. 4 vols. Freiburg = (1987–2013) *Christ in Christian Tradition. II: From the Council of Chalcedon (451) to Gregory the Great (590–604).* 4 vols. Louisville, KY.

Günther, L.-M. (2007) 'Raumwahrnehmung in der spätantiken Hagiographie und Historiographie', in *Wahrnehmung and Erfahrung geographischer Räume in der Antike*, ed. M. Rathmann. Mainz: 231–41.

Gyselen, R. (1989) *Res Orientales. I La géographie administrative de l'empire sassanide. Les témoignages sigillographiques.* Paris.

(2002) *Nouveaux matériaux pour la géographie historique de l'empire sassanide: Sceaux administratifs de la collection Ahmad Saeedi.* Studia Iranica Cahier 24. Paris.

Hage, W. (1964) *Die syrisch-jakobitische Kirche in frühislamischer Zeit nach orientalischen Quellen.* Wiesbaden.

Hainthaler, T. (1990) 'Die Ausbildung zweier Hierarchien' in *Jesus der Christus im Glauben der Kirche* II 4, ed. A. Grillmeier. Freiburg: 60–90.

Haldén, P. (2012) 'From Empire to Commonwealth(s): Orders in Europe 1300–1800', in *Universal Empire: A Comparative Approach to Imperial Culture and Representation in Eurasian History*, ed. P. Bang and D. Kołodziejczyk. Cambridge: 280–303.

Haldon, J. (2007) 'Citizens of Ancient Lineage . . . '? The Role and Significance of Syrians in the Byzantine Elite in the Seventh and Eighth Centuries', in *Syriac Polemics: Studies in Honour of Gerrit Jan Reinink*, ed. W. Van Bekkum, J.-W. Drijvers and A. Klugkist. Leuven: 91–102.

(2016) *The Empire That Would Not Die: The Paradox of East Roman Survival, 640–740.* Cambridge, MA.

Hänger, C. (2001) *Die Welt im Kopf. Raumbilder und Strategie im römischen Kaiserreich.* Göttingen.

Harich-Schwarzbauer, H. (2013) 'Die "Mauern" Roms in Claudians De bello Gildonico und de bello Getico – Diskurse der Angst in den Jahren 398–402', in *Der Fall Roms 410 und die Wiederauferstehungen der ewigen Stadt*, ed. H. Harich-Schwarzbauer and K. Pollmann. Berlin: 37–52.

Harrak, A. (1999) *The Chronicle of Zuqnīn.* Medieval Sources in Translation 36. Toronto.

(2009) 'La victoire arabo-musulmane selon le chroniqueur de Zuqnin (VIIIe siècle)', in *L'historiographie syriaque.* ed. M. Debié. Etudes syriaques 6. Paris: 89–105.

Hartmann, U. (2014) '" . . . und die Pronoia hat die Menschheit noch nicht verlassen." Die Konstruktion der Geistesgeschichte als pagane Gegenwelt in Eunaps Philosophenviten', in *Griechische Profanhistoriker des fünften nachchristlichen Jahrhunderts*, ed. B. Bleckmann and T. Stickler. Stuttgart: 51–84.

Hengel, M. (1983) 'Der Historiker Lukas und die Geographie Palästinas in der Apostelgeschichte', *Zeitschrift des Deutschen Palästina-Vereins* 99: 147–83.

Hermann, T. (1923) 'Bemerkungen zu den Regeln des Mar Abraham und Mar Dadischo vom Berge Isla', *Zeitschrift für die neutestamentliche Wissenschaft* 22: 286–99.

(1928) 'Patriarch Paul von Antiochia und das alexandrinische Schisma vom Jahre 575', *Zeitschrift für die neutestamentliche Wissenschaft* 27: 263–304.

Herrin, J. (2013) *Margins and Metropolis: Authority across the Byzantine Empire.* Princeton, NJ.

Hewsen, R. H. (1992) *The Geography of Ananias of Širak Ašxarhac'oyc': The Long and Short Recensions.* Beihefte zum Tübinger Atlas des Vorderen Orients Reihe B 77. Wiesbaden.

(1997) 'An Ecclesiastical Analysis of the Naxarar System: A Re-examination of Adontz's Chapter XII', in *From Byzantium to Iran. Armenian Studies in Honour of Nina G. Garsoïan*, ed. J.-P. Mahé and R. W. Thomson. Atlanta: 97–149.

Hezser, C. (2011) *Jewish Travel in Antiquity.* Texte und Studien zum antiken Judentum 144. Tübingen.

Hilkens, A. (2015) 'Andronicus et son influence sur la présentation de l'histoire postdiluvienne et pré-Abrahamique de la Chronique anonyme jusqu'à l'année 1234', in *Historiographie tardo-antique et transmission des savoirs*, ed. P. Blaudeau and P. Van Nuffelen. Berlin: 55–81.

(2018) *The Anonymous Syriac Chronicle of 1234 and Its Sources.* Orientalia Lovaniensia Analecta 272. Bibliothèque de Byzantion 18. Leuven.

Hillgarth, J. N. (1966) 'Coins and Chronicles: Propaganda in Sixth-Century Spain and the Byzantine Background', *Historia* 15: 483–508.

Hillner, J. (ed.) (2016) *Clerical Exile in Late Antiquity.* Early Christianity in the Context of Antiquity 17. New York.

Honigmann, E. (1939) 'L'histoire ecclésiastique de Jean d'Ephèse', *Byzantion* 14: 15–625.

(1954) *Le couvent de Barsauma et le patriarcat jacobite d'Antioche et de Syrie.* Paris.

Horn, C. B. (2004) 'Weaving the Pilgrim's Crown: John Rufus's View of Peter the Iberian's Journeys in Late Antique Palestine', in *Journal of Eastern Christian Studies* 56: 171–90.

(2006) *Asceticism and Christological Controversy in Fifth-Century Palestine: The Career of Peter the Iberian.* Oxford Early Christian Studies. Oxford.

Horton, H. M. (2012) *Traversing the Frontier: The Man'Yoshu Account of a Japanese Mission to Silla in 736–737.* Harvard East Asian Monographs 330. Cambridge, MA.

Howard-Johnston, J. (2010) *Witness to a World Crisis: Historians and Histories of the Middle East in the Seventh Century.* Oxford.

Humfress, C. (2007) *Orthodoxy and the Courts in Late Antiquity.* Oxford.

Humphreys, M. (2014) *Law, Power and Imperial Ideology in the Iconoclast Era.* Oxford.

Humphries, M. (2007) 'A New Created World: Classical Geographical Texts and Christian Contexts in Late Antiquity', in *Texts and Culture in Late Antiquity: Inheritance, Authority and Change*, ed. J. H. D. Scourfield. Swansea: 33–67.

(2008) 'Rufinus's Eusebius: Translation, Continuation, and Edition in the Latin *Ecclesiastical History*', *Journal of Early Christian Studies* 16: 143–64.

(2017) 'Late Antiquity and World History: Challenging Conventional Narratives and Analyses', *Studies in Late Antiquity* 1: 8–37.

Hunt, E. D. (1982) *Holy Land Pilgrimage in the Later Roman Empire, AD 312–460*. Oxford.

Huyse, P. (1999) *Die dreisprachige Inschrift Šābuhrs I. an der Ka'ba-i Zardušt (ŠKZ)*. 2 vols. London.

Ineeme, K. (2016) 'Dayr al-Suryan: New discoveries', in *Claremont Coptic Encyclopedia*, www.academia.edu/21718087/Dayr_al-Suryan_New_Discoveries

Ineeme, K. and Van Rompay, L. (1998) 'La présence des Syriens dans le Wadi al-Natrun (Égypte). À propos des découvertes récentes de peintures et de textes muraux dans l'Église de la Vierge du Couvent des Syriens', *Parole de l'Orient* 23: 167–206.

Inglebert, H. (2001) *Interpretatio christiana: les mutations des savoirs (cosmographie, géographie, éthnographie, histoire) dans l'antiquité chrétienne (30–630 après J.-C.)*. Collection des études augustiniennes Sér. Antiquité 166. Paris.

(2014) *Le monde, l'histoire: essai sur les histoires universelles*. Paris.

(2015) 'Les discours de l'unité romaine au quatrième siècle', in *East and West in the Roman Empire of the Fourth Century: An End to Unity?*, ed. R. Dijkstra, S. van Poppel and D. Slootjes. Leiden, The Netherlands: 9–25.

Isele, B. (2010) *Kampf um Kirchen: Religiöse Gewalt, heiliger Raum und christliche Topographie in Alexandria und Konstantinopel (4. Jh.)*. Münster.

Jacobs, A. S. (2004) *Remains of the Jews: The Holy Land and Christian Empire in Late Antiquity*. Divinations. Stanford, CA.

(2017) 'The Lost Generation', in *Melania: Early Christianity through the Life of One Family*, ed. C. M. Chin and C. T. Schroeder. Oakland, CA: 207–21.

Jacobs, M. (2014) *Reorienting the East: Jewish Travelers to the Medieval Muslim World*. Jewish Culture and Contexts. Philadelphia.

Janiszewski, P. (2006) *The Missing Link: Greek Pagan Historiography in the Second Half of the Third Century and in the Fourth Century AD*. Warsaw.

Janković, M. A. (ed.) (2014) *The Edges of the Roman World*. New Castle upon Tyne.

Jankowiak, M. (2012) 'Travelling across Borders: A Church Historian's Perspective on Contacts between Byzantium and Syria in the Second Half of the Seventh Century', in *Arab-Byzantine Coins and History*, ed. A. Goodwin. Washington, DC: 13–25.

(2013) 'The Invention of Dyotheletism', *Studia Patristica* 63: 335–42.

Jeffreys, E., et al. (1986) *The Chronicle of John Malalas*. Melbourne.

Johnson, A. P. (2006) *Ethnicity and Argument in Eusebius' Praeparatio Evangelica*. Oxford.

Johnson, S. F. (ed.) (2006) *Greek Literature in Late Antiquity: Dynamism, Didacticism, Classicism.* Aldershot, UK.

(2011) 'Apostolic Geography', *Dumbarton Oaks Papers* 64: 5–25.

(2012) 'Travel, Cartography, and Cosmology', in *The Oxford Handbook of Late Antiquity*, ed. S. F. Johnson. Oxford: 562–94.

(2015) 'The Social Presence of Greek in Eastern Christianity, 200–1200 CE', in *Languages and Cultures of Eastern* Christianity: *Greek*, ed. S. F. Johnson. Farnham, UK: 1–122.

(2016a) *Literary Territories: Cartographical Thinking in Late Antiquity.* Oxford and New York.

(2016b) '"The Stone the Builders Rejected": Liturgical and Exegetical Irrelevancies in the Piacenza Pilgrim', *Dumbarton Oaks Papers* 70: 43–70.

Jullien, F. (2006) 'Rabban-Šāpūr, un monastère au rayonnement exceptionnel: La réforme d'Abraham de Kaškar dans le Bēth-Huzāyē', *Orientalia Christiana Periodica* 72: 333–48.

(2008a) 'Aux sources du monachisme oriental: Abraham de Kashkar et le développement de la légende de Mar Awgin', *Revue de l'histoire des religions* 225: 37–52.

(2008b) *Le monachisme en Perse: la réforme d'Abraham le Grand, père des moines de l'Orient.* Corpus scriptorum Christianorum Orientalium 622. Subsidia 121. Leuven.

Kaegi, W. (1968) *Byzantium and the Decline of Rome.* Princeton, NJ.

Kaldellis, A. (2003) 'The Religion of Ioannes Lydos', *Phoenix* 57: 300–16.

(2005a) 'Republican Theory and Political Dissidence in Ioannes Lydos', *Byzantine and Modern Greek Studies* 29: 1–16.

(2005b) 'The Works and Days of Hesychios the Illoustrios of Miletos', *Greek, Roman, and Byzantine Studies* 45: 381–403.

(2007) *Hellenism in Byzantium: The Transformations of Greek Identity and the Reception of the Classical Tradition.* Cambridge.

(2009) 'The Date and Structure of Prokopios' *Secret History* and His Projected Work on Church History', *Greek, Roman, and Byzantine Studies* 49: 585–616.

(2010) 'The Corpus of Byzantine Historiography: An Interpretive Essay', in *The Byzantine World*, ed. P. Stephenson. London: 211–22.

(2013) *Ethnography after Antiquity: Foreign Lands and Peoples in Byzantine Literature.* Philadelphia.

(2015a) *Byzantine Readings of Ancient Historians.* London and New York.

(2015b) *The Byzantine Republic: People and Power in New Rome.* Cambridge, MA.

Kelly, C. (2009) *Attila the Hun: Barbarian Terror and the Fall of the Roman Empire.* London.

(2013) *Theodosius II: Rethinking the Roman Empire in Late Antiquity.* Cambridge.

Kelly, G. (2003) 'The New Rome and the Old: Ammianus Marcellinus' Silences on Constantinople', *Classical Quarterly* 53: 588–607.

(2008) *Ammianus Marcellinus: The Allusive Historian.* Cambridge.

(2012) 'Claudian and Constantinople', in *Two Romes: Rome and Constantinople in Late Antiquity*, ed. G. Kelly and L. Grig. Oxford: 241–64.

Key Fowden, E. (1999) *The Barbarian Plain: Saint between Rome and Iran.* Berkeley, CA.

Kofsky, A. (1997) 'Peter the Iberian: Pilgrimage, Monasticism and Ecclesiastical Politics in Byzantine Palestine', *Liber Annuus* 47: 209–22.

König, J. and Woolf, G. (eds.) 2013. *Encyclopaedism from Antiquity to the Renaissance.* New York.

Krallis, D. (2014) 'Greek Glory, Constantinian Legend: Praxagoras' Athenian Agenda in Zosimos' *New History*?', *Journal of Late Antiquity* 7: 110–30.

Kruse, M. (forthcoming) *The Politics of Roman Memory: From the Fall of Rome to the Age of Justinian.* Philadelphia.

Kulikowski, M. (2004) *Late Roman Spain and Its Cities.* Baltimore.

Külzer, A. (1994) *Peregrinatio graeca in terram sanctam: Studien zu Pilgerführern und Reisebeschreibungen über Syrien, Palästina und den Sinai aus byzantinischer und metabyzantinischer Zeit.* Studien und Texte zur Byzantinistik 2. Frankfurt.

Lançon, B. (2004) 'Chronique et hagiographie. Les traces de l'émergence des saints dans les chroniques latines des IV-VI siècles', in *Saint Jérôme, Chronique*, ed. B. Jeanjean and B. Lançon. Rennes: 195–206.

Lane Fox, R. (1997) 'The Itinerary of Alexander: Constantius to Julian', *Classical Quarterly* 47: 239–52.

Lang, D. M. (1976) *Lives and Legends of the Georgian Saints.* 2nd ed. London.

Laurence, P. (ed.) (2002) *La vie latine de Sainte Mélanie.* Jerusalem.

Lee, A. D. (1993) *Information and Frontiers: Roman Foreign Relations in Late Antiquity.* Cambridge.

(2007) 'Episcopal Power and Perils in the Late Sixth century: The Case of Gregory of Antioch', in *Wolf Liebeschuetz Reflected: Essays by Colleagues, Friends and Pupils*, ed. J. Drinkwater and B. Salway. London: 99–106.

Lenski, N. (2002) *Failure of Empire: Valens and the Roman State in the Fourth Century A.D.* Berkeley, CA.

(2014) 'Constantine and the Tyche of Constantinople', in *Contested Monarchy: Integrating the Roman Empire in the Fourth Century AD*, ed. J. Wienand. Oxford: 330–52.

Leppin, H. (1996) *Von Constantin dem Großen zu Theodosius II.: Das christliche Kaisertum bei den Kirchenhistorikern Socrates, Sozomenus und Theodoret.* Hypomnemata 110. Göttingen.

(2003) 'The Church Historians I. Socrates, Sozomenus, and Theodoretus', in *Greek and Roman Historiography: Fourth to Sixth Century*, ed. G. Marasco. Leiden, The Netherlands and Boston: 219–54.

(2009) 'Theodoret und Evagrius Scholasticus: Kirchenhistoriker aus Syrien zwischen regionaler und imperialer Tradition', in *Jenseits der Grenzen. Beiträge zur spätantiken und frühmittelalterlichen Geschichtsschreibung*, ed. A. Goltz, H. Leppin and H. Schlange-Schöningen. Millennium-Studies 25. Berlin: 153–68.

(2011) *Justinian: Das christliche Experiment*. Stuttgart.

(2012) 'Roman Identity in a Border Region: Evagrius and the Defence of the Roman Empire', in *Visions of Community in the Post-Roman World: The West, Byzantium and the Islamic World, 300–1100*, ed. W. Pohl et al. London: 241–58.

(2017) 'Skeptische Anmerkungen zur Mission des Johannes von Ephesos in Kleinasien', in *Die Christianisierung Kleinasiens* (Asia Minor Studien 87), ed. W. Ameling and K. Zimmermann. Bonn: 49–59.

Leyerle, B. (1996) 'Landscape as Cartography in Early Christian Pilgrimage Narratives', *Journal of the American Academy of Religion* 64: 119–43.

Liddel, P. P. and Fear, A. (eds.) (2010) *Historiae Mundi: Studies in Universal History*. London.

Liebeschuetz, J. H. W. G. (1990) *Barbarians and Bishops: Army, Church, and State in the Age of Arcadius and Chrysostom*. Oxford.

(2015) 'Arab Tribesmen and Desert Frontiers in Late Antiquity', *Journal of Late Antiquity* 8: 62–96.

Limor, O. (2006) 'Holy Journey: Pilgrimage and Christian Sacred Landscape', in *Christians and Christianity in the Holy Land: From the Origins to the Latin Kingdoms*, ed. O. Limor and G. Stroumsa. Cultural Encounters in Late Antiquity and the Middle Ages 5. Turnhout: 321–53.

Lounghis, T. (1980) *Les ambassades byzantines en Occident, depuis la fondation des états barbares jusqu'aux Croisades (407–1096)*. Athens.

Lozovsky, N. (2000) *The Earth Is Our Book: Geographical Knowledge in the Latin West Ca. 400–1000*. Recentiores. Ann Arbor, MI.

(2006) 'Roman Geography and Ethnography in the Carolingian Empire', *Speculum* 81: 325–64.

Maas, M. (1992) *John Lydus and the Roman Past: Antiquarianism and Politics in the Age of Justinian*. London.

(2003) '"Delivered from Their Ancient Customs": Christianity and the Question of Cultural Change in Early Byzantine Ethnography', in *Conversion in Late Antiquity and the Early Middle Ages*, ed. K. Mills and A. Grafton. Rochester, NY: 152–88.

(2007) 'Strabo and Procopius: Classical Geography for a Christian Empire', in *From Rome to Constantinople: Studies in Honour of Averil Cameron*, ed. H. Amirav and B. ter Haar Romeny. Leuven: 67–83.

(2012) 'Barbarians in Late Antiquity: Problems and Approaches', in *The Oxford Handbook of Late Antiquity*, ed. S. F. Johnson. Oxford: 60–91.

Macrides, R. (2002) *Travel in the Byzantine World*. Aldershot, UK.

Madden, T. F. (1992) 'The Serpent Column of Delphi in Constantinople: Placement, Purposes, and Mutilations', *Byzantine and Modern Greek Studies* 16: 111–45.

Magdalino, P. (2005) 'Ο οφθαλμός της οικουμένης και ο ομφαλός της γης', in *Το Βυζάντιο ως Οικουμένη*, ed. E. Chrysos. Athens: 107–23.

(2010) 'Byzantium = Constantinople', in *A Companion to Byzantium*, ed. L. James. Malden, MA, and Chichester, UK: 43–54.

Maier, F. K. (2016) 'Chronotopos. Erzählung, Zeit und Raum im Hellenismus', *Klio* 98: 465–94.

Maier, H. O. (2011) 'Dominion from Sea to Sea: Eusebius of Caesarea, Constantine the Great, and the Exegesis of Empire', in *The Calling of the Nations: Exegesis, Ethnography, and Empire in a Biblical-Historic Present*, ed. M. Vessey. Toronto: 149–75.

Mango, C. (1988–9) 'The Tradition of Byzantine Chronography', *Harvard Ukrainian Studies* 12–13: 360–72.

Mango, C. and Scott, R. (1997) *The Chronicle of Theophanes Confessor*. Oxford.

Maraval, P. (1985) *Lieux saints et pèlerinages d'orient: Histoire et géographie des origines à la conquête arabe*. Paris.

(1998) 'L'échec en Orient. Le développement des Églises dissidentes dans l'Empire', in *Les Églises d'Orient et d'Occident*, ed. L. Piétri. Histoire du christianisme des origines à nos jours 3. Paris: 458–81.

(2002a) *Égérie, journal de voyage: Itinéraire*. 2nd ed. Sources chrétiennes 296. Paris.

(2002b) 'The Earliest Phase of Christian Pilgrimage in the Near East (before the 7th Century)', *Dumbarton Oaks Papers* 56: 63–74.

Marsham, A. (2013) 'The Architecture of Allegiance in Early Islamic Late Antiquity: The Accession of Mu'āwiya in Jerusalem, ca. 661 CE', in *Ceremonies and Rituals of Power in Byzantium and the Medieval Mediterranean: Comparative Perspectives*, ed. A. Beihammer, S. Constantinou and M. Parani. Leiden, The Netherlands: 87–114.

Martínez Díez, G. and Rodríguez, F. (eds.) (1992) *La colección canónica hispana*. Tomo V. *Concilios hispanos. Segunda parte*. Madrid.

McCormick, M. (1998) 'The Imperial Edge: Italo-Byzantine Identity, Movement and Integration', in *Studies on the Internal Diaspora of the Byzantine Empire*, ed. H. Ahrweiler and A. Laiou. Washington, DC: 17–52.

(2001) *Origins of the European Economy: Communications and Commerce, A.D. 300–900*. Cambridge.

McDonough, S. J. (2006) 'A Question of Faith? Persecution and Political Centralization in the Sasanian Empire of Yazdgard II (436–57 CE)', in *Violence in Late Antiquity: Perceptions and Practices*, ed. H. A. Drake. Aldershot, UK: 69–81.

(2011) 'Were the Sasanians Barbarians? Roman Writers on the "Empire of the Persians"', in *Romans, Barbarians, and the Transformation of the Roman World: Cultural Interaction and the Creation of Identity in Late Antiquity*, ed. R. Mathisen and D. Shanzer. Farnham, UK: 55–65.

Meier, M. (2003) *Das andere Zeitalter Justinians: Kontingenzerfahrung und Kontingenzbewältigung im 6. Jahrhundert n. Chr.* Hypomnemata: Untersuchungen zur Antike und zu ihrem Nachleben 147. Göttingen.

(2009) *Anastasios I. Die Entstehung des Byzantinischen Reiches*. Stuttgart.

(2014) 'Candidus: um die Geschichte der Isaurier', in *Griechische Profanhistoriker des fünften nachchristlichen Jahrhunderts*, ed. B. Bleckmann and T. Stickler. Stuttgart: 171–94.

Mellon Saint-Laurent, J.-N. (2015) *Missionary Stories and the Formation of the Syriac Churches*. Berkeley, CA.

Menze, V.-L. (2008) *Justinian and the Making of the Syrian Orthodox Church*. Oxford and New York.

Merrills, A. H. (2000) *Geography in Early Christian Historiography*. Cambridge.

(2004) 'Monks, Monsters, and Barbarians: Re-Defining the African Periphery in Late Antiquity', *Journal of Early Christian Studies* 12.2: 217–44.

(2005) *History and Geography in Late Antiquity*. Cambridge Studies in Medieval Life and Thought. Fourth Series. Cambridge.

Milani, C. (ed.) (1977) *Itinerarium Antonini Placentini: Un viaggio in Terra Santa del 560–570 d.C.* Scienze filologiche e letteratura 7. Milan.

Miles, R. (1999) 'Introduction: Constructing Identities in Late Antiquity', in *Constructing Identities in Late Antiquity*, ed. R. Miles. London: 1–15.

Millar, F. (2006) *A Greek Roman Empire: Power and Belief under Theodosius II (408–450)*. Sather Classical Lectures 64. Berkeley, CA.

(2010) 'Rome's "Arab" Allies in Late Antiquity', in *Commutatio et Contentio: Studies in the Late Roman, Sasanian and Early Islamic Near East. In Memory of Zeev Rubin*, ed. H. Börm and J. Wiesehöfer. Düsseldorf: 199–226.

(2013) 'The Evolution of the Syrian Orthodox Church in the Pre-Islamic Period: From Greek to Syriac?', *Journal of Early Christian Studies* 21: 43–92.

Mingana, A. (1917) 'Some Early Judaeo-Christian Documents in the John Rylands Library', *Bulletin of the John Rylands Library* 4: 59–118.

Minov, S. (2010) 'The Story of Solomon's Palace at Heliopolis', *Le Muséon* 123: 61–89.

Momigliano, A. (2012) *Essays in Ancient and Modern Historiography*, rev. ed. Chicago.

Mommsen, Th. (ed.) (1894) *Chronica Minora 2. Monumenta Germaniae Historica. Auctores antiquissimi* 11. Berlin.

Montgomery, J. A. (1927) *The History of Yaballaha III, Nestorian Patriarch, and of His Vicar, Bar Sauma, Mongol Ambassador to the Frankish Courts at the End of the Thirteenth Century*. Records of Civilization, Sources and Studies 8. New York.

Moorhead, J. (1981) 'Monophysite Responses to the Arab Invasions', *Byzantion* 51: 579–91.

Morony, M. G. (1984) *Iraq after the Muslim Conquest*. Princeton, NJ.

(2012) 'Religious Communities in the Early Islamic World', in *Visions of Community in the Post-Roman World: The West, Byzantium and the Islamic World, 300–1100*, ed. W. Pohl, C. Gantner and R. E. Payne. Farnham, UK: 155–64.

Moss, Y. (2016) *Incorruptible Bodies: Christology, Society and Authority in Late Antiquity*. Oakland, CA.

Mounayer, J. (1963) *Les synods syriens jacobites*. Beirut.

Muehlberger, E. (2015) 'The Legend of Arius' Death: Imagination, Space and Filth in Late Ancient Historiography', *Past and Present* 227: 3–29.

Muhlberger, S. (1981) *The Fifth-Century Chroniclers: Prosper, Hydatius, and the Gallic Chronicler of 452.* Leeds, UK.

Müller-Wiener, W. (1977) *Bildlexikon zur Topographie Istanbuls: Byzantion, Konstantinupolis, Istanbul bis zum Beginn d. 17. Jh.* Tübingen.

Mullett, M. (2002) 'Travel Genres and the Unexpected', in *Travel in Byzantium*, ed. R. Macrides. Aldershot, UK: 259–84.

Mund-Dopchie, M. (2009) *Ultima Thulé: Histoire d'un lieu et genèse d'un mythe.* Genève.

Nabe-von Schonberg, I. (1977) 'Die Westsyrische Kirche im Mittelalter (800–1150)'. PhD Diss. Ruprecht-Karls-Universität Heidelberg.

Nasrallah, L. S. (2005) 'Mapping the World: Justin, Tatian, Lucian, and the Second Sophistic', *Harvard Theological Review* 98: 283–314.

Natal, D. (2018) 'Putting the Roman Periphery on the Map: The Geography of Romanness, Orthodoxy, and Legitimacy in Victricius of Rouen's *De Laude Sanctorum*'. *Early Medieval Europe* 26: 304–26.

Nau, F. (1917) 'Andronicus le philosophe', *Revue de l'Orient chrétien* 10: 462–71.

Nechaeva, E. (2014) *Embassies, Negotiations, Gifts: Systems of East Roman Diplomacy in Late Antiquity.* Stuttgart.

Newbold, R. F. (1983) 'Patterns of Communication and Movement in Ammianus and Gregory of Tours', in *History and Historians in Late Antiquity*, eds. B. Croke and A. M. Emmett. Oxford: 66–81.

Nicolet, C. (1991) *Space, Geography, and Politics in the Early Roman Empire.* Jerome Lectures 19. Ann Arbor, MI.

Olbrich, K. (2006) '*Constantiniana Daphne*: Die Gründungsmythen eines anderen Rom?', *Klio* 88: 483–509.

Palmer, A. (1991) 'The History of the Syrian Orthodox in Jerusalem', *Oriens Christianus* 75: 16–43.

(2009) 'Les chroniques brèves Syriaques', in *L'historiographie syriaque*. ed. M. Debié. Etudes syriaques 6. Paris: 57–87.

Palmer, A., Brock, S. P. and Hoyland, R. (1993) *The Seventh Century in the West Syrian Chronicles.* Translated Texts for Historians 15. Liverpool, UK.

Panagiotopoulos, I. (2003) *The Patriarchal Institution in the Early Church: The Pentarchy of the Patriarchs. The Presuppositions, the Evolution and the Function of the Institution.* Athens.

Papaconstantinou, A. (2010) 'Administering the Early Islamic Empire: Insights from the Papyri', in *Money, Power and Politics in Early Islamic Syria: A Review of Current Debates*, ed. J. Haldon. Farnham, UK: 57–74.

Parry, K. (2017) 'Byzantine-Rite Christians (Melkites) in Central Asia in Late Antiquity and the Middle Ages', *History and Theology at Macquarie University* 2: 91–108.

Payne, R. E. (2015) *A State of Mixture: Christians, Zoroastrians, and Iranian Political Culture in Late Antiquity.* Oakland, CA.

Payne Smith, J. (1903) *A Compendious Syriac Dictionary Founded upon the Thesaurus Syriacus of R. Payne Smith.* Oxford.

Payne-Smith, R. (1860) *The Ecclesiastical History of John of Ephesus.* London.

Peeters, P. (1913) 'Saint Hilarion d'Ibérie', *Analecta Bollandiana* 32: 243–69.

Peri, V. (1988) 'La pentarchia: instituzione ecclesiale (IV–VII siecolo) e teoria canonico-teologica', *Bisanzio, Roma e l'Italia nell 'Alto Medievo* 34: 209–311.

Perrin, M.-Y. (1997) 'Grégoire de Tours et l'espace extra-gaulois: le gallocentrisme grégorien revisité', in *Grégoire de Tours et l'espace gaulois. Actes du congrès international, Tours, 3–5 novembre 1994*, ed. N. Gauthier and H. Galinié. Tours: 35–45.

(2001) 'Théodoret de Cyr et la représentation de l'espace ascétique: imaginaire classique et nouveauté socio-religieuse', in *Pensiero e istituzioni del mondo classico nelle culture del Vicino Oriente. Atti del Seminario Nazionale di studio (Brescia, 14–16 ott. 1999)*. Alessandria, Italy: 211–35.

Perrone, L. (2009) 'Pierre l'Ibère ou l'exil comme pèlerinage et combat pour la foi', in *Man Near a Roman Arch: Studies Presented to Prof. Yoram Tsafrir*, ed. L. Di Segni et al. Jerusalem: 190–204.

Pfeilschifter, R. (2013) *Der Kaiser und Konstantinopel: Kommunikation und Konfliktaustrag in einer spätantiken Metropole*. Millennium-Studien 44. Berlin.

Pierre, S. (2017) 'Les tribus arabes chrétiennes de Haute-Mésopotamie (Ier/VIIe–Ie/VIIIe s.)'. PhD Diss. Paris I: Sorbonne.

Pohl, W. (2013) 'Introduction – Strategies of Identification: A Methodological Profile', in *Strategies of Identification: Ethnicity and Religion in Early Medieval Europe*, ed. W. Pohl and G. Heydemann. Turnhout: 1–64.

Pohl, W., Wood, I. N. and Reimitz H. (eds.) (2001) *The Transformation of Frontiers from Late Antiquity to the Carolingians*. Leiden, The Netherlands.

Pollmann, K. (2011) 'Unending Sway: The Ideology of Empire in Early Christian Latin Thought', in *The Calling of the Nations: Exegesis, Ethnography, and Empire in a Biblical-Historic Present*, ed. M. Vessey. Toronto: 176–99.

Praet, R. (2018) 'From Rome to Constantinople: Antiquarian Echoes of Cultural Trauma in the Sixth Century'. PhD Diss. Ghent University and University of Groningen.

Purves, A. C. (2010) *Space and Time in Ancient Greek Narrative*. New York.

Racine, F. (2007) 'Geography, Identity and the Legend of Saint Christopher', in *Religious Identity in Late Antiquity*, ed. R. Frakes and E. DePalma Digeser. Toronto: 105–25.

Rapp, C. (2005) *Holy Bishops in Late Antiquity: The Nature of Christian Leadership in an Age of Transition*. Berkeley, CA.

Rebenich, S. (1994) 'Review of Burgess 1993', *Gnomon* 71: 437–48.

Reed, A. Y. (2009) 'Beyond the Land of Nod: Syriac Images of Asia and the Historiography of "the West"', *History of Religions* 49: 48–87.

Reimitz, H. (2015) *History, Frankish Identity and the Framing of Western Ethnicity, 550–850*. Cambridge Studies in Medieval Life and Thought. Fourth Series 101. Cambridge.

Reinink, G. (1993) 'The Beginning of Syriac Apologetic Literature in Response to Islam', *Oriens Christianus* 77: 165–83.

Renoux, C. A. (1989) *Le lectionnaire de Jérusalem en Arménie: I. Introduction et liste des manuscrits.* Patrologia Orientalis 44.4. Turnhout.

(1999) *II: Edition synoptique des plus anciens témoins.* Patrologia Orientalis 48.2. Turnhout.

Revanoglou, A. M. (2005) *Geōgraphika kai ethnographika stoicheia sto ergo tu Prokopiu Kaisareias.* Byzantina keimena kai meletai 39. Thessaloniki.

Reydellet, M. (1970) 'Les intentions idéologiques et politiques dans la *Chronique* d'Isidore de Séville', *Mémoires et études de l'Ecole française de Rome. Antiquité* 82: 363–400.

(1981) *La royauté dans la littérature latine de Sidoine Apollinaire à Isidore de Seville.* Rome.

Richter, S. G. (2002) *Studien zur Christianisierung Nubiens.* Sprachen und Kulturen des christlichen Orients 11. Wiesbaden.

Rimell, V. and Asper, M. (eds.) (2017) *Imagining Empire: Political Space in Hellenistic and Roman Literature.* Bibliothek der klassischen Altertumswissenschaften 153. Heidelberg.

Robinson, C. (1996) 'Tribes and Nomads in Early Islamic Mesopotamia', in *Continuity and Change in Northern Mesopotamia from the Hellenistic to the Early Islamic Period,* ed. K. Bartl and S. Hauser. Berlin: 429–52.

Romm, J. S. (1992) *The Edges of the Earth in Ancient Thought: Geography, Exploration, and Fiction.* Princeton, NJ.

Rosen, K. (2001) 'Iustinus II', *Reallexikon für Antike und Christentum* 19: 778–801.

(2016) *Attila: der Schrecken der Welt.* Munich.

Rubin, B. (1952) 'Art. Prokopios von Kaisareia', *Paulys Realencyclopedie der classischen Altertumswissenschaft* 45: 273–599.

Rundgren, F. (1996) 'From Pancatantra to Stephanites and Ichnelates: Some Notes on the Old Syriac Translation of Kalila wa-Dimna', in *Leimōn: Studies Presented to Lennart Rydén on His Sixty-Fifth Birthday,* ed. J.-O. Rosenqvist. Acta Universitatis Upsaliensis: Studia Byzantina Upsaliensia 6. Uppsala: 167–80.

Ryssel, V. (1888) *Ein Brief Georgs, Bischofs der Araber, an den Presbyter Jesus, aus dem Syrischen übersetzt und erläutert. Mit einer Einleitung über sein Leben und seine Schriften.* Gotha.

Saint-Laurent, J.-N. (2015) *Missionary Stories and the Formation of the Syriac Churches.* Oakland, CA.

Salibi, K. (1962) 'The Traditional Historiography of the Maronites', in *Historians of the Middle East,* ed. B. Lewis and K. Holt. Oxford: 212–25.

Salway, B. (2005) 'The Nature and Genesis of the Peutinger Map', *Imago Mundi* 57: 119–35.

Sarantis, A. (2009) 'War and Diplomacy in Pannonia and the Northwest Balkans during the Reign of Justinian: The Gepid Threat and Imperial Responses', *Dumbarton Oaks Papers* 63: 15–40.

(2010) 'The Justinianic Herules: From Allied Barbarians to Roman Provincials', in *Neglected Barbarians,* ed. F. Curta. Studies in the Early Middle Ages 32. Turnhout: 361–402.

(2016) *Justinian's Balkan Wars: Campaigning, Diplomacy and Development in Illyricum, Thrace and the Northern World A.D. 527–65.* ARCA: Classical Medieval Texts, Papers, and Monographs 53. Prenton, UK.

Schleicher, F. (2014) *Cosmographia Christiana: Kosmologie und Geographie im frühen Christentum.* Paderborn.

Schönfelder, J. M. (1862) *Die Kirchengeschichte des Johannes von Ephesus.* Munich.

Schulthess, F. (ed.) (1911) *Kalila und Dimna.* 2 vols. Berlin.

Schuster, M. (1940) 'Die Hunnenbeschreibungen bei Ammianus, Sidonius und Iordanis', *Wiener Studien* 58: 119–30.

Scott, R. (1985) 'Malalas, *The Secret History*, and Justinian's Propaganda', *Dumbarton Oaks Papers* 39: 99–109.

Selb, W. and Kaufhold, H. (2002) *Das syrisch-römische Rechtsbuch.* 3 vols. Vienna.

Shahîd, I. (1984) *Byzantium and the Arabs in the Fourth Century.* Washington, DC.

(1995) *Byzantium and the Arabs in the Sixth Century.* 3 vols. Washington, DC.

Shaked, S. (2008) 'Religion in the Late Sasanian Period: Eran, Aneran and Other Religious Designations', in *The Sasanian Era: The Idea of Iran Vol. 3*, ed. V. S. Curtis and S. Stewart. London: 103–17.

Shoemaker, S. (2017) 'Sing, O Daughter(s) of Zion', in *Melania: Early Christianity through the Life of One Family*, ed. C. Chin and C. T. Schroeder. Oakland, CA: 222–39.

Signes-Codoñer, J. (2014) *The Emperor Theophilos and the East, 829–842: Court and Frontier in Byzantium during the Last Phase of Iconoclasm.* Farnham, UK.

Silverstein, A. (2009) 'The Medieval Islamic Worldview: Arabic Geography in Its Historical Context', in *Geography and Ethnography: Perceptions of the World in Pre-Modern Societies*, ed. K. Raaflaub and R. Talbert. Chichester, UK: 273–90.

Simonsohn, U. (2013) 'Blessed Are the Peacemakers: An Ecclesiastical Definition of Authority in the Early Islamic Period', in *Meditations on Authority*, ed. D. Shulman. Jerusalem: 101–27.

Singh, D. (2015) 'Eusebius as Political Theologian: The Legend Continues', *Harvard Theological Review* 108: 129–54.

Sivan, H. S. (1988a) 'Holy Land Pilgrimage and Western Audiences: Some Reflections on Egeria and Her Circle', *Classical Quarterly* n.s. 38: 528–35.

(1988b) 'Subversive Pilgrimages: Barsauma in Jerusalem'. *Journal of Early Christian Studies* 26: 53–74.

(1988c) 'Who Was Egeria? Piety and Pilgrimage in the Age of Gratian', *Harvard Theological Review* 81: 59–72.

Skjærvø, P. O. and Humbach, H. (1983) *The Sasanian Inscription of Paikuli.* Wiesbaden.

Slater, C. (1986) *Trail of Miracles: Stories from a Pilgrimage in Northeast Brazil.* Berkeley, CA.

Soukry, A. (1881) *Géographie de Moïse de Khorène d'après Ptolémée.* Venice.

Staab, F. (1976) 'Ostrogothic Geographers at the Court of Theoderic the Great: A Study of Some Sources of the Anonymous Cosmographer of Ravenna', *Viator* 7: 27–64.

Stein, E. (1949) *Histoire du Bas–Empire. Tome II: De la disparition de l'empire d'Occident à la mort de Justinien (476–565)*. Paris and Bruges.

Steinacher, R. (2010) 'The Herules: Fragments of a History', in *Neglected Barbarians*, ed. F. Curta. Studies in the Early Middle Ages 32. Turnhout: 319–60.

Stenger, J. R. (2016) 'Eusebius and the Representation of the Holy Land', in *Brill's Companion to Ancient Geography*, ed. H.-J. Gehrke, M. Cataudella and S. Bianchetti. Leiden, The Netherlands: 381–98.

Steppa, J.-E. (2002) *John Rufus and the World Vision of Anti-Chalcedonian Culture*. Piscataway, NJ.

Stevenson, W. (2002–3) 'Sozomen, Barbarians, and Early Byzantine Historiography', *Greek, Roman and Byzantine Studies* 43: 51–75.

Stocking, R. L. (2000) *Bishops, Councils, and Consensus in the Visigothic Kingdom, 589–633*. Ann Arbor, MI.

Svennung, J. (1967) *Jordanes und Scandia. Kritisch-exegetische Studien*. Stockholm.

Tacoma, L. E. (2016) *Moving Romans Migration to Rome in the Principate*. Oxford.

Talbert, R. and Broderson, K. (eds.) (2004) *Space in the Roman World*. Münster.

Talbert, R. and Unger, R. W. (eds.) (2008) *Cartography in Antiquity and the Middle Ages: Fresh Perspectives, New Methods*. Technology and Change in History 10. Leiden, The Netherlands.

Tamcke, M. (2007) 'Abraham of Kashkar's Pilgrimage', *ARAM* 19: 477–82.

Tang, L. (2014) *East Syriac Christianity in Mongol-Yuan China (12th–14th Centuries)*. Wiesbaden.

Tannous, J. (2009) Between Christology and Kalam: The Life and Letters of George Bishop of the Arabs (d. AD, 724). Piscataway, NJ.

(2014) 'In Search of Monotheletism', *Dumbarton Oaks Papers* 68: 29–67.

(2018) 'Romanness in the Syriac East', in *The Transformations of Romanness: Early Medieval Regions and Identities*. ed. W. Pohl. Millennium Studies 71. Berlin: 457–79.

(forthcoming) *The Life of Theodota of Amid*.

Tardy, R. (1999) *Najrân: Chrétiens d'Arabie avant l'islam*. Beirut.

Tausend, K. (1984) 'Die Darstellung der Hunnen bei Ammianus Marcellinus, Priskos, Iordanes und den lateinischen Dichtern und Panegyrikern'. PhD Diss. Karl-Franzens-Universität Graz.

Taylor, D. (2009) 'The Psalm Commentary of Daniel of Salah and the Formation of Sixth-Century Syrian Orthodox Identity', *Church History and Religious Culture* 89: 65–92.

Tchekhanovets, Y. (2011) 'Early Georgian Pilgrimage to the Holy Land', *Liber Annuus* 61: 453–71.

Teillet, S. (2011) *Des Goths à la nation gothique. Les origines de l'idée de nation en Occident du Ve au VIIe siècle*. Paris.

Terian, A. (2008) *Macarius of Jerusalem: Letter to the Armenians AD 335*. AVANT Series 4. Crestwood, NY.

Teule, H. (1994) 'The Perception of the Jerusalem Pilgrimage in Syriac Monastic Circles', in *VI Symposium Syriacum 1992*, ed. R. Lavenant. Orientalia Christiana Analecta 247. Rome: 311–21.

(2005) 'Syrian Orthodox Attitudes to the Pilgrimage to Jerusalem', *Eastern Christian Art* 2: 121–5.

Thompson, E. A. (1980) 'Procopius on Brittia and Britannia', *Classical Quarterly* 30: 498–507.

Thomson, R. W. (1967) 'A Seventh-Century Armenian Pilgrim on Mount Tabor', *The Journal of Theological Studies* 18: 27–33.

(1985) 'Jerusalem and Armenia', in *Studia Patristica: Papers of the Ninth International Conference on Patristic Studies, Oxford 1983* vol. 18.1. Leuven: 77–91.

(1991) *The History of Łazar Pʻarpecʻi*. Occasional Papers and Proceedings 4. Atlanta.

(2001) *The Armenian Adaptation of the Ecclesiastical History of Socrates Scholasticus*. Hebrew University Armenian Studies 3. Leuven.

(2010) *Agathangelos: The Lives of Saint Gregory*. Ann Arbor, MI.

(2012) *Saint Basil of Caesarea and Armenian Cosmology: A Study of the Armenian Version of Saint Basil's Hexaemeron and Its Influence on Medieval Armenian Views about the Cosmos*. Corpus Scriptorum Christianorum Orientalium 646. Subsisia 130. Louvain.

Thomson, R. W. and Howard-Johnston, J. D. (1999) *The Armenian History Attributed to Sebeos*. Translated Texts for Historians 31. Liverpool, UK.

Toepel, A. (2008) *Die Mönche des Kublai Khan: Die Reise der Pilger Mar Yahballaha und Rabban Sauma nach Europa*. Darmstadt.

Toral-Niehoff, I. (2014) *Al-Ḥīra. Eine Arabische Kulturmetropole im spätantiken Kontext*. Leiden, The Netherlands.

Traina, G. (2013) 'Mapping the World under Theodosius II', in *Theodosius II: Rethinking the Roman Empire in Late Antiquity*, ed. C. Kelly. Cambridge: 115–71.

(2015) 'Mapping the New Empire: A Geographical Look at the Fourth Century', in *East and West in the Roman Empire of the Fourth Century: An End to Unity?*, ed. R. Dijkstra, S. Van Poppel and D. Slootjes. Leiden, The Netherlands: 49–62.

Treadgold, W. (2007) *The Early Byzantine Historians*. New York.

(2013) *The Middle Byzantine Historians*. Basingstoke, UK.

Trimingham, J. (1979) *Christianity among the Arabs in Pre-Islamic Times*. London.

Trombley, F. R. and Watt, J. W. (2000) *The Chronicle of Pseudo-Joshua the Stylite*. Translated Texts for Historians 7. Liverpool, UK.

Turner, V. W. and Turner, E. L. B. (1978) *Image and Pilgrimage in Christian Culture: Anthropological Perspectives*. Lectures on the History of Religions 11. New York.

Van Dam, R. (2007) *The Roman Revolution of Constantine*. Cambridge.

(2010) *Rome and Constantinople: Rewriting Roman History during Late Antiquity*. Waco, TX.

(2014) '"Constantine's Beautiful City": The Symbolic Value of Constantinople', *Antiquité tardive* 22: 83–94.

Vanderspoel, J. (2012) 'A Tale of Two Cities: Themistius on Rome and Constantinople', in *Two Romes: Rome and Constantinople in Late Antiquity*, ed. L. Grig and G. Kelly. Oxford: 223–40.

van der Vliet, J. (2006) 'Bringing Home the Homeless: Landscape and History in Egyptian Hagiography', *Church History and Religious Culture* 86: 39–55.

Van Donzel, E. J. and Schmidt, A. B. (2010) *Gog and Magog in Early Eastern Christian and Islamic Sources: Sallam's Quest for Alexander's Wall*. Brill's Inner Asian Library 22. Leiden, The Netherlands, and Boston.

Van Ginkel, J. J. (1994) 'John of Ephesus on Emperors: The Perception of the Byzantine Empire by a Monophysite', in *VI Symposium Syriacum, 1992*, ed. R. Lavenant. Orientalia Christiana Analecta 247. Rome: 323–33.

(1995) 'John of Ephesus: A Monophysite Historian in Sixth-Century Byzantium'. PhD Diss. University of Groningen.

(1998) 'Making History: Michael the Syrian and His Sixth-Century Sources', in *Symposium Syriacum VII*, ed. R. Lavenant. Orientalia Christiana Analecta 256. Rome: 351–8.

(2006a) 'The Perception and Presentation of the Arab Conquest in Syriac Historiography', in *The Encounter of Eastern Christianity with Early Islam*, ed. E. Grypeou, M. N. Swanson and D. Thomas. Leiden, The Netherlands: 171–84.

(2006b) 'Michael the Syrian and His Sources: Reflections on the Methodology of Michael the Great as a Historiographer and Its Implications for Modern Historians', *Journal of the Canadian Society for Syriac Studies* 6: 53–60.

(2010) 'A Man Is Not an Island', in *The Syriac Renaissance*, ed. H. Teule, C. Tauwinkl, B. ter Haar Romeny and J. Van Ginkel. Leuven: 113–21.

Van Hoof, L. (2011) 'Libanius and the EU Presidency: Career Moves in the Autobiography', in *Libanios: Le premier humaniste*, ed. P.-L. Malosse and O. Lagacherie. Salerno, Italy: 193–206.

(2019) 'Vergilian allusions in the Getica of Jordanes', *Latomus* 78: 171–85.

Van Hoof, L. and Van Nuffelen, P. (2011) 'Pseudo-Themistius, Pros Basilea: A Panegyric for Justinian?', *Byzantion* 81: 412–23.

(2017) 'The Historiography of Crisis: Jordanes, Cassiodorus and Justinian in Mid-Sixth-Century Constantinople', *Journal of Roman Studies* 107: 275–300.

(forthcoming a) *Jordanes: Romana and Getica*. Translated Texts for Historians. Liverpool, UK.

(forthcoming b) *The Fragmentary Latin Histories of Late Antiquity (AD 300–650): Edition, Translation and Commentary*. Cambridge.

Van Nuffelen, P. (2004) *Un héritage de paix et de piété: étude sur les histoires ecclésiastiques de Socrate et de Sozomène*. Leuven.

(2010) 'Theology vs. Genre? Tradition as Universal Historiography in Late Antiquity', in *Universal Historiography in Antiquity and Beyond*, ed. P. Liddel and A. Fear. London: 190–212.

(2012) *Orosius and the Rhetoric of History*. Oxford Early Christian Studies. Oxford.

(2013) 'Olympiodorus of Thebes and Eastern Triumphalism', in *Theodosius II: Rethinking the Roman Empire in Late Antiquity*, ed. C. Kelly. Cambridge: 130–52.

(2015) 'Not Much Happened: 410 and All That', *Journal of Roman Studies* 105: 322–9.

(2018) *Penser la tolérance durant l'Antiquité tardive*. Paris.

Van Schaik, S. and Galambos, I. (2012) *Manuscripts and Travellers: The Sino-Tibetan Documents of a Tenth-Century Buddhist Pilgrim*. Studies in Manuscript Cultures 2. Berlin.

Vergin, W. (2013) *Das Imperium Romanum und seine Gegenwelten: Die geographisch-ethnographischen Exkurse in den 'Res Gestae' des Ammianus Marcellinus*. Millennium-Studien zu Kultur und Geschichte des ersten Jahrtausends n. Chr. 41. Berlin and Boston.

Verrycken, K. (1998) 'Johannes Philoponos', *Reallexikon für Antike und Christentum* 18: 534–53.

Vööbus, A. (1975–6) *The Synodicon in the West Syrian Tradition*. Louvain.

Walker, J. T. (2006) *The Legend of Mar Qardagh*. Berkeley, CA.

Wallinga, T. (1992) 'The Date of Joannes Lydus' *De magistratibus*', *Revue internationale des droits de l'antiquité* (ser. 3) 39: 359–80.

Washburn, D. A. (2012) *Banishment in the Later Roman Empire, 284–476 CE*. Routledge Studies in Ancient History 5. New York.

Watts, E. (2006) *City and School in Late Antique Athens and Alexandria*. Berkeley, CA.

(2014) *The Final Pagan Generation*. Berkeley, CA.

Weltecke, D. (2003) *Die 'Beschreibung der Zeiten' von Mōr Michael dem Grossen (1126–1199): eine Studie zu ihrem historischen und historiographiegeschichtlichen Kontext*. Leuven.

(2017) 'Space, Etanglement and Decentralization: How to Narrate a Transcultural History of Christianity (550 to 1350 CE)', in *Locating Religions: Contact, Diversity and Translocality*, ed. R. Glas and N. Jaspert. Leiden, The Netherlands: 315–44.

Whitby, L. M. (2000) 'The Successors of Justinian', in *The Cambridge Ancient History Volume 14.2.*, ed. A. Cameron et al. Cambridge: 86–111.

(2011) 'Imperial Christian Historiography', in *The Oxford History of Historywriting. Vol. I: Beginnings to AD 600*, ed. A. Feldherr and G. Hardy. Oxford: 346–68.

Whitby, M. and Whitby, M. (1989) *Chronicon Paschale, 284–628 AD*. Liverpool, UK.

Wickham, C. (2010) *The Inheritance of Rome: A History of Europe from 400 to 1000*. London.

Wiesehöfer, J. and Huyse, P. (2006) *Ērān ud Anērān. Studien zu den Beziehungen zwischen dem Sasanidenreich und der Mittelmeerwelt.* Oriens et Occidens 13. Munich.

Winterhager, P. (2016) 'Rome in the Seventh-Century Byzantine Empire: A Migrants' Network Perspective from the Circle of Maximos the Confessor', in *From Constantinople to the Frontier: The City and the Cities*, ed. N. Matheou, T. Kampianaki and L. Bondioli. Leiden, The Netherlands: 191–206.

Witakowski, W. (1987) *The Syriac Chronicle of Pseudo-Dionysius of Tel-Mahre: A Study in the History of Historiography.* Studia Semitica Uppsaliensia 9. Uppsala, Sweden.

(1990) 'Malalas in Syriac', in *Studies in John Malalas*, ed. E. Jeffreys et al. Sidney: 299–310.

(1991) 'Sources of Pseudo-Dionysius for the Third Part of His Chronicle', *Orientalia Suecana* 40: 252–75.

(1993) 'The Division of the Earth between the Descendants of Noah in Syriac Tradition', *ARAM* 5: 635–56.

(1996) *Pseudo-Dionysius of Tel-Mahre, Chronicle.* Translated Texts for Historians 22. Liverpool, UK.

(2007) 'Geographical Knowledge of the Syrians', in *The Professorship of Semitic Languages at Uppsala University 400 Years*, ed. M. Eskhult, B. Isaksson and G. Ramsay. Acta Universitatis Upsaliensis: Studia Semitica Upsaliensia 24. Uppsala, Sweden: 219–46.

Wolf, K. B. (1999) *Conquerors and Chroniclers of Early Medieval Spain.* Translated Texts for Historians 9. 2nd ed. Liverpool, UK.

Wolfram, H. (1979) 'Gotisches Königtum und römisches Kaisertum von Theodosius dem Grossen bis Justinian I', *Frühmittelalterliche Studien* 13: 1–28.

(2009) *Die Goten: von den Anfängen bis zur Mitte des sechsten Jahrhunderts; Entwurf einer historischen Ethnographie.* 5. Aufl. Munich.

Wolska-Conus, W. (1978) 'Geographie', in *Reallexicon für Antike und Christentum.* Stuttgart: 155–222.

Wood, J. (2010) 'Defending Byzantine Spain: Frontiers and Diplomacy', *Early Medieval Europe* 18: 292–319.

(2012) *The Politics of Identity in Visigoth Spain: Religion and Power in the Histories of Isidore of Seville.* Leiden, The Netherlands, and Boston.

(2013) '*Religiones* and *gentes* in Isidore of Seville's *Chronica maiora*: The Visigoths as a Chosen People', in *Post-Roman Transitions: Christian and Barbarian Identities in the Early Medieval West*, ed. W. Pohl and G. Heydemann. Turnhout: 125–68.

Wood, P. (2010) '*We Have No King but Christ': Christian Political Thought in Greater Syria on the Eve of the Arab Conquest (c. 400–585).* Oxford.

(2012) 'The Chorepiscopoi and Controversies over Orthopraxy in Sixth Century Mesopotamia', *Journal of Ecclesiastical History* 63: 446–57.

(2013) *The Chronicle of Seert: Christian Historical Imagination in Late Antique Iraq.* Oxford Early Christian Studies. Oxford.

(forthcoming) *Christian Networks in the Abbasid Jazira, c. 740–840.*

Woolf, G. (2011) *Tales of the Barbarians: Ethnography and Empire in the Roman West.* Blackwell-Bristol Lectures on Greece, Rome and the Classical Tradition. Malden, MA.

Wright, W. (ed.) (1884) *The Book of Kalilah and Dimnah, Translated from Arabic into Syriac.* Oxford.

Yarrow, L. M. (2006) *Historiography at the End of the Republic: Provincial Perspectives on Roman Rule.* Oxford.

Zadeh, T. E. (2011) *Mapping Frontiers across Medieval Islam: Geography, Translation, and the 'Abbāsid Empire.* Library of Middle East History 27. London and New York.

Zimmermann, M. (1999) 'Enkomion und Historiographie: Entwicklungslinien der kaiserzeitlichen Geschichtsschreibung vom 1. bis zum frühen 3. Jh. n. Chr', in *Geschichtsschreibung und politischer Wandel im 3. Jh. n. Chr., Kolloquium zu Ehren von Karl-Ernst Petzold (Juni 1998) anlässlich seines 80. Geburtstags,* ed. M. Zimmermann. Stuttgart: 17–56.

Index